CW00486922

THEMES IN ROMAN S

Niall Rudd

Duckworth

First published in 1986 by
Gerald Duckworth & Co. Ltd.
The Old Piano Factory
43 Gloucester Crescent, London NW1

© 1986 by Niall Rudd

All rights reserved. No part of this
publication may be reproduced, stored in a
retrieval system, or transmitted, in any
form or by any means, electronic, mechanical,
photocopying, recording or otherwise, without
the prior permission of the publishers.

ISBN 0 7156 2014 2

British Library Cataloguing in Publication Data

Rudd, Niall,
    Themes in Roman satire.—(Classical life
    and letters)
    1. Satire, Latin—History and criticism
    I. Title   II. Series
    877'.01'09   PA6056

    ISBN 0-7156-2014-2

Photoset in North Wales by
Derek Doyle & Associates, Mold, Clwyd
Printed and Bound in Great Britain by
Unwin Brothers Limited, Old Woking.

To my wife Nancy

sine qua non

Contents

Preface

After talking of Greek antecedents and the original meaning of *satura*, books on Roman satire go on to describe the various writers and their work – first Ennius, then Lucilius, and so on. That is the most natural and straightforward way of proceeding, and it has produced at least two learned and comprehensive descriptions of the genre.[1] The same method has been followed in two useful collections of essays;[2] and, in addition, there has been a handful of books on the individual satirists.[3] I have thought for some time, however, that there was need for a different kind of book – one which, instead of treating the satirists vertically, man by man, studied them in a series of horizontal bands, each band representing a particular theme or topic. That, in effect, is what the present book does.

The method has entailed certain limitations. I have said nothing on the writings of Varro, Seneca, and Petronius. Even within the Lucilian tradition I have not attempted to give a full account of each poet's work; nor have I repeated the story of its transmission and influence. But there have, I believe, been certain gains. It has been possible to pay more attention to the satirists' historical environment, to offer more in the way of quotation and illustration, and by setting out what each writer says on a particular subject to provide the reader with a more solid basis for comparative comment.

A little thought will show that the six themes I have chosen overlap. So it was necessary to make certain decisions of a somewhat arbitrary kind. In the first chapter, under 'Aims and Motives', I have described the satirists' areas of attack, but personal details have been reserved for Chapter Two ('Freedom and Authority'). In that second chapter I have also discussed, where relevant, the poet's position *vis-à-vis* his patron, in so far as that related to political power. Other aspects of patronage are examined in Chapter Four ('Class and Patronage'). In Chapter Three ('Style and Public') I talk about the poets' own style, whereas in Chapter One I indicate the kinds of style which they satirised. The only exception to this has to do with neoteric or neo-Callimachean material, which

---

[1] Those by U. Knoche and M. Coffey (for these and other references see the Bibliography).

[2] Those edited by J.P. Sullivan and by E.S. Ramage, D.L. Sigsbee, and S.C. Fredericks.

[3] E.g. N. Terzaghi's *Lucilio*, my own *The Satires of Horace*, G. Highet's *Juvenal the Satirist*, and J. Gérard's *Juvénal et la réalité contemporaine*. A new book, by M. Morford, on Persius has been recently announced.

appears under the heading 'Greece and the Greeks'. That material could, indeed, have gone elsewhere, but it seemed to provide the best balance when placed in Chapter Five. As for the opening chapter, that is meant to offer a way of orienting oneself to the genre as a whole. Before beginning it, readers might be wise to cover, say, a quarter of Horace, Persius, and Juvenal in translation, a task which could be completed in two or three evenings. Having done so, they will be less likely to feel that they have been thrown in at the deep end.

Quis leget haec? 'Who is going to read this?' That very pertinent question was put to Persius by a speaker in *Satire* 1. The reply was short and unambitious: *nemo* 'No one'. I am a little more optimistic, but it would be well to indicate whom I have in mind. As the last paragraph implied, the book is meant primarily for students; but I hope it may also be of some use to teachers of Latin who are not specialists in satire, and to others who take a literary interest in the genre. Those who *have* made a study of Roman satire will find various defects, and no doubt will say so; but although the book owes a debt to their work, it is not really meant for them (*Persium non curo legere*).

For reasons of space I have not printed Latin quotations, except in the case of very short extracts. This has favoured Lucilius, since he exists only in that form. But as readers are less likely to have their own copies of his text, perhaps the advantage is not unfair. The rule I have just mentioned is relaxed in Chapter Three, because it did not seem sensible to suppress the Latin in a chapter largely devoted to style. The translations of Lucilius and Juvenal are new; those of Horace and Persius are based on the Penguin Translation (1979), but differ in numerous points of detail. Most of these points have to do with rhythm, but in a few instances I have introduced corrections. Except in the case of Persius' Prologue, a few verses of Horace's *Epodes* and *Odes*, and some fragments of early Lucilius, the lines contain six stresses and are intended to recall the movement of the Latin hexameter. Needless to say, I am aware of their shortcomings and offer them with the usual reservations. The texts employed are, in the main, those of Warmington (*ROL*, vol. 3) for Lucilius, Klingner (Teubner 1959) for Horace, and Clausen (Oxford 1959) for Persius and Juvenal.

In the case of Lucilius the textual difficulties are severe. But, although I have been conscious of specific problems and have occasionally preferred the reading of Terzaghi / Mariotti (Florence 1966) to that of Warmington, I have not as a rule presented any discussion. This refusal may be put down to lack of time, space, and competence, and to the unlikelihood of any significant progress. I can only hope that the literary points which I have tried to make would not be seriously affected by adopting different readings. As Housman said, 'Cautious men do not edit Lucilius', and even writing about him as a satirist is a risky undertaking. But the alternative is to ignore one of the most distinctive and arresting voices that ever spoke Latin.

As Horace was more than a satirist, it seemed right to make some reference to his other works. The *Epodes* were composed in the same period as the *Satires*, but in quite a different tradition. When they attack people, whether individuals or types, there is no moral-didactic intention. The *Epistles*, of which Book 1 appeared after the first collection of *Odes*, are written in the same metre as the *Satires*.[4] Dialogue has now given way to letter, and the amount of direct speech has been greatly reduced. Censure is much less prominent than affirmation, and in general the moralist may be said to have absorbed the satirist. Nevertheless, the satirical spirit does appear from time to time, and in any general discussion of Roman satire the *Epistles* ought not to be neglected.

Although I have learned something, I hope, from various kinds of critical writing over the last thirty-odd years, the opinions behind this book are traditional. I mention five. First, that while every work no doubt embodies (more, or less, satisfactorily) the creator's view of the art which he is practising, it is merely confusing to say that every statue 'is really about sculpture' and every poem 'is really about poetry'. Above all else, Roman satire is about Roman life. Second, that provided it is not distorted by textual corruption a poet's meaning, in its most basic sense, can be rightly or wrongly apprehended. Disagreements are a matter for rational debate. Third, that although an important poet can say several things at the same time, he is not entitled to praise if he contradicts himself. This, of course, obliges us to ask whether such-and-such a passage really is a contradiction, and if so how much it matters. Fourth, that in spite of our very imperfect evidence we can gain some idea of how the Romans thought and felt. This does not imply that they all thought and felt alike. It means, rather, that we are not so trapped in our Anglo-Saxon bourgeois ethos (or whatever) as to be incapable of reaching outside it. Fifth, that when some Roman custom or attitude seems objectionable in the light of our own moral beliefs, we are permitted to say so. Rome is not exempt from criticism just because it happens to be another culture. Naturally, there will be disagreements. A National Front supporter will not react to Juvenal's attack on Greek immigrants in the same way as a progressive liberal. But if they both react, it shows they have read the satire instead of merely noticing it. Those five opinions, though briefly and crudely stated, are accepted as truisms within the humanist tradition. Outside it they are widely contested.

The circumstances in which the book was written made it difficult to

---

[4] According to the scholiasts in their introduction to *Sat.* 1.1, Horace entitled the two books of satires *Sermones* and the epistles *Epistulae*. He also referred to the epistles as *sermones* (*E.* 2.1.250). For the sake of clarity I have reserved *sermones* for the hexameter poems as a whole. *E* stands for the *Epistles*, and the *Satires* are referred to simply by the appropriate numbers.

send out drafts for criticism. But I should like to thank Professor John Crook for helping me with certain questions in Roman law. He is not, of course, responsible for my errors. Finally, at a time of great strain in British universities, caused by a sterile and hostile government, my departmental colleagues made it possible for me to take a term's leave in order to complete the book. I thank them most warmly.

N.R.

CHAPTER ONE

Aims and Motives

Roman satirists may be thought of as functioning within a triangle of which the apices are (a) attack, (b) entertainment, and (c) preaching. If a poem rests too long on apex (a) it passes into lampoon or invective; if it lingers on (b) it changes into some form of comedy; and if it remains on (c) it becomes a sermon. In this triple function preaching appears to have a less important status than the other two. For a poem which has its position somewhere along the line (b) – (c) does not count as a satire. (Many of Horace's *Epistles* are on or near that line.) Likewise a poem located wholly on the line (a) – (c) does not count as a satire. (Some passages in Persius are only kept off that line by the intriguing novelty of their language.) On the other hand a large number of satires are situated along the line (a) – (b). They seem to have no didactic purpose, unless one takes the unsatisfactory view that every witty attack is by implication a sermon. Still, a great many satires do have a didactic element, and so to study the genre as whole we need to think of an area rather than a line. Within this triangle the function of a satirist's work may change from poem to poem, so that neat generalisations about 'Horatian' and 'Juvenalian' types tend to mislead. There is sometimes movement even within a single piece. And of course 'attack', 'entertainment', and 'preaching' are themselves very loose and flexible terms.

In examining a writer's aim we shall be asking how he wished to affect his audience and readers; and in considering his motives we shall be speculating about the feelings or state of mind which prompted him to write. On each of these questions the satirists have provided a certain amount of evidence. But this must be checked where possible against the testimony of other writers and, more important, against the poems themselves. Where there is conflict, or apparent conflict, the critic must pause. He may, of course, obtain clarification from commentaries and articles, but he will find (particularly in the case of Juvenal) that on some of the central issues there has been disagreement since the Renaissance. All he can do then is to plot what seems to him the most probable path followed by the satirist within the triangle. In doing so he will discover that other readers have produced rather different diagrams, and his own may have to be altered on a subsequent reading.

(i) Lucilius

We all get our first impressions of Lucilius from somebody else. Horace begins by speaking of his *libertas* – the frankness with which he attacked wrong-doers (1.4.5) – and later he pictures him tearing away people's disguises (2.1.64-5) and denouncing the whole community tribe by tribe (2.1.69). Persius says he bit the city, breaking his molar on Lupus and Mucius (1.114-5). To Juvenal he is the great son of Aurunca who drove his team across the plain (1.19-20) and went roaring through the city, sword in hand (1.165-6). After looking at the fragments we realise that these pictures are incomplete and arise in part from a polemical or rhetorical context. In justifying their work the three later satirists are claiming the right to criticise others, and are appealing to Lucilius, the inventor of the genre, as their great exemplar: 'Look at what he did; surely I can do something too.' Fair enough, but *libertas* was not Lucilius' only quality. Other writers, including Horace, admired his wit, his learning, his easy way of talking about himself.[1] Some even admired his style.[2] Nevertheless, it is natural to start with his censorious ridicule, for that element in his work not only gave *satura* a new meaning but also appeared increasingly remarkable as memories of the free republic faded.[3]

In 131 B.C. Scipio Aemilianus was trapped by a fiendishly clever question from the tribune C. Papirius Carbo. 'What is your opinion,' asked Carbo, 'about the death of Tiberius Gracchus?' Scipio tried to hedge: 'If he intended to seize control of the state, I think he deserved to die.' The crowd fastened on the last four words and roared its disapproval.[4] Later, when the *comitia tributa* met to appoint a general to deal with the rebellion of Aristonicus in the east, there was a heavy majority in favour of P. Licinius Crassus Mucianus, the father-in-law of Gaius Gracchus. Only two of the thirty-five tribes voted for Scipio, in spite of his recent victory at Numantia. Cichorius (336) surmises that, in anger at his friend's defeat, Lucilius proceeded to arraign each tribe in turn, starting from the Papirian: *prima Papiria Tusculidarum* (1132) 'first the Papirian tribe of the Tusculans', and then going on to the Ufentine:

---

[1] See Cicero, *De Orat.* 1.72; Horace 1.4.1-6; Quintilian 10.1.94.

[2] Varro in Gellius 6.14.6; Fronto, Loeb vol. 2, 48.

[3] *Satura* (stressed on the first syllable) was originally a dish full of first fruits offered to the gods, or else a kind of stuffing with various ingredients. It then acquired the meaning 'medley' as in the *saturae* of Ennius and Pacuvius. See Van Rooy, ch. 1 and Coffey, ch. 2. The existence of stage medleys (Livy 7.2) is a matter of dispute. Knoche (9-11) and Coffey (18-21) are sceptical; I tend towards belief (Penguin trans. of Horace's *Satires* and *Epistles*, 10); so also Jocelyn (2.13).

[4] See Cicero, *De Orat.* 2.106 and the other sources cited by Astin, 264-5.

Priuerno Oufentina uenit fluuioque Oufente (1133)

The Ufentine tribe comes from Privernum and the river Ufens.

Whether or not this clever conjecture is right, it is certain that Lucilius attacked the tribes, singling out the foremost men in each: *primores populi arripuit populumque tributim*, says Horace (2.1.69), adding that he showed indulgence only to Excellence and its friends: *scilicet uni aequus Virtuti atque eius amicis* (2.1.70). *Virtus* is surely a reference to Scipio; this is confirmed two lines later by the phrase *uirtus Scipiadae* 'the excellent Scipio'. The association was encouraged by Scipio himself, who built a temple to *Virtus*.[5] A few of Scipio's enemies appear in the fragments; their names will be mentioned in the next chapter. Here we need only note that Roman political quarrels were usually conducted in terms of moral vituperation. This should be borne in mind when we read in Horace that Lucilius branded crooks, thieves, rakes, and cut-throats (1.4.1-5). No doubt in many cases their chief offence was to have opposed *Virtus*.

With the luxurious dinner-parties of the auctioneers Gallonius (203-7) and Granius (448-9 and before 595) we seem to be moving away from political attacks. Yet Gallonius presumably had public figures at his table, and we know that Granius entertained L. Licinius Crassus, who was tribune of the plebs in 107 B.C. It is likely that a role in public life was also played by the unappealing L. Trebellius, who *arcessit febris senium uomitum pus* (532) 'brings on fever moroseness retching and pus'. Other victims are even more shadowy, since their names are not preserved, e.g. *sacer ille tocoglyphos ac Syrophoenix* (540) 'that cursed scrooge of a Syrophoenician', *carcer uix carcere dignus* (1176) 'a jailbird for whom the cage is almost too good', or the man addressed as *senium atque insulse sophista* (1210) 'you dotard, you witless quibbler'. But whatever their identity, they all serve to illustrate the range of the satirist's abuse.

Another of Lucilius' targets was literary: the grand style of epic and tragedy, or at least the faults of that style. According to Aulus Gellius (17.21.49), he was well known for his satirical comments, and his activity as a critic is acknowledged by the scholiasts on Horace and Persius.[6] One, rather trivial, example is the remark he made about Ennius' line

sparsis hastis longis campus splendet et horret (*Scipio* 6, *ROL* 1, 396)

The plain, with long spears scattered upon it, shines and bristles.

The phrase *campus horret* was a reminiscence of Homer's *ephrixen de*

---

[5] See Plutarch, *De Fortuna Romanorum* 5 (*Moralia*, Loeb vol. 4).

[6] See Porphyrio's note on Horace 1.10.53; the *Life* of Persius (Suetonius, vol. 2.499); Pliny the elder said Lucilius was the first critic of style: *primus condidit stili nasum* (*NH. praef.* 7).

machê (*Il.* 13.339) 'The battle-line bristled'. That did not deter Lucilius. He fastened on *horret* which often meant 'shivers with cold', and suggested that Ennius ought to have written *horret et alget* 'shivers and freezes'.[7] This carried the further implication that the line was *frigidus*, i.e. flat and tasteless. In general, however, Lucilius used epic more as an *instrument* of satire, and so additional examples will be reserved for Chapter Two. He seems to have been rather harder on tragedy, perhaps because it was a more public genre and more high-flown in its diction. A few fragments are drawn from Ennius' *Thyestes* and have to do with the curses called down by Thyestes on his brother Atreus: may he not be blessed with favourable breezes (882-3) but suffer shipwreck

> *latere pendens saxa spargens tabo sanie et sanguine atro* (885)

> hang by his flank and spatter the rocks with serum, pus, and blackish blood –

a clear case of verbal over-kill; for, as Cicero points out (*Tusc.* 1.107), Atreus was already drowned and so would not have felt these agonies. Pacuvius fared no better. Apart from a reference to his contorted prologues (879) we have fragments from parodies of his *Chryses* (880), his *Armorum Iudicium* (731-4), and his *Antiopa*. The last-named heroine is described as

> *squalitate summa ac scabie summa in aerumna obrutam,*
> *neque inimicis inuidiosam, neque amico exoptabilem* (729-30)

> crushed by appalling filth and eczema, and in appalling misery,
> not resented by her enemies, not sought after by her friends.

Another character in need of soap and water was, perhaps, Telephus in Accius' play of that name:

> *hic cruciatur fame*
> *frigore inluuie inbalnitie inperfunditie incuria* (727-8)

> He is tortured by uncleanliness
> hunger cold unbathfulness unwashfulness uncaredforness.

There may also have been a more personal element in the gibes at Accius. One refers to his size: *qua re pro facie pro statura Accius* (844). According to the elder Pliny (*NH* 34.19), Accius was rather short. So Lucilius may have contrasted his height with his style. Alternatively, the contrast m ıy have been with the large statue, also mentioned by Pliny, which Accius placed in the temple of the Muses. In any case we do have a little to confirm what the ancients say about Lucilius' criticisms of tragedy.

---

[7] Lucilius, 413. For Ennius' metre see Jocelyn (1) 146-9.

There are also some fragments which can be construed as being part of a controversy between Lucilius and one or more tragic poets.[8] Perhaps Lucilius claimed that, since such writers had their ideas upside down, to them the low style was something 'strange and monstrificacious': *nunc ignobilitas his mirum ac monstrificabile* (726). The writers perhaps reply that by composing tragedies they wanted to win the public's esteem (720-1).[9] Lucilius:

> *nisi portenta anguisque uolucris ac pinnatos scribitis* (723)

> [You think you cannot win esteem]
> save you write of prodigies and winged serpents in the air.

The two sides have incompatible tastes. Lucilius:

> *ut ego effugiam quod te in primis cupere apisci intellego* (702)

> so I shun what you, I gather, are most eager to attain.

Opponent:

> *et quod tibi magno opere cordi est mihi uehementer displicet* (701)

> and what you so greatly cherish I emphatically dislike.

Lucilius:

> *summis nitere opibus, et ego contra ut dissimilis siem* (703)

> You press on, but I shall strive to be as different as I can.

In spite of this interchange, one doubts if there was much real harshness in Lucilius' criticisms of tragedy. Rather than drawing moral conclusions (as Persius did) from its turgid style, he probably poked fun at it for taking itself too seriously. Like Aristophanes before him, he obviously enjoyed writing parodies, and whatever he may have said about the unpretentious style of his own *sermones*, he clearly admired the tragedians for their verbal audacity. Some of his comic fragments, too, are a long way from the level of conversation. In their exuberance and fantasy they recall the high spirits of Plautus.

In other passages Lucilius seems to have conducted a much more general kind of attack. One thinks of the lines on superstition (524-9):

---

[8] See Krenkel (1) 193-200; Christes 103-40.

[9] Frag. 721 reads *uoluimus capere animum illorum*; but the text of 720 is unclear, and the meaning of the fragment as a whole is uncertain; see Christes, 123.

As for the goblins and witches established by Fauns and by humans
like Numa Pompilius, he dreads them and thinks them all-important.
As children believe that bronze statues are all alive
and men, those people think that products of fancy are real;
they believe that bronze statues contain a living intelligence.
A picture gallery, nothing real, each thing a figment,

or of the squalid miser (278-81):

One who has neither beast nor slave nor any companion;
he keeps his bag, and whatever cash he has, beside him;
he eats sleeps and washes with his bag; the fellow's possessions
are all in a single bag; the bag is tied to his arm,

or of the lively fragment on the rat-race (1145-51):

But as it is, from dawn to dusk, on feast-days and work-days,
the whole community together, people and senate alike,
mill about in the city square and never leave it.
They all engage in one and the same craft and endeavour –
to cheat with the maximum cunning, fight with the utmost guile,
compete in charming words, pretending they're excellent fellows,
and laying traps as if they were all each other's foes.

The purpose of such writing was, in a broad sense, moral; and this moves
it in the direction of apex (c). The longest passage of this kind is the
definition of *uirtus* (1196-1208):

Excellence is, my dear Albinus, being ready to pay
what is truly due in our business dealings and daily life;
excellence is knowing what every issue involves for a person;
excellence is knowing what is right, useful, and noble for a person;
what is good and bad, what is useless, wrong, and disgraceful;
excellence is knowing the end and limit of acquiring possessions;
excellence is being prepared to pay what is due to wealth;
excellence is giving what in actual fact is owed to honour,
being a foe and opponent of wicked men and behaviour,
a staunch defender, however, of good men and behaviour,
prizing the latter, wishing them well, and showing them friendship;
it means, moreover, putting our fatherland's interests first,
then those of our parents, and thirdly and lastly our own.[10]

Clearly, then, Lucilius enjoyed preaching. But however salutary his
aims may have been, he inevitably made enemies – not just among his
victims, but among those who regarded him as a busybody, a

---

[10] Albinus cannot be identified with any certainty, and we do not know whether he was
being exhorted or admonished. Whatever the context, there is nothing in the passage itself
to suggest that it is anything other than a straightforward Stoic affirmation.

scandal-monger, and a conceited prig. Some of these feelings are represented in fragments of Book 30:

> *nunc, Gai, quoniam incilans nos laedis, uicissim* (1075)

Now, Gaius, because you abuse and wound us, in turn ...

> *quid tu istuc curas ubi ego oblinar atque uoluter?* (1082)

What business is it of yours where I wallow and roll?

> *quid seruas quo eam, quid agam? quid id attinet ad te?* (1083)

Why do you watch where I go, what I'm doing? What's that to you?

> *gaudes cum de me ista foris sermonibus differs* (1085)

You enjoy spreading abroad in your talks those tales about me

> *et maledicendo in multis sermonibus differs* (1086)

and in your libellous talks you often tear me to pieces

> *quin totum purges deuellas me atque deuras*
> *exultes et sollicites* (1088-9)

[It seems nothing can stop you]
from totally cleaning me, plucking me smooth, singeing me bare,
jumping upon me, tormenting me.

In the face of such criticism two courses were open. The first was to do nothing. ('Never apologise, never explain.') The second was to offer some kind of justification. Merely by recording the complaints Lucilius had committed himself to the second. What he actually said is less easy to determine. One argument, probably, was that in every society there are some rotten people who deserve to be exposed (cf. Horace 1.4.25ff.):

> *hic in stercore humi fabulisque fimo atque sucerdis* (1081)

He in the dung on the ground, in the goat-turds, shit and pig-muck.

Another, probably, was that if the critic lived a good life he was out of the satirist's reach (cf. Horace 1.4.67-8):

> *nolito tibi me male dicere posse putare* (1069)

You mustn't imagine that I possess the power to defame you.

Another was to accuse the critic of wanting to whitewash everything:

> *omnes formonsi fortes tibi, ego improbus; esto* (1077)

To you everyone's fine and brave; I am a villain.
Very well ...

Another, possibly, was that when a citizen committed some minor misdemeanour Lucilius was not the sort to fly at him with teeth bared, glaring like a dog:

> *inde canino rictu oculisque*
> *inuolem* (1000-1).[11]

Another, possibly, was that the really dangerous person was someone on close terms with the critic:

> *quem scis scire tuas omnes maculasque notasque* (1070)

who, as you know, has knowledge of all your stains and blemishes.

Another, probably, was that the critic was simply jealous of Lucilius' success:

> *et sua perciperet retro rellicta iacere* (1090)

perceiving his own creations were ignored and cast aside,

> *et sola ex multis nunc nostra poemata ferri* (1091)

whereas mine alone, of the many produced, were now in demand.

These defences can, with varying degrees of plausibility, be inferred from the fragments. There is nothing to show, however, that they were all employed on the same occasion.

There were some areas of Lucilius' work in which satire seems to have played at the most a minor role. We know he took a keen interest in language and dealt, at least in passing, with usage (398-400: distinguish *intro* from *intus* and *apud* from *ad*), vocabulary (after 1141; avoid dialect words), accent (232: rustic pronunciations are laughable), etymology (1215: praetors precede; 1271: *uita* is a *uis*), and rhythm (after 412: final monosyllables are only permissible when they refer to small animals). Other topics were treated at greater length. Some words were acknowledged to be musical (after 418); some sounds were ugly, e.g. the letter 'r', which resembled the snarl of a dog (389). Accius had written about orthography, recommending that a long 'a' should be represented by 'aa' and 'ng' by 'gg'; that 'y' and 'z' should be abandoned; and that Greek names should always be spelt in the Greek form (*ROL* 2, xxii-iv). Lucilius rejected the first suggestion (369-72), and probably ignored the others. But he did advance some ideas of his own (with what degree of seriousness we cannot tell), proposing, e.g., that the nominative plural of *puer* should be spelt *puerei* to distinguish it from the genitive singular

---

[11] Cf. Ennius, *Sat.* 22; or Lucilius may be saying that when he sees a crime he behaves like a good watch-dog.

(377-9). Lucilius also dealt with certain technical terms of literary criticism, e.g. the difference between *poema* (either a short poem or part of a long one) and *poesis* (a long work seen as a whole, like the *Iliad* or the *Annals*).[12] He discussed the choice and arrangement of words (417-18) and the shape of dramatic programmes (414-15). And several fragments suggest that his pronouncements on literary forms and styles were firmly based on historical scholarship. So we can begin to see why Cicero and Quintilian both admired the satirist's learning. But he was certainly no cloistered intellectual. He aired his opinions freely on a wide range of practical subjects. Frag. 149 and perhaps 150-1 give information about constructing a bed; 678-87 describes the diagnosis and treatment of an illness; in 1053-7 advice is offered to someone setting up house: he must engage various kinds of staff, including weavers and a bakeress; and several fragments reveal an interest in horseflesh, e.g. 511-13:

> A clattering jolter bred in Campania may get the better
> of this one over a mile or two, but will never hold him
> in a longer race; he'll look as if he's galloping backwards.[13]

It is a fair guess, however, that the largest proportion of Lucilius' work was designed primarily to entertain, and was therefore situated in the neighbourhood of apex (b). Such entertainment took many forms – fables, anecdotes, comic scenes. Just occasionally we gatch a glimpse of their liveliness, as in the pre-fight interview with Pacideianus, who in his day was 'The Greatest' (174-5):

> 'I'll darned well kill him,' he said, 'and win the fight, I can tell you.
> But I guess it'll be like this: I'll take it first on the face;
> then I'll sink my sword in the dummy's belly and lungs.
> I hate the guy; it's a grudge fight; we don't mean to hang round –
> just long enough for one of us to get his sword in his hand.
> I hate the fellow's guts and can't wait to get at him (176-81).'

For Lucilius life did not always have to be criticised or interpreted; it could simply be observed in all its fascinating variety. It could also be lived, as we see from his report of a journey south in Book 3.[14] Some of the fragments will be quoted later; here it is enough to note a few of the main features: e.g., a drive down the Via Appia to Capua, a row round Cape Palinurus in the middle of the night, and the crossing to Sicily. We hear of steep hills, muddy roads, and heavily-laden horses; we glimpse an encounter between two gladiators and overhear some colourful abuse; we are told of an inn with a Syrian hostess and miserable food; and most

---

[12] 401-10. See Greenberg, 263-89; Brink (1), index p. 293.
[13] Cf. 152-5; 343-4; 505-6.
[14] For a discussion of Lucilius' journey see Fiske, 306-16.

spectacular of all, we hear of Stromboli erupting at night. As far as we know, this verse-diary had no precedent in Greek or Latin. Just as new, in a Roman context, were Lucilius' poems about girls, which will be discussed in Chapter Six. One fragment (898-9) implies an unwelcome interruption in the middle of a love-scene. If the victim was Lucilius himself that would have been quite characteristic, for he took a comic view of sex, and in general was not afraid to recount his own misfortunes (Horace, 2.1.31). The same ironic objectivity is seen in 929-30:

> *amicos hodie cum inprobo illo audiuimus*
> *Lucilio aduocasse*

> We hear your dinner-guests today include
> that awful man, Lucilius.

In another passage the poet has been ill but is now well enough to remonstrate with a friend for not coming to see him. The lines begin thus:

> *quo me habeam pacto, tam etsi non quaeris, docebo,*
> *quando in eo numero mansi quo in maxima non est*
> *pars hominum* (186-8)

> I'll tell you how I am, although you never enquire,
> since I'm still in the group to which the great majority
> do not belong.

As a final illustration we will take a fragment in which, after complaining about his finances and the condition of his estates, he resigns himself to being what he is – the alternatives are worse:

> *publicanus uero ut Asiae fiam, ut scripturarius*
> *pro Lucilio, id ego nolo et uno hoc non muto omnia* (650-1)

> Me, become a tax-collector, farming Asian revenues
> rather than Lucilius? Never! That's one thing I will not change.

The aim of such writing, then, was to entertain. But these fragments are so dominated by Lucilius' personality that one also looks for a psychological motive. And that surely is to be found in the exuberant ego of the poet himself. He felt, quite rightly, that someone as interesting as he was should be made known to the world at large. No doubt if we had more material we could make proper allowance for his comic inventiveness; it would also be strange if the more personal satires were never one-sided or tendentious. Nevertheless, no Roman had put so much of himself into his writings, and Horace's enthusiastic exaggeration is wholly understandable:

ille uelut fidis arcana sodalibus olim
credebat libris neque, si male cesserat, usquam
decurrens alio neque, si bene; quo fit ut omnis
uotiua pateat ueluti descripta tabella
uita senis (2.1.30-4)

He in the past would confide intimate facts to his books
which he trusted like friends; and whether things went well or badly,
he'd always turn to them. So the whole of the old man's life
is laid before us as if it were painted on a votive tablet.

The concluding words formed an apt motto for Boswell's *Life of Johnson*.

(ii) Horace

Qui fit, Maecenas – how is it, Maecenas, that people envy each other's
occupations; make themselves miserable through greed; ruin themselves
by extravagance, gluttony, and sexual infatuation; frighten themselves
by superstition; and wear themselves out in the pursuit of power and
prestige? How very silly it all is!

It is here, in the perception of human incongruities, that we find the
roots of Horatian satire. Happiness, as most people acknowledged, was
the common goal of man. But one had only to look around to see that
happiness was not ensured by wealth, power, or social status. Therefore
the frantic pursuit of those ends must be due to a misconception; it was
in some way irrational. But to call it irrational suggested that it ought to
be amenable to reason. And so, to an extent, it was. Sensible behaviour,
in Horace's view, could be learned – by obeying one's parents (1.4.105ff.),
by listening to the advice of candid friends (1.4.132), by observing other
people's faults (1.4.109ff.), by introspection (1.4.133ff.), and by reading
the right books (*E.* 1.1.34ff.). One sort of book was that which called
attention to men's follies and vices. But simple sermons, however well
meant, were not enough. They had to be readable, and that called for
style and wit. In 1.1.25-6 Horace compares his homilies to the biscuits
(*crustula*) by which children are taught their ABC (*elementa*). It is a
splendid simile; for *elementa* means not only the letters of the alphabet
but also the basic principles of an art (most generally the art of living);
and the *crustula* are not simply rewards for learning the letters; they *are*
the letters. The teaching (the *utile*) and the pleasing (the *dulce*) are parts
of the same process.[1]

One has to be clear about the didactic function; for in recent times
there has been an attempt to persuade us that Horace had no intention of
influencing behaviour: he chose to write about ethics because that was a

---

[1] The Lucretian idea of smearing the bitter cup of philosophy with the honey of poetry
(*DRN* 4.11-22) is no less subtle; for what the reader imbibes is an atomic mixture of the
wholesome and the sweet.

subject of great variety and interest, and one on which he could produce lively amusing verse; he did not expect to modify our attitudes or make us better, any more than he hoped to make us all poets by writing the *Ars Poetica*. That view has a certain attraction in our own age, when so many educated people want to deny that art has any effect on behaviour; but it runs counter to several of Horace's own statements. We have just referred to a passage of 1.1 which sets the tone for the *Satires*. Another passage, also about *elementa*, prepares us for the *Epistles*:

> *restat ut his ego me ipse regam solerque elementis* (*E.* 1.1.27)
>
> For the present I'll find guidance and comfort in these principles.

This does not mean that Horace aspired to anything so pompous as 'reforming society'. All his homilies could do was to sharpen the reader's moral awareness, and (who knows?) that might eventually modify his conduct. There was no question of converting people to a supernatural religion with a divine leader who promised personal immortality. Even the earthly commandment 'Love thy neighbour' implied a different emphasis. For the wisdom affirmed by Horace (and by more thoroughgoing ancient philosophers) was based, not on altruism, but on enlightened self-interest. A life dedicated to making money, he argued, was in the end a poor one; power involved constant effort and was inseparable from danger; glory was vain and transitory; romantic infatuation brought ruin, disgrace, and sometimes death. One should therefore set a limit to desire and ambition, and study the things that really mattered, like friendship, poetry and ethics.

But now we are in danger of forgetting that the homilies are satires. While the positive text is clear enough, the sermon is largely focussed on what *not* to do. The examples held up for our inspection are *exempla stultitiae*, human nature in all its short-sightedness and perversity. As many of the *exempla* are named, this involves a degree of aggressiveness. Granted, the figures concerned do not constitute the reason for the satire. Unlike some of Lucilius' victims, they and their shortcomings are rarely given more than a couple of lines, and they function mainly as illustrations of the argument. They are seldom people of any importance in public life, which is another point of contrast with Lucilius. Nevertheless, Horace's misers, spendthrifts, careerists, gluttons, and debauchees are subjected to ridicule; and this accounts for much of our pleasure, for we enjoy seeing our fellow-creatures depicted as fools. At the same time Horace hoped that at least occasionally, when we caught ourselves smiling, we would pause and listen to an inner voice which murmured *de te fabula narratur* 'You are the subject of the story' (1.1.69-70). The following passage will illustrate his manner:

Richman, a poor fellow in spite of his hoard of silver
and gold, would drink on holidays coarse Veientine wine
from a Campanian mug; his normal drink was fermented must.
Once he was sunk in so deep a coma that his heir had already
grabbed the keys and was prancing delightedly round his coffers.
The doctor, who was a quick thinker and a loyal friend,
revived him so: he had a table brought in and some bags of coins
poured on top of it; then he asked some people to come
and count them. Bringing the patient to, he added 'If you don't
look after your property, your greedy heir will make off with the lot!'
'Over my dead body!'
                          'Wake up then and live. Now here –'
'What's this?'
                          'You're weak. Your pulse is low, and your whole system
will collapse if it's not sustained by food and a strong tonic.
What are you waiting for? Come on, take a sip of this rice gruel.'
'How much was it?'
                          'Not much.'
                                        'Well *how* much?'
                                                       'Tuppence.'
                                                                  'Ah dear!
What matter whether I die from illness or from theft and pillage' (2.3.142-57).

That little scene (at least in the original) exhibits the kind of wit which
Cicero describes as *aequabiliter in omni sermoni fusum* 'evenly
distributed throughout a speech' (*De Orat*. 2.218). It is, he says, a natural
gift, possessed by good mimics and raconteurs. And no doubt when
Horace read that passage he used an appropriate voice for the man who
found the cost of living too high. If, then, we think once more of our
satirical triangle, we will probably want to place Horace's *sermones*
about half way between (b) entertainment and (c) preaching, and about
a third of the way up towards (a) attack, though some of the pieces, like
1.2 and 2.5 would go higher.

What has been said so far applies mainly to the homilies or diatribes.
Those are the poems by which Horatian satire must in the end be judged.
But there are other, slighter, pieces where much the most important
function is to entertain. Sometimes Horace indicates his intention quite
clearly. *Sat*. 1.7 (Rex v. Persius) is introduced as an amusing anecdote –
the story is known in all the barbers' shops. That, indeed, is the simplest
case. There is no moral message. The incident took place several years
before and in another country. The punch-line, though doubtless less
feeble in the year after Caesar's death, carried little political resonance
when it was published in 35 B.C. The poem's main justification lies in the
clever mock-heroic style. In 1.8 the intention again is comic:

Once I was the trunk of a fig-tree, a useless lump of wood.
Then the carpenter, wondering whether to make a bench or a Priapus,
decided I should be a god. So a god I am.

Here one may also infer other, secondary, purposes – to ridicule superstition, to amuse Maecenas, and perhaps even to annoy the woman (or type of woman) who lay behind Canidia. Both 1.5 (the journey to Brundisium) and 1.9 (the encounter with the pest) tell us something about Horace's relations with his powerful friends; 2.4 (the disquisition of Catius) is a satire on gastronomy, and 2.8 (Nasidienus' dinner-party) exposes the vulgarity of a *nouveau riche*. But in all these cases the humorous element predominates.

The literary pieces (1.4, 1.10, 2.1) are best treated together. They have a moral purpose in so far as they deal with the spirit and function of satire; and they are didactic in as much as they aim to create a taste receptive to Horace's new, classical, way of writing. They are also entertaining in characteristically Horatian ways. But since they are satires, they proceed by criticising the work of predecessors and contemporaries. That will be our concern here.

At the outset we note that nearly all the assertions are made from a defensive position. This usually leads to ironic exaggeration or understatement. In 1.10.40-8, for instance, Horace says Fundanius was writing comedies, Pollio tragedies, Varius epic, and Virgil pastoral; satire was the one genre capable of improvement; so he chose satire. At first, perhaps, we imagine him trying a series of literary compartments and, with mounting exasperation, finding each one occupied. But things can hardly have happened quite like that. The main function of the lines, apart from paying a compliment to the poet's friends, is to make it clear that *aemulatio* was an important factor in Horace's decision:

> *hoc erat, experto frustra Varrone Atacino*
> *atque quibusdam aliis, melius quod scribere possem*

> This form had been tried by Varro of Atax and others
> without success and was therefore one which I could develop.

Horace's contribution turned out not to be a development in the sense, say, that Virgil's *Eclogues* were a development of Theocritus' *Idylls*. It rather took the form of an artistic refinement. Lucilius had blazed the trail and cleared the ground; Horace was the cultivator. As Cicero said, *nihil est simul et inuentum et perfectum* (*Brutus*, 71), 'Nothing is brought to perfection at the time of its discovery'.

At the beginning his path was not smooth. To judge from 1.4.91-3, his early piece (1.2) had caused a certain amount of offence (Rudd, 1). It is easy to imagine some people, after reading stray copies of that bawdy and personal satire, saying 'Who does this fellow think he is?' At any rate a defence was presented in 1.4 along the following lines: Old Comedy and Lucilius branded criminals (1-7); unlike Crispinus, I write very little (13-8); unlike Fannius, I do not seek publicity (21-3); the innocent have nothing to fear (67-8); real malice is backbiting one's friends (81-103); I was taught to notice wicked behaviour by my father; he used individuals as examples of vice (103-31); I am really quite a good-humoured fellow (91-2, 103-4); my observations are just amusing exercises for my own improvement (137-9). These arguments are not wholly consistent with one another, but they are engagingly presented. Horace uses every means to assure his readers that he has no intention of becoming a scurrilous libeller. At the same time he avoids any promise that he will refrain from attacking his fellow-citizens in future. That would have meant abandoning satire altogether.

In justifying his own satire Horace made some derogatory remarks about Lucilius' style:

> As a *tour de force* he would often
> dictate two hundred lines an hour standing on his head.
> He was a muddy river with a lot of stuff that should have been removed.
> A man of many words, he disliked the effort of writing –
> writing properly, that is; I don't care a hoot for quantity.

Lucilius' admirers objected to this, and so Horace wrote again, stating his position more clearly:

> True, I did say that Lucilius' verses lurched
> awkwardly along. Which of his admirers is so perverse
> as not to admit it? But he is also praised on the same page
> for scouring the city with caustic wit. While granting him this,
> however, I cannot allow the rest as well, for then
> I should have to admire Laberius' mimes for their poetic beauty (1.10.1-6).

Decimus Laberius, a writer of mimes or farces, had died a few years before, in 43 B.C. According to Macrobius (*Sat.* 2.7.2) he was a sharply outspoken man (*asperae libertatis*); Aulus Gellius gives examples of his recklessness in coining new words and forms (16.7); and a fragment of his *Lacus Auernus* may indicate indifference to qualities of rhythm: *uersorum non numerorum numero studuimus.*[2] So, like Crispinus and Fannius in 1.4, and Cassius the Etruscan in 1.10, Laberius provides a more recent and unfavourable illustration of Lucilius' characteristics – in this case his stylistic irresponsibility, and perhaps by implication his coarseness. For Gellius also mentions Laberius' obscenity, and when Horace goes on to say

> *ergo non satis est risu diducere rictum*
> *auditoris*

> So it's not enough to make your listener bare his teeth
> in a grin,

[2] Bonaria, vol. 1, 47.

it is hard not to think that he has in mind the vulgarity of the mime as well as its undisciplined style.

A little later on, after deprecating the excessive use of Greek, Horace repeats and amplifies his remarks about Lucilius' prolixity:

> But I said he was a muddy river and that in the stuff he brought down
> there was often more to be removed than retained ...
> ... he resembles a man whose only concern is to force
> words into a framework of six feet, and who gaily produces
> two hundred lines before dinner and as many after (1.10.50-4).

A possible defence of Lucilius was to say that he had written to satisfy the tastes of his own age. Horace grants that; but with the confidence of an artist writing in a classical period he asserts that modern standards are superior; Lucilius would not get away with such carelessness now:

> ... If fate had postponed his birth till our own day,
> he would file his work drastically down and prune whatever
> rambled beyond the proper limit, and in shaping his verses
> he would often scratch his head and nibble his nails to the quick
> (1.10.68-71).

An attempt has been made elsewhere to illustrate these criticisms with the aid of the fragments.[3] Here we need only refer to the lines on *uirtus* quoted earlier (p. 6). While the vocabulary is unexceptionable, Horace would not have approved of *uirtus ... uirtus* reiterated *ad nauseam*; he would have marked lines 5 and 10 as otiose, and removed all those monotonous effects of rhyme and alliteration; he would also have got rid of the archaic *potesse* (2), *re* (6) and *patriai* (12) and reduced the number of elisions in v.9.

Among Lucilius' admirers was a small group of literary men who favoured the Alexandrian manner established in the previous generation by Calvus and Catullus. These men are slightingly mentioned in 1.10, but in view of their critical stance it will be more convenient to consider them in Chapter Five. One other poet, however, should be noted here. He is designated by the nickname Alpinus in a passage which provides a transition between Horace's misguided attempts at Greek and Fundanius' Latin comedies:[4]

> So while the turgid Alpman murders Memnon and plasters
> the head of the Rhine with mud, I write these entertainments
> which will never ring out in the hall where Tarpa judges the entries,
> nor be revived again and again for a theatre audience (1.10.36-9).

[3] Rudd (2), 97-118.
[4] The Alpman is naturally identified with the Furius of 2.5.40-1. Whether this Furius is the same as Furius Bibaculus remains uncertain; see Bardon, vol. 1, 347-53 and 363-6; Rudd (2), 289-90.

The first of these poems was a Latin version of the story treated by Arctinus in his *Aethiopis*; it told how the African Memnon, who had come to fight on Priam's side, was slain by Achilles. To Horace another cyclic poem was a tedious irrelevance, and this one, it seems, was undistinguished. Nothing certain is known about the Rhine epic, but the gibe certainly implies that the verse was muddy – a quality it shared with Lucilius' satires and the effusions of Cassius (60-4).

Unlike Lucilius, then, Horace makes few criticisms of recent poetry. Although his own preferences at this stage were for iambic and satire, he could speak with approval of Pollio's tragedy and Varius' epic (1.10.42-4). Later on, in view of what Virgil had accomplished in the *Aeneid*, he could describe the authentic poem as 'flowing strong and clear, like an unpolluted river' (*E.* 2.2.120).

In 2.1 Horace discusses for the last time his motives in writing satire. Earlier he had hinted at the labour and frustration of composing (1.10.70-1); here he admits it is a pleasure: *me pedibus delectat claudere uerba* (28). The admission is made in five words of casual understatement – as if Mozart had remarked that he enjoyed putting notes between bars. But it contains, of course, a central truth about Horace's motives. And when in other passages he decries various forms of effort and recommends a life of ease and serenity, we should not forget that for him this leisure included the arduous pleasures of creating poetry.

Since by now most of the book had been finished he knew there was little danger of causing offence; so the elaborate consultation with the lawyer Trebatius is something of a charade. Lucilius recurs again at strategic points of the argument: he was the first satirist (62-3); he attacked important figures without embarrassing his friends (64-70); and he wrote engagingly about his private life (30-4). Horace had always been aware of this last point; no doubt it was partly Lucilius' example that helped him to make poetry out of his own experiences. But in reading the personal sections of the *sermones* we have to use our common sense. Total credulity and total rejection are equally naive. When, in a non-dramatic context, Horace makes a statement about people or events in his life, we are not justified in dismissing it as fiction. Yet it seems clear that in every case the autobiographical material has been selected and processed so as to serve a poetic or rhetorical purpose. The description of his father's teaching in 1.4.105ff. may well owe something to Terence's *Adelphi*.[5] But to say that the method of Horace senior was for all the world like that of stern old Demea does not imply that the later passage is a mere fabrication. By supplying a gentle comic framework the allusion actually enhances our sense of reality. Still, the glimpses of

---

[5] In Terence, *Adelphi* 414ff. Demea describes how he trains his son: 'I tell him to look into everybody's life as into a mirror and to draw from others an example for himself.'

Horace's father are very fleeting. We do not hear where he came from, what he looked like, or what kind of home he provided. And surely he must occasionally have laughed? Alas, such speculations are irrelevant; for the character is included primarily for the sake of the argument. That is, he provides one further excuse for Horace's habit of criticising his fellow men. In 1.6 he is used for another rhetorical purpose: to substantiate the claim that the poet, although from a humble background, has been decently brought up and given an excellent education.

In regard to Horace's feelings and opinions, as distinct from people and events in his life, the question of 'reality' becomes more difficult. Yet the same sort of approach seems right. When, for example, in an early satire Horace tells us that he likes easy and available sex (1.2.119), how literally do we take him? To a young Roman male, abstinence seemed unnecessary, but the seduction of citizens' wives and daughters was dangerous and anti-social; so occasional recourse to the demi-monde seemed the obvious answer. That does not mean, however, that Horace's relations with girls were conducted with the crass cynicism described in 1.2. What Horace has done is to select an element or aspect of his real personality and adjust it to the requirements of the context, in this case a diatribe against adulterous affairs. A different, more sensitive, attitude is projected in the *Odes*.

Since, in delivering his homilies, Horace did not wear special regalia or speak from a pulpit, there was always the risk of someone saying 'What about yourself?'. This problem was met head on in 1.3, where Horace admitted his own defects and then turned the poem into a plea for tolerance. But that device could not be used again. Also Horace wanted to extend the range of his *sermones*, and this could not be done as long as the preacher was likely to be identified with Q. Horatius Flaccus. So in 2.2 he gave the discourse on the simple life to Ofellus, confining himself to a few comments at the end. In 2.4 he became the respectful listener, allowing Catius to make himself ridiculous by his disquisition on gastronomy. In 2.6 the country mouse wins the day, a victory which may have been decisive for the narrator Cervius, but hardly for Horace. In 2.3 and 2.7 the procedure of the earlier diatribes is reversed; instead of delivering the homily, the poet becomes the butt of an attack, first from an earnest Stoic and then from a dangerously outspoken slave. We must therefore allow for some comic exaggeration. In 2.8 it is Fundanius the playwright who describes Nasidienus' dinner-party; Horace merely sets the account in motion and offers a prompt later on. Perhaps he felt that laughter at an upstart would not have come well from the son of a freedman. In 2.5 he has withdrawn altogether; the moral conclusions are left to emerge obliquely from the conversation in Hades.

By the time he came to write the *Epistles* Horace's chief aim was no longer to satirise vice and folly. So the danger of seeming self-righteous was reduced, and the poet himself could safely return as the main speaker, functioning sometimes as the point of departure, and sometimes as a focus, for the ethical discussion. The context of the discussion is friendship, and the tone varies according to the age and status of the recipient. In *E.* 1.3 Horace takes a kindly interest in the young members of Tiberius' staff – are they writing and behaving as they ought? In *E.* 1.4 he compliments Tibullus on his personal qualities, reminds him of his good fortune, urges him to be cheerful, and finishes with a joke at his own expense: Horace the Epicurean pig. In *E.* 1.8 he gently warns Celsus against arrogance, after first confessing how poorly he is managing his own moral life. In *E.* 1.9 he respectfully commends Septimius to Tiberius, but only after a contorted examination of his own motives. Throughout the book Horace is either preparing to take up the study of philosophy or else is already searching for 'what is true and proper'. By his own admission he is wavering and fallible; he is receptive to other people's advice; he is never the sage.

As a final illustration of how Horace projects himself, let us consider the famous passage from *E.* 2.2 beginning *Romae nutriri mihi contigit* (41-54). The poet, it seems, has been the helpless puppet of circumstances: it happened that he was brought up in Rome, Athens made its contribution, the times uprooted him, the surge carried him into battle, Philippi discharged him, and finally Poverty compelled him to write. This amusingly ineffectual figure fails to become the subject of a single main verb. He is well-meaning enough, but his training has been of a rather rudimentary kind. At school he was given 'the essential *Iliad*' with a definite moral slant. (Anger is wrong: look at the damage done by the resentful Achilles.) Athens added a 'a little more in the way of a liberal education'. He wanted to be able to tell right from wrong (perhaps an over-simple ambition for a student of ethics), and to seek truth amidst the woods of the Academy (*inter siluas Academi quaerere uerum*). Perhaps the trees had grown again after the depredations of Sulla;[6] but whether real or figurative, a *silua* is not a place where one expects to find anything very easily. The soldier was no more impressive than the scholar – a raw recruit swept into action on the losing side. After defeat, discharge; and suddenly there was a need to earn money. The high flier had been brought down to earth with a bump. Clearly the events of 42 B.C. were a shattering experience. So why the flippant, self-depreciating tone? Because, not for the first time, Horace is in a jam. He has failed to deliver the *carmina* which he had promised to Florus, and excuses must be found. Surely the great man will appreciate that his poems have always been the product of necessity. Now that he has enough to live on, what madness it would be to spend the night pen-in-hand instead of enjoying his sleep! But of course the explanation for his inability to write

[6] Plutarch, *Sulla* 12.3. The lecturer was probably Theomnestus (Plutarch, *Brutus* 24, 1).

poetry is itself a long and immensely accomplished poem. The excerpt reminds us that the method of *ridentem dicere uerum* is not confined to the *Satires*. And, as always, to assess the *uerum* one must take account of the *risus*.

(iii) Persius

As Persius has kindly supplied a prologue to account for his 'sudden appearance on the poetic scene' (3), we expect it to tell us something about his intentions. It does not do that, but it does purport to explain his motives. Although he is not a 'proper poet', he has to write because he needs the money. This represents a clever combination of two Horatian passages: (a) the lines where, for tactical reasons, Horace disclaims the title of poet (1.4.39-41), and (b) his assertion that it was poverty that impelled him to write (*E.* 2.2.51-2). Unlike Horace, who at the time in question had lost his property and was earning a modest salary in the treasury, Persius was comfortably off. (At his early death in A.D. 62 he left a sum of two million sesterces.[1]) But it was important that poets should be poor, especially if they intended to complain about the power of money. And there was, in fact, a long-standing convention to that effect. If a poet was rich he kept quiet about it, just as it would now be a breach of decorum for a farmer to admit that he wasn't ruined.

To learn more about the satirist we move on to the scene at the beginning of 3.[2] It is 11 a.m. and a student is still asleep after a late-night drinking session. An older companion bursts in and proceeds to lecture him on his lazy habits; such behaviour, he adds, is not excused by the fact that the young man has plenty of money and is a knight from a respectable Tuscan family. These details strongly suggest that the figure of the student is a comic profile of Persius himself. This is confirmed when, after recalling his own thoughtless youth, the companion goes on to speak of the young man's familiarity with Stoicism:

> But you're no novice at spotting crooked behaviour and grasping
> the doctrines of the learned Porch with its mural of trousered Persians –
> doctrines swotted to the small hours by sleepless crew-cut
> students sustained by lentil soup and thick porridge (52-5).

A moment later, however, it becomes clear that the audience has nodded off again:

> Still snoring! Your head's lolling, neck-joints undone
> and jaws unfastened at both sides, yawning off yesterday.

---

[1] *Life* (Suetonius, vol. 2, 496).
[2] For discussion of the *mise en scène* see Jenkinson, Appendix B.

Whether or not the historical Persius was over-fond of Falernian and suffered from incapacitating hangovers, he was apparently capable of viewing his student days with a certain amount of detached amusement. Perhaps he had acquired that perspective, like so much else, from Horace.

In the first thirty lines of that opening scene all three functions of satire are well exploited. But then the companion goes on to warn the student about the terrors of remorse:

> O mighty father of the gods, when sadistic lust with its dagger
> dipped in fiery poison incites dictators to crime,
> may it please thee to punish their cruelty in this and no other way:
> let them see Goodness and waste with remorse at having betrayed her.

Though undeniably powerful,[3] those lines can hardly be regarded as satire. They are also rather lost on a congregation of one sleepy student. In vv. 66-72 the preacher again comes to the fore:

> Listen, you wretches, and learn the purpose of human existence –
> what we are, what kind of life we were born to live,
> which lane we have drawn, where we begin to turn for home,
> how much money's enough, what prayers are right, what advantage
> are crisp notes, how much should be set aside for the state
> and for your nearest and dearest; what role the Lord has asked you
> to play, what post you have been assigned in the human service.

That, however, is immediately followed by a prohibition which draws the thought back within the triangle of satire:

> Learn *this*; never mind those jars piled in a barrister's larder
> as rewards for defending some greasy Umbrians, rotting beside
> the pepper and hams ('tokens of gratitude' from a Marsian client)
> while the first tin of sardines still contains a survivor.

In other words, the proceeds of success should not be envied.

We have just looked at one autobiographical passage. The sketch presented in 5 is altogether more earnest. In a thirty-line section of almost embarrassing respect and gratitude we are told how, after assuming the *toga uirilis*, the young Persius was instructed by the philosopher Cornutus. Here is an excerpt:

---

[3] See Milton, *PL* 4.846ff.

> You lifted my tender years
> in your Socratic arms, Cornutus. With quiet dexterity
> you laid your ruler down to straighten my erratic behaviour.
> My mind struggled to submit as it felt the pressure of reason,
> and under your thumb it took on the right form and features.
> Together, I remember, we enjoyed those long and sunny days;
> together we spent the early part of the night at supper.
> The two of us planned a single scheme of work and rest,
> and relaxed our common concerns as we ate a simple meal (36-44).

Perhaps it was natural for a boy who had lost his father at the age of six to lean for support on older men. (We are told in the *Life* that he also looked on Servilius Nonianus as a father.) Yet one cannot help contrasting this cloistered and rather airless scene with the experience of the young Horace in Rome and Athens. It is also true that Horace's description of his education in 1.4 and 1.6 contributes directly to his polemical purpose, namely to vindicate himself against his detractors, whereas Persius' lines do not have that function. They nevertheless have an important place in the poem's structure. First, Cornutus and his tuition represent the point to which the first twenty lines lead up. Those are twenty lines of hard-hitting literary satire. The sequence of thought goes like this: 'Poets conventionally ask for a hundred tongues.' 'Yes, but surely your verse is of a less pretentious kind.' 'It is, but I would gladly have a hundred tongues to express my gratitude to you, Cornutus.'

The satire opens thus:

> This is the poet's age-old cry: 'Give me a hundred
> voices, a hundred mouths, and a hundred tongues for my songs!'
> whether they're writing a play to be mouthed by a dismal tragedian,
> or showing a wounded Parthian pulling a spear from his groin.

The interlocutor pretends to misunderstand:

> 'What's the point of all this? What lumps of nutritious verse
> are you cramming in, that you need a hundred throats to ingest them?
> Bards committed to the elevated style may gather mists
> on Helicon – those who would bring Thyestes' or Procne's saucepan
> to the boil to provide a regular supper for tasteless Sweetman.

Persius has chosen the stories of Thyestes and Procne, not only because they are horrible, but because they enable him to continue the food metaphor: the dinner consumed by the actor (Sweetman), who is playing the character (Thyestes), is prepared by the dramatist. Such a subject calls for an outlandish style. Persius' own subject, however, is real life, and so the speaker encourages him to write accordingly:

Draw your material from there. Leave to Mycenae
its menus of heads and feet, and get used to common food.'

Another metaphor is one of sound:

You don't squeeze air from a bellows which gasps
as the furnace smelts the ore, or go in for hoarse and pent-up
muttering, inanely cawing to yourself some deep observation,
nor do you strain to blow up your cheeks until they go bang.

Another again is one of dress:

You keep to the dress of everyday speech.

Persius answers:

It's certainly not my aim to swell my page with frivolities
dressed in mourning in the hope of lending weight to smoke (19-20).

So the Cornutus passage, itself non-satirical, is preceded by a lively attack on tragedy as being pretentious, hypocritical, and ridiculous.[4] Furthermore (looking ahead) it prepares us for the main body of the poem, which is a Stoic sermon on moral freedom. The preparation is not just thematic. By describing his studies Persius convinces his readers that he is qualified to preach and sincerely committed to his philosophy. The message itself, though primarily didactic, is enlivened by satirical wit, as when a sluggard is pulled in opposite directions by greed and pleasure. Here is the intervention of greed (5.132-9):

Daylight, and you're lying snoring. 'Get up,' says Lady Greed,
'Hey, get up!' You refuse. She persists, 'Up!'
                                        'I'm unable.'
'Up!'
        'What for?'
                'What a question! Go and fetch kippers from Pontus,
plus beaver-musk, oakum, ebony, frankincense, slippery silk.
The pepper's arrived; unload it before the camel's had a drink.
Do a shady deal, then swear you haven't.'
                                        'But God will hear.'
'Ha! Listen, you numskull, if you want to have God on your side,
you'll spend your days happily scraping the bottom of the barrel.'

[4] There is a good discussion of the opening of Persius 5 in Bramble, ch. 1.

In 1, as in 5, the critique of modern poetry is connected with Persius'
moral preaching, but the implications are much wider, and the satire is
given a quasi-mythical framework. To apprehend that framework we
have to remember that in Greek mythology King Midas showed his
incompetence as a judge of literature by declaring Pan superior to Apollo.
As a punishment he was given ass's ears. With the aid of a turban he
managed to conceal his ears from everyone except his barber. The latter,
bursting with the secret, whispered it into a hole in the ground. Now
early in 1 we hear that Persius is possessed of a truth (8) – a truth which
finally turns out to be the fact that everyone in Rome has ass's ears (121).
He is cautioned not to make this public, for it would be dangerous to
offend the great. So after wistfully recalling the outspokenness of Lucilius
and the more indirect criticism of Horace, he resolves to bury the secret
in his book. More will be said of this decision in Chapter Three.

At first sight the truth perceived by the satirist is purely literary: the
various kinds of poetry applauded by the rich elite and by the general
public are all, in their different ways, frivolous and artificial. Theme,
style, and presentation bear witness to the fact that poetry has ceased to
be 'a criticism of life' and has become a vehicle of exhibitionism or an
after-dinner entertainment. The possible dangers of such complaints are
discussed in Chapter Two.

Again (still considering what Persius says purely in literary terms) one
may observe that the focus of his concern is quite different from
Horace's. The Augustan believed that over the years Latin poets had
shown a considerable degree of talent; what they lacked was patience and
self-criticism; they hated the business of revision (the *limae labor*), and
as a result their work lacked form and finish (*AP* 285-94). One
contemporary group was in a different category, namely the uncritical
admirers of Calvus and Catullus. They were open to objection, not
because they were technically crude, but because they upheld the
neoteric interest in the sentimental and sometimes morbid themes of
Greek myth, and cared little for the moral issues of metropolitan life.
Whereas Horace's involvement with this group was fairly limited (they
figure in 1.10, but not in the epistles of Book 2, where the historical
perspective is much longer), it is clear that the taste and attitude which
they represented still flourished a century later, at which time they
became a major target for Persius. Hence, although Horace and Persius
were not far apart in their literary theory, the prevailing fashions caused
them to say very different things about smoothness. For Horace it was a
desideratum; for Persius it was a symptom of viciousness, a technique
which enabled poets to say things that didn't matter in a very fluent
style.

This brings us to another, more important, change of emphasis. While
both satirists held that poetry was, or should be, closely related to life,
Persius gave this belief a special application. Like other Stoics, he

maintained that as 'the style is the man' so the community's literary taste is an index of its moral condition. Seneca developed the idea in *Ep.* 114: 'Just as an individual's actions resemble his speech, so a rhetorical style sometimes reflects the mores of society – if the community's moral standards have gone slack and it has given itself over to frivolous pleasures. A lack of discipline in speech, if it is not just confined to one or two people but is widely approved and accepted, is a sign of general corruption' (2). Again, 'you should not be surprised that such rottenness is adopted by the more educated class as well as by the coarser elements of the public; for the distinction between them is one of dress, not of taste' (12). So the Rome of Nero is morally corrupt. Persius repeatedly hammers this message home with allegations of gluttony and perversion. Thus the grandees at the dinner-table are *saturi* (31) and *crudi* (51) – they have over-eaten and the food lies undigested in their stomachs. One of them has a fat pot-belly – *pinguis aqualiculus* (57), which is doubtless related to his fondness for sows' udders – *sumen* (53). As for perversion, one need only recall the recitation in vv.15-21:

> You will finally read the product
> from a public platform, carefully combed, in a new white toga,
> with a birthday gem on your finger, rinsing your supple throat
> with a clear preparatory warble, your eyes swooning in ecstasy.
> Then, what a sight! The mighty sons of Rome in a dither,
> losing control of voice and movement as the quivering strains
> steal under the spine and scratch the secret passage.

This unpleasant description, paralleled at other points in the poem, makes it plain that in their morals, as in their taste, the Romans had abandoned *uirtus*.

The examples quoted above may help us to compare Persius' preaching with that of Horace. When Persius makes an ethical assertion he does so, one feels, because the principle has been laid down by Chrysippus and appears in all the best text-books. Horace finds the principle cogent because it can be tested against the experience of any sensible man. Persius' more academic approach reveals itself in various details. Apart from recurrent references to classes and tutorials, there is a difference of attitude. In 3, for example, the speaker delivering the diatribe is a serious, if shadowy, figure, whereas in Horace 2.3 the corresponding preacher is a ruined antique-dealer who has become a Stoic convert. In 5 Persius is earnestly committed to the paradox that 'all fools are slaves, only the wise are free'.[5] In Horace 2.7 the same doctrine is given an ironic framework which saves the poet from full involvement; for the sermon is preached by the slave Davus, who got it from another

---

[5] For this and other Stoic paradoxes see Cicero, *Paradoxa Stoicorum* (printed with *De Orat.* 3 in the Loeb translation) and Horace 2.7.

slave, who apparently heard it by listening at the keyhole of Crispinus' lecture-room (2.7.45). The immediate recipient of the sermon, moreover, and its ostensible object, is Horace himself.

The last point has a far-reaching significance. Horace kept in touch with the people he criticised, largely because he did not pretend to be unusually virtuous. Now, a century later, the distance between the satirist and his foolish and vicious targets has noticeably increased. No rapprochement seems possible, and there are very few on Persius' side. In 4.27-32 we have this comment on a wealthy landowner who is rather close with his money:

> Oh *that* damned creature. Even his own mother couldn't love him.
> On a public holiday he hangs up his yoke at the cross-road shrines;
> reluctantly scraping the dirty old seal off his little wine-jar
> he groans 'Cheers!' and downs the shrivelled dregs of his senile
> vinegar, munching an onion in its jacket with a pinch of salt.
> His slaves cheer excitedly at getting a bowl of porridge.

Good vivid stuff, we think; typical of Persius at his most pugnacious. But actually we are being asked to *condemn* this attack. We should, says the satirist, be more critical of our own faults and less eager to carp at our neighbours' (23-4). All very well, but the spirit of tolerance does not emerge from the poem, as it does from Horace 1.3. Similarly in 6, the least puritanical of Persius' satires, where he is advocating a sensible attitude to the spending of money, 'he fails to convince us that enlightened self-indulgence is a true facet of his character' (Nisbet, 67). This failure can be seen in the altercation with the greedy heir (41ff.) which, though trenchant and clever, becomes increasingly harsh (66-74):

> [Don't call me to account, saying] 'Put down
> the sum inherited, add the interest, subtract the expenditure,
> what's the remainder?'
> *Remainder*? Come on, boy, drown the cabbage,
> drown it in oil and damn the expense! Shall I on my holiday
> eat boiled nettles and a smoked pig's cheek with a hook-hole in the ear,
> so that one day your young wastrel may gorge on goose's liver,
> and when the fastidious vein throbs in his roving cock
> relieve himself into an upper-class pouch? Am I to be left
> with transparent skin while his priest-belly wobbles with fat?

Persius could, of course, derive comfort from the teachings of a dogmatic philosophy. Most of his themes are Stoic, though not exclusively so, e.g. the degraded conception of divinity implied by immoral prayers (2), the terrors of a guilty conscience (3.35ff.), vice as a form of disease (3.88ff.), the ever-present need of self-examination (4), and sin as slavery (5.73ff.). But that philosophy, at least in the rigorous form presented by Persius, tended to see people in simple terms of wise and foolish.[6] Since the great majority are, of course, foolish, this means that, like the preacher Crispinus at the end of Horace 1.3, the satirist comes over as a rather lonely figure. He despises men for their folly, and at the same time realises with sardonic resignation that his preaching is greeted with derision. On two occasions (3.77ff. and 5.189ff.) the man who rejects it is a brutal centurion – a character whom we instinctively dislike. But even a more sympathetic listener might have found the sermons rather abrasive. Persius knew this. In his view most people were morally unhealthy, and the right treatment was bound to cause discomfort. Hence his intention was *pallentis radere mores* (5.15) 'to scrape pale forms of conduct' or *teneras mordaci radere uero / auriculas* (1.107-8) 'to scrape tender ears with biting truth'. This involved a somewhat harsh kind of wit. In 5.16 Persius is praised for his ability 'to nail guilt with sophisticated play' (*ingenuo culpam defigere ludo*) – a strange phrase, which seems to imply that the old idea of liberal humour inherited from the Greeks through Panaetius and transmitted by Cicero (*De Off.* 1.103-4) is now being used with a new sharpness. The change is already apparent in 1. Like Midas' barber, Persius alone has seen Rome's asininity, and because he has 'an unruly spleen' (*petulanti splene*) he is compelled to guffaw (*cachinno* in v.12). The compulsive expression of contempt may remind us of a later phrase: *rigidi censura cachinni* 'the condemnation of a severe guffaw'.[7] Horace's gentle teachers with their tempting biscuits have been left behind. We are moving towards Juvenal.

(iv) Juvenal

Although the first three satirists trace different paths within the triangle, it is usually possible to tell where they are at any given moment. Lucilius, of course, poses problems; but those arise from the state of his text, not from the nature of his writing. Juvenal is more elusive. Let us start from apex (c) – preaching; for though it tends to be overlooked there *is* a didactic element in Juvenal. We first encounter it in 8, where Ponticus, a governor designate, is urged to match his noble birth with noble conduct (74-145). The passage contains some typically sardonic hints, e.g. 'Be sure above all not to inflict a great injustice / on men who are brave and wretched' (121-2). But most of the section gives positive encouragement, based on the aphorism *nobilitas sola est atque unica uirtus* (20) 'the one and only nobility is goodness.' In 11, in the course of a lecture on extravagance, we hear of the simple hospitality offered by

---

[6] The Stoic *prokoptôn*, who strives to improve and therefore occupies an intermediate position between the sage and the fool does not appear in Persius. One wonders what Persius thought of the saying, often repeated by his friend Thrasea, *qui uitia odit, homines odit* (Pliny, *Ep.* 8.22) 'Whoever hates faults hates people.'

[7] Juvenal 10.31.

Juvenal (56-76). *Satire* 13 dilates on the terrors of a guilty conscience (192-239). In 14 (a condemnation of parents who fail to set a good example) the preaching is couched in negative terms, but one might still argue that it had a positive aim.

Can we, then, attribute the same purpose to the satires as a whole? The main scholarly tradition emphatically says yes. In other words, those indignant tirades, which inveigh against every aspect of Roman life and therefore seem to start from apex (a), were intended ultimately to promote moral reform. Mancinelli, in his commentary of 1492, under the heading *Iuvenalis Commoda*, described Juvenal as 'a divine poet and the best imaginable censor of morals'. In 1501 Britannicus commended him as (of all things) an ideal school text, because 'as though with whip and sword he hunts down the vices of sinners, showing by the most wholesome style of his poetry that one should turn aside from the path of depravity and lay hold on righteousness'.[1] Lubinus in 1603 claimed, perhaps rightly, that the satires contained 'more wisdom, more precepts for reforming life and conduct, than are to be found in all ten books of Aristotle's *Ethics*'.[2] In 1802 Gifford was even more exalted: '... fixing all his soul on the eternal distinctions of moral good and evil, he laboured ... to set forth the loveliness of virtue and the deformity and horror of vice in full and perfect display.' On the subject of indecency he added: 'When I find that his views are to render depravity loathsome; that everything which can alarm and disgust is directed at her in his terrible page, I forget the grossness of the execution in the excellence of the design.'[3] In our own century the Loeb editor writes: 'An ardent admirer of the simple and hardy virtues of ancient Rome, he holds up a mirror to every part of the private life of the Rome of his day, and by the most caustic and trenchant invective seeks to shame her out of her vices.'[4]

This is all rather disconcerting. The quotations, which are typical of the editorial tradition, come from scholars who were familiar with all the satires, not just with edifying passages contained in florilegia, and who were in general superior to us in their command of Latin. Perhaps, on the basis of their biblical education, they assumed that anyone who attacked a heathen society with such vehemence *must* have had a high moral purpose. Or did they feel, half consciously, that if their author was fit to be read he *had* to be justified in these terms? Certainly if learned men had not taken that view, Juvenal would not have survived the middle ages.

Nevertheless, the central tradition may, for whatever reasons, be

[1] Britannicus, in his prefatory address.
[2] Lubinus, *Apolog.* p. 3.
[3] Introduction to his translation pp. li and lix.
[4] Ramsay, Loeb Translation, xxxiii-iv.

misleading. To reach our own conclusions we have to ask questions like the following: Was the portrait of Virro (5) intended to bring about an improvement in the manners of hosts? Were Roman ladies supposed to become more virtuous on reading 6? Were new and enlightened patrons expected to emerge as a result of 7? Again, after reading 3, was the emperor meant to expand the fire brigade, impose a new set of regulations for the construction of tenements, and perhaps start a programme for the repatriation of Greek immigrants? It all seems very unlikely. Most of the features of Roman life attacked by Juvenal were the result of a long and irreversable process. The decay of the nobility, the impoverishment of the class to which Juvenal belonged, the success of energetic freedmen, the sexual frivolity – these were developments which could not possibly have been altered by a poet; and Juvenal knew it:

> *nil erit ulterius quod nostris moribus addat*
> *posteritas, eadem facient cupientque minores* (1.147-8)

Nothing more will remain for future ages to add
to our behaviour; they'll be the same in their values and conduct.

Later, though philosophy and experience are said to teach wisdom, it is the wisdom of resignation:

> *rari quippe boni: numera, uix sunt totidem quot*
> *Thebarum portae uel diuitis ostia Nili* (13.26-7)

Good men indeed are rare: count them, they're barely as many
as are the gates of Thebes or the mouths of the wealthy Nile.

Yet if he is rarely a reformer, Juvenal need not on that account forfeit the name of moralist; for it is possible to express indignation and disgust without cherishing any illusions about human improvement. 'Look, my friends,' we might imagine him saying, 'we have inherited this monstrous city; it is not of our making and we cannot hope to change it. Let us therefore apprehend it in all its horror and absurdity, and demonstrate our integrity by repudiating its values. That may at least help us to survive with some degree of self-respect.' If Juvenal's satire represents that kind of emotional catharsis, one naturally wonders what could have happened to him to produce such resentment. Unfortunately Juvenal himself tells us nothing. This reticence stands in sharp contrast to the easy familiarity of Horace, who like Lucilius before him was happy to talk about his career and the way he lived. The difference can be described in rhetorical terms by contrasting the intimacy of the *sermo* with the distance implied by a *declamatio*, or by distinguishing *ethos*, which had to do with the agreeable presentation of the speaker's self, from *pathos*, which was primarily connected with the feelings of the audience.[5] But these different forms and techniques were matters of choice, and in the end the choice rested with the writer. Even when, quite late in his career, Juvenal composed a more relaxed and Horatian type of poem (11), he still did not take the opportunity to present a self-portrait.

So far, then, taking account of the small number of didactic passages, and assuming the more limited kind of moral intention just described, we are still on the line (a) – (c), i.e. attack and preaching, but somewhat closer to (a). To see how this position should be further modified we turn to 1. The opening lines have a function analogous to that of Persius' prologue. Persius alleged that his reason for writing was financial. Juvenal doesn't say that. (Perhaps in his case the joke would not have been funny.) What he does is to claim the right to retaliate for all the boredom he has suffered. There have been too many *togatae* – comedies which, though supposedly about Roman life, were essentially trivial; too many elegies – a genre already despised by Persius. Then come the satirist's traditional *bêtes noires*, the epic poets and tragedians. Finally there is a swipe at exponents of romantic epic like Valerius Flaccus, who had written on the Argonautic expedition. Juvenal's next claim is that he has had the requisite rhetorical training. This too is described in humorous terms – the classroom beatings, the hackneyed *suasoria* giving advice to Sulla. Then another throw-away joke: it is misguided mercy to spare paper which is doomed anyway – doomed, because if Juvenal doesn't waste it someone else will. Last of all, why write satire? The answer is self-evident: when the laws of nature are being flouted in so many ways, it's hard *not* to write satire (30). The wickedness of Roman life does not allow indifference:

si natura negat, facit indignatio uersum (79).

The line is a general statement: if nature says no (i.e., if a man has no natural talent), indignation composes verse. Persius had said that if expressions were refused by nature, the belly could procure them (*Prol.* 10-11). In Juvenal's case the creativity comes not from hunger but from anger. But, as with Persius, the result is said to be nothing wonderful in the way of poetry: *qualemcumque potest, quales ego uel Cluuienus* (80). Whether he came from life or literature, Cluvienus was clearly a third-rate blusterer. The bathos is an ironic device to forestall criticism.

In view of these passages, we are obliged to change Juvenal's position again, moving him in the direction of apex (b) – entertainment. There is no problem about this, so long as the humour backs up the satirical thrust.

[5] For *ethos* and *pathos* see Quintilian 6.2.8-20.

When a soft eunuch marries, and Mevia takes to sticking
a Tuscan boar, spear poised by her naked breast;
when a fellow who made my stiff young beard crunch with his clippers
can challenge with his millions singlehanded the whole aristocracy;
when Crispinus, a blob of Nilotic scum, bred in Canopus,
hitches a cloak of Tyrian purple onto his shoulder
and flutters a simple ring of gold on his sweaty finger
(in summer he cannot bear the weight of a heavier stone),
it's hard *not* to write satire (22-30).

Here sexual scorn, social snobbery, xenophobia, jealousy, physical revulsion – one is piled on the other until the satirist explodes with exasperation and contempt. The indignation, however prejudiced and illiberal, is enforced by the rhetorical wit, and the result is powerfully effective. The same is true of the vignettes of the obese lawyer and the vulture-like informer (31-6). But the tone begins to waver in 37ff.

> *cum te summoueant qui testamenta merentur*
> *noctibus, in caelum quos euehit optima summi*
> *nunc uia processus, uetulae uesica beatae*

When you're shouldered aside by people who earn bequests at night,
people who reach the top by a form of social climbing
that now ensures success – through a rich old female's funnel.

Shocking, but effective. The point has been made, so Juvenal will move on. But no.

> *unciolam Proculeius habet, sed Gillo deuncem,*
> *partes quisque suas ad mensuram inguinis heres*

Proculeius obtains a single twelfth, but Gillo eleven:
each heir's reward is assessed by the size of his organ.

Whether we relish or deplore the wit, does not our attention begin to stray from the *moral* point? And Juvenal hasn't finished yet:

> *accipiat sane mercedem sanguinis et sic*
> *palleat ut nudis pressit qui calcibus anguem*
> *aut Lugudunensem rhetor dicturus ad aram*

Very well. Let each receive the price of his life-blood, becoming
as pale as a man who has stepped on a snake in his bare feet
or is waiting to speak in that grim competition at the altar of Lyons.[6]

---

[6] An altar to Rome and Augustus was set up at Lyons by Drusus in 12 B.C. Caligula held a contest in oratory there in A.D. 39-40. Those who fared worst were compelled to erase their work with their tongues or else be flogged or flung into the Rhone (Suetonius, *Cal.* 20).

Here the pallor of debauchery has been illustrated by the pallor of fear,
and the examples (one from *Aeneid* 2.379-80, the other from the reign of
Caligula) are far-fetched and disparate. But a more serious problem is
the fact that the passage actually modifies our indignation, since it shows
that the gigolo will pay a heavy price for his success.[7]

Comparable examples can be found in every period of Juvenal's work.
In 3, after opposing 'sycophantic Greek' to 'honest Roman', the satirist
sees a further possibility of comic elaboration and adds '*We* may flatter
just as intensively; they are believed (92-3)', thus destroying the
antithesis which he has so carefully built up. In 10.188ff. Juvenal
demonstrates in depressingly vivid detail that long life is no blessing.
Speaking of the old man's many ailments, he says:

> If you asked their names,
> I could sooner tell how many fancy-men Oppia loved,
> how many patients Themison killed in a single autumn,
> how many partners were cheated by Basilus, how many orphans
> by Hirrus, how many men are drained in a single day
> by the tall Maura, how many schoolboys Hamillus bends over (219-24).

Again, the increasingly drastic illustrations lead our attention away from
the old man. Half way through 15 we are told the appalling and pathetic
story of the Vascones in Spain, who under siege conditions were reduced
to cannibalism. Although such an action was excusable, and was in fact
permitted by the Stoics (see Rankin), Juvenal makes a patronising and
flippant comment:

> We know better
> thanks to the teaching of Zeno, but who would expect a Spaniard
> to be a Stoic, at least in the days of old Metellus?
> Now the entire world has its Graeco-Roman culture;
> smooth-tongued Gaul has been coaching lawyers from Britain, and now
> they're talking of hiring a rhetoric-teacher in Timbuctoo! (106-12)

The same disconcerting habit sometimes blurs the distinction between
more and less serious offences. In 6.379ff. we have the following sequence:
if your wife is musical she will commit adultery with professional singers;
but that is better than being a chatterbox in male company; just as bad
is the sadist who thrashes her less fortunate neighbours; but worst of all
is the bluestocking who holds forth on literature and corrects her friends'
grammar. The sixth satire, in fact, raises the question of Juvenal's
intention in its most acute form. The poem as a whole cannot be taken
seriously – there is too much comedy (a great deal of it enjoyable);
equally, it cannot be regarded as an elaborate joke – there is too much

[7] Courtney thinks that v.42 comes after v.36, and that vv.37-41 come before v.55 or v.58.

that is serious. However it is read, some passages are absurdly
hyperbolical, and others are revolting. The problem has long been
recognised. In 1629 Daniel Heinsius asked in his *De Satyra Horatii Liber*
(115) why Juvenal had written 6: *quo fine? sane ut mores emendet. quam
uero est indignum et foedum ita castitatem suadere ut a castis legi non
possis!* 'To what purpose? To improve people's behaviour, I presume.
But how unseemly and disgraceful it is to commend purity in a manner
which prevents the pure from reading you!' The anonymous editor of
1784 says (*Pref.* p. x): 'It is indeed a very extraordinary phenomenon in
the moral world that a man who is supposed to have censured vice with
the sincerest abhorrence would use expressions and display scenes so
extremely indelicate as to promote the very vices which he professed and
intended to discountenance.' That is going too far. One doubts whether 6
has ever made lechery attractive, or whether 2 and 9 have encouraged
perversion. Nevertheless, the problem remains.

One way of dealing with it is to point to the influence of rhetoric. That
influence is undeniable, and has been demonstrated with great
thoroughness by De Decker. But if we maintain that Juvenal was
primarily a declaimer intent on giving a display of rhetorical virtuosity,
then we encounter other difficulties. First, to what class of rhetoric
should the satires be assigned? Clearly not to the *genus iudiciale* (the
poet is not arguing a case in court or appealing to any particular law); nor
to the *genus deliberatiuum* or its school version the *suasoria*, for only a
minority of the satires can be seen as *suasoriae*, and even then the
resemblance is only formal. Juvenal's work comes closest to the *genus
demonstratiuum*, which was largely concerned with praise and blame;
but the standard examples of vituperative oratory, like Caesar's *Anticato*
and Cicero's *In Pisonem*, were composed for particular occasions and
directed at specific people. They have no counterpart in Juvenal.[8]

Perhaps, however, if we interpret 'rhetoric' in a much broader sense, so
as to include all aspects of Juvenal's style – his wild hyperbole, his
obscenity, his surprise effects, and so on – it may still be possible to see
his aim as primarily rhetorical; in which case his work will have to be
approached from apex (b), that of entertainment or amusement. About
twenty years ago strong support was given to this position by H.A.
Mason's brilliant essay entitled 'Is Juvenal a Classic?'. Mason starts
from the contention that 'the key to Juvenal's art lies in the study of
Martial. The two poets appeal to the same taste and presuppose the
same habits in their listening and reading public' (96). He also refers to
the younger Pliny who defended his own risqué verses by saying that men
of great learning and probity had composed pieces of that kind. There
was no serious intention or effect (Pliny, *Ep.* 4.14.4, 5.3.2). Mason then
cites cases where Juvenal has, as it were, used stones from Martial's

[8] These points are developed by Anderson, 429-44.

epigrams to construct the more elaborate edifices of his own satires. Thus in 4.5 Martial writes:

> Good and poor as you are, sincere in tongue and heart,
>   what do you mean, Fabianus, by coming to Rome?
> You cannot expect to find acceptance as pimp or boozer,
>   nor to summon trembling prisoners in threatening tones.
> You are not able to seduce the wife of your dearest friend,
>   nor rise to meet the demands of freezing hags,
> nor hawk the emperor's airy promises round the palace,
>   nor applaud Canus' or Glaphyrus' musical skill.
> How will you live?
>   'A staunch man, a reliable friend –'
> Sorry; that's no way to become a Philomelus.

Several of these ideas are built into Juvenal's third satire in the section beginning *quid Romae faciam*? (41ff.).

When the approaches of De Decker and Mason are combined, as they can be, they add up to a very substantial case, one which stresses the pleasure derived from Juvenal's artistry and wit, and minimises his moral and social concern. Further support is available from a point which is well known to everyone but seldom mentioned in studies of Juvenal, namely that some people complain, not because they are deeply offended or because they seriously hope to effect change, but because at bottom they *enjoy* complaining; that is their chief way of communicating with the world. On this view, Juvenal was just such a person. He needed Rome, with all its hideous disfigurements, because Rome defined his identity as a writer. Without it he was nothing.

Yet if we place our conception of Juvenal too close to apex (b), we shall find it hard to take account of the other elements in his work. Perhaps, to begin with, he was not always quite so close to Martial. Whereas Martial's epigrams on the hypocrisy and sterility of male 'brides' are specimens of cool, satirical, wit (1.24 and 12.42), in Juvenal 2 the same ideas become part of a long indignant tirade which deplores the decay of Roman *uirtus*. A similar change takes place with *Epig.* 4.5 (quoted above) when it is embodied in Juvenal 3 (Anderson, 380-1). There are other more general differences of tone between the two poets. It appears, for instance, that 'Martial preferred the basic obscenities to their substitutes, metaphorical or euphemistic' (Adams, 220); the opposite tendency is found in Juvenal. More far-reaching is the fact that, when such weight is placed on Juvenal's linguistic brilliance, the satires begin to part company with actuality; they are no longer thought of as presenting a vivid caricature of Roman life, and they cease to offer any serious judgment on it. Towards the end of his summing up, De Decker writes: ' le poète déclame souvent avec cette chaleur factive, cette colère de tête, qui animait les rhéteurs, quand ils fulminaient contre des crimes abominables ... mais imaginaires' (203). Nisard had rightly remarked that it was only after a long sojourn in the schools of rhetoric that Juvenal thought of turning his attention to the heap of corruption that surrounded him. De Decker adds: 'On peut faire un pas de plus et douter de la réalité de cette "fange de vices" ...' (204). Mason accepts the reality of Roman corruption but maintains that Juvenal draws us away from it. 'The effect of [9] is to direct our attention into a region remote from that of a social commentator' (96). *Satire* 3 'is not a topical poem written with an eye on actual conditions, and it does not exhibit moral earnestness' (132). More generally, '[Juvenal] was more interested in literature than social conditions and ... he lacks any consistent standpoint or moral coherence. Indeed his whole art consists in opportunism and the surprise effects obtainable from deliberate inconsistency' (107).

Now, as we have seen, Juvenal's moral earnestness does seem to waver, and he does go in for clever effects which compromise his consistency. The question is whether these features or tendencies are so frequent and so prevalent as to justify our putting them at the centre of our critical picture. I think myself that if they are given that position of centrality they upset the balance. If, for example, Juvenal was primarily an entertainer, it is hard to see what he was doing in long sections of 8, 11, and 14, which are not triumphs of wit. Even within the better-known satires, where the wit is unmistakable, it may direct our attention to, rather than away from, social conditions. Mason himself is so impressed by Juvenal's complaints about poverty in 3 that, much to his credit, he makes an exception of that passage, saying it is 'not open to the charge of unreality' (129). But as soon as we grant that the satire is sometimes serious, other passages will also claim attention. In brief, it seems that if Juvenal is assessed primarily in terms of bathos, paradox, hyperbole and the rest he has to pay too high a price.

Can we frame a hypothesis which will include both the moral commentator (as distinct from the reformer), who reacts to the social and ethical realities of Rome, and the wit who normally supports that reaction but sometimes undermines it or goes shooting off at a tangent? Perhaps we can, if we think of Juvenal as having two attitudes or roles, the chief one being that of the upright citizen who denounces the evils of his day, convinced that mankind in general and Rome in particular have declined from the standards of an earlier age, and the secondary one being that of a cynic who enjoys witty excursions and knows that the past too was far from perfect. The first role gave scope for impassioned rhetoric, but it was vulnerable to the charges of self-righteousness and simple-mindedness. From time to time it seems that Juvenal tried to take account of those charges by stepping out of his chief role and making some dry, unsentimental, comment. In 2, for instance, which is a fairly homogeneous poem, Juvenal realised that the stern old Romans of the past would provide an excellent foil to the hypocritical perverts of today.

So he asks

> What does Curius feel,
> or the Scipios twain? What Fabricius and the shade of Camillus?
> What Crémera's legion and the valiant lads who fell at Cannae –
> the dead of all those wars – when a ghost like this descends
> from the world above? (153-7)

Yet for fear he might appear naive or (heaven help us) religious, he reminds us in advance that Hades is a ridiculous fantasy in which no adult could possibly believe (149-53), and he goes on to answer his own question in a less sombre tone:

> They'd insist on purification, if sulphur
> and torches were to be had and a laurel-twig dipped in water.

In 10 the stance is different, that of a disenchanted observer reflecting on man's futile and misguided aspirations; but at a number of points a similar process of 'correction' can be seen taking place. Near the end Juvenal asks if there is nothing for which we should pray (346). In reply he composes those famous lines beginning *orandum est ut sit mens sana in corpore sano* (356) 'pray for the boon of a healthy mind in a healthy body'. But as if to assure everyone that he has not gone soft, he prefaces those lines with two others:

> *ut tamen et poscas aliquid uoueasque sacellis*
> *exta et candiduli diuina tomacula porci*
>
> If you must have something to ask for, some reason to burn in the chapels
> a white little piggy's offal and sausages fit for the gods ...

And he follows them with the Epicurean assertion: *monstro quod ipse tibi possis dare*, 'I'm showing you what you can grant to yourself'.[9] So apparently even virtuous prayers are unnecessary.

As a moralist Juvenal deplores the corruption of modern Rome; but as a realist he is careful to take some of the shine off the golden age. In his picture of the world as it was before the departure of Pudicitia and Astraea (6.1-20) he modifies our nostalgia by mentioning the huge-breasted wife 'often more rough than her acorn-belching husband' (10). And in 13, as he addresses Calvinus in a half-chiding, half-bantering, manner, he paints that blessed time in a memorably comic passage beginning

> That was what life was like among the native inhabitants
> before the coup which ousted Saturn and made him exchange

---

[9] Bailey, 116 (*Sent. Vat.* 65).

his crown for a farmer's sickle; then Juno was still a wee lassie,
and Jove a caveman on Ida without official status (38-41).

This ambiguity of tone sometimes complicates the task of distinguishing Juvenal's targets. In 5 the wretched clients are castigated for their servility, and most of the comic effects are at their expense. Yet the host Virro comes off worse. He is selfish, greedy, arrogant, and sadistic – a veritable monster of malevolence. While the guests are subjected to Juvenal's ridicule, his hatred is reserved for Virro. In 7 our attention is focussed on the men of learning, whose misfortunes are treated with a rather uncharitable humour ('poor miserable blighters'). Yet in vv.30-2, 36-47, 74-8, and 178-85 enough is said about those who ought to be providing patronage to make it clear that their meanness is responsible for the intellectuals' plight.[10] In 13 Calvinus, who has been swindled by someone he trusted, receives a Juvenalian consolation. He is teased for over-reacting, reminded that his loss is relatively small, and told that his feelings of outrage are naive and childish: what else did he expect in a world like this? But although Calvinus' leg is pulled rather heavily, especially in the first half of the poem, that does not mean he is the villain of the piece, any more than the guests are the villains of 5 or the intellectuals of 7. Granted, Juvenal has now adopted a position of weary cynicism from which an honest man is seen as a freak, and justifiable indignation is mocked. Nevertheless, throughout the poem we are constantly reminded of the wickedness of modern society. Calvinus *has* been wronged, and Juvenal knows it: What do you think everyone feels about this recent crime? (5-6). But being Juvenal, he cannot write a straightforward consolation. Pure sympathy is not his stock in trade.[11]

Satire 9 is more complex. At the centre is a patron who employs a gigolo to satisfy both his wife and himself. The immorality of this arrangement passes almost without comment; it is the patron's meanness and ingratitude which are criticised. This quaintly biassed protest is understandable since it comes from the one who up to recently has completed the *ménage à trois*. Now his occupation is gone. Although such a creature is really in no position to feel aggrieved about anything, he receives, or rather *thinks* he receives, the satirist's sympathetic concern. Here, then, Juvenal the wit is very much to the fore; the satire is one of his most brilliant performances. So is Naevolus simply meant to be funny? I think not. What Juvenal has done is to *assume* the moral

[10] See Rudd (3), 84-118 and Wiesen, 464-83. (Wiesen's article was evidently written at the same time as ch. 4 of my *Lines of Enquiry*. The article appeared when I was writing another chapter of that book, and much to my shame I failed to notice it before the book went to the press.)

[11] For 13 see Morford and his references. I do not share the view that the poem is a satire on the genre of the *consolatio*, though that genre is certainly used as a means to the poet's end.

dimension, and then to pretend it isn't there, as Swift did in *A Modest Proposal*. If the solid base of contempt and disgust is removed, the satire loses its *point d'appui*.[12]

In 12 Juvenal prepares to celebrate the return of Catullus, a merchant who has narrowly escaped drowning. But instead of conjuring up the horror of his friend's experience, he adopts an ironical manner: when the sea rose and the lightning struck it was like a storm in a poem; the skipper had to jettison his cargo, as a beaver abandons his precious testacles; all kinds of priceless valuables went overboard – a tribute to Catullus, for who else these days would put his life above his possessions? Finally it was necessary to hack the ship to pieces in order to remain afloat.[13] The conventions of the address of welcome are well known.[14] This one is distinctly odd. Should we therefore turn the interpretation around and assume that Juvenal is really criticising Catullus for his greed? That will hardly do. Of the 92 verses under discussion 26 are devoted to the celebration and 21 to the ship's safe return; even the sarcastic jokes about Catullus' cargo (37-49) do not amount to anything like an indictment of wealth. So just as 13 is a satirical consolation, 12 is a satirical welcome – the only sort a friend could expect from Juvenal. After v.92 the satirist goes on to contrast his own motives in celebrating Catullus' return with those of a legacy-hunter. The last forty-odd lines are unimpressive, and their connexion with the rest of the poem is rather artificial.[15] It is almost as if they were added in order to re-assert the satirist's chief role and to give the poem, belatedly, some ethical point.

The tensions in 15 are different. As the cannibalistic orgy is from one point of view horrible and from another ludicrous, we may find some effort is needed to regard it as both horrible and ludicrous at the same time. Still, that problem is not unfamiliar in the literature of our own century. More disconcerting is the tension between two lines of thought. Most of the time Juvenal seems to be saying 'The compassion which we see about us in everyday life is what distinguishes us from the beasts; so this act of cannibalism was a monstrous perversion of nature.' That allows a strong contrast between civilised and savage behaviour; but Juvenal does not hold that contrast steadily throughout the poem,

---

[12] Mason disagrees: 'Juvenal appears here without the faintest moral concern' (96).

[13] A modern version of this comic motif was employed by the Marx Brothers in *Go West*. A train crossing the prairie came under attack and was running out of fuel. Disaster was averted by chopping up the carriages. One shot showed Harpo sharpening an axe on the bogey-wheels.

[14] Cairns, 21-3.

[15] The two parts of the poem are not effectively connected by the name Corvinus (1 and 93), even if we suppose that the name was chosen for its associations with legacy-hunting (Courtney, 517). The first part has nothing to do with legacy-hunting. Granted, the *captator*'s elaborate offerings on behalf of his friend are contrasted with Juvenal's offerings on behalf of Catullus. But the digression on elephants is clumsy, and the hypothetical comparison of the *captator* to Agamemnon is strained.

perhaps because he is reluctant to grant that contemporary Rome is civilised. In vv.147-57 he sees communal values as emerging in the remote past; since then mankind has deteriorated, and the Egyptians are just an extreme instance of what has happened. The same point is hinted at earlier, when we are told that god *ridet et odit* (71). One might assume that this Juvenalian deity was laughing at and loathing the Egyptians; but no, he is reacting to the sight of modern man. It is doubtful if these tensions can be satisfactorily resolved. Nor can the poem be made consistent by treating it all as a joke. At several points, especially in the long passage on tenderness (131-58), Juvenal does invite a serious reaction in moral terms. The satire is not merely a *jeu d'esprit*.

We have argued that Juvenal's usual purpose was to evoke indignation, contempt, and disgust, and that this purpose was normally furthered by his satirical wit. Granted, not every poem displays the same intensity of feeling; why should it? There are also some passages where the satirist seems to waver or become distracted. Where such cases really deflect the moral thrust they should be acknowledged as anomalies or even contradictions. One can only speculate on what caused them. From time to time, as I have suggested, Juvenal may step outside his role of critic in order to protect himself against sophisticated laughter. Other anomalies may arise from the writer's comic energy breaking away from the theme in hand and asserting itself as an independent force (e.g., 1.40-4, 3.92-3, 4.18-21, 10.220-4). Others again may come simply from a lapse of concentration or a lack of critical revision (e.g., 12.102-10, 15.84-7). For whatever reasons, we have to do with a writer who sometimes turned aside from his main business, and who on occasions did not make it clear how he wished to be taken. Perhaps he was not always sure himself.

CHAPTER TWO

Freedom and Authority

(i) Lucilius

All satire contains an element of attack, and it is a nice question whether hostile feelings of fear, envy, anger, or contempt can ever be wholly absent from it. Often, of course, such feelings are overlaid by something happier and more benevolent; often too they become attenuated to a point where they lose their name and are scarcely recognisable. Then they cease to cause offence, and simply add a kind of spice to whatever is said or done. In the context of early Roman society the complexity of such matters can be indicated by asking whether the raillery directed at brides and bridegrooms on their wedding-night – a raillery which was essentially good-natured and aimed to promote prosperity – was wholly devoid of envy; and whether the bawdy songs which accompanied triumphant generals did not in part represent a release of fear.

Those two types of utterance were rather exceptional in that they belonged to occasions of joyful ritual when it was important to ward off the attention of malevolent powers. There was therefore no official restraint on what was said, even though the victims may well have felt that the joking at times went too far. But when no traditional licence was in operation,and when abusive attacks were made in such a way as to injure a person's status or reputation, that was a different matter. Such behaviour then came within the scope of the Twelve Tables, a legal code which had been framed as early as the fifth century B.C.

St Augustine (*Civ. Dei* 2.9) cites a chapter of Cicero's *Republic* (4.12) which said that one of those laws imposed the death penalty on 'anyone who chanted hostile words or composed a *carmen* so as to bring ill repute or disgrace on another' – *si quis occentauisset siue carmen condidisset quod infamiam faceret flagitiumue alteri*.[1] There is no sufficient reason to doubt that this quotation of the old law is substantially correct; Cicero, after all, had learned the Twelve Tables as a schoolboy (*Leg.* 2.59). And the likelihood that it was intended to take account of slanderous abuse delivered in public is supported by Festus, writing in the second century A.D., who says that in former times *occentare* was used for *conuicium facere* 'to insult'.[2] Another provision of the Twelve

---

[1] *ROL* 3, Table 8, 1a.

[2] Festus, 196.12, quoted at loc. cit. (n. 1 above). Festus provided a synopsis of Verrius Flaccus' *De Significatu Verborum*, written in the time of Augustus. Festus in his turn was summarised by the eighth-century scholar Paulus.

Tables is quoted in part by the elder Pliny: *qui malum carmen incantassit* (*NH* 28.18), 'anyone who pronounces an evil spell'. Although there has been much controversy about the question, it seems best to assume that the two provisions were distinct, and that magic and defamation were treated separately.[3] As for defamation, that could have had a serious effect on a man's position in the community; it could also have presented a threat to public order. Such behaviour, therefore, was forbidden. As time went by, the law was apparently extended so as to include insults spoken on the comic stage. That at any rate was the context which Cicero and Augustine had in mind.

According to tradition, a similar law once existed in Athens.[4] The Greek references are late and unsatisfactory, and the issue is complicated by an attempt on the part of the ancient commentators to make the law responsible for the decline of the chorus in Middle and New Comedy. But whatever the truth may have been, the tradition was accepted by Horace, perhaps on the authority of Varro:

> Old Comedy followed, winning a lot of acclaim;
> but its freedom exceeded the proper limit and turned to violence,
> which needed a law to control it. The law was obeyed, and the chorus
> preserved a mortified silence having lost its licence to wound (*AP* 281-4).

Greece, then, seemed to provide an analogy to what happened in Rome where

> at last a law was enacted
> involving penalties; no one, it said, should be traduced
> in scurrilous verse. They changed their tune, and in fear of the cudgel
> returned to decent language and the business of giving pleasure
> (*E.* 2.1.152-5).

Granted that such a law did exist in early Roman times, its effects remain uncertain. Many scholars, however, believe that it can still be seen operating in the case of Naevius. This poet, who was born in Campania about 270 B.C. and served in the first Punic war (264-241), subsequently wrote a long poem in Saturnians on the struggle with Carthage, thus giving Rome her first national epic. He also wrote a couple of serious dramas, including *Clastidium*, which celebrated the victory of M. Claudius Marcellus over the Gauls in 222 B.C.[5] But he was particularly successful in comedy, and it was there that his forthright spirit was most in evidence. In one play a character proclaims his intention of speaking freely:

[3] The various opinions are set out and discussed by Manfredini, chs. 1 and 2. The view adopted in the text is based on Fraenkel.

[4] See Maidment, 9-11 and Halliwell, 87.

[5] *ROL* 2, Naevius, *Historical Plays in Roman Dress*, 1.

libera lingua loquemur ludis Liberalibus[6]

Liber's festival will let us loose our tongues in liberty.

In the prologue of the *Tarentilla* ('The Girl from Tarentum') Naevius speaks of winning applause in the theatre and thus defying the power of any *rex*.[7] In another place he mentions a great man whose father once dragged him away from his mistress in a state of undress. The lines were widely believed to refer to Scipio Africanus. Whether the story was true is another question; Aulus Gellius remains agnostic (7.8.5). Finally Naevius took one chance too many by asserting

fato Metelli Romae fiunt consules[8]

'Tis fate that makes Metelli consuls here.

We cannot tell how the gibe was shaped, but the satirical point seems plain enough: such men reached high office without merit, simply through family influence. Q. Caecilius Metellus, who was consul in 206 B.C. and whose brother was praetor, made the following rejoinder:

dabunt malum Metelli Naeuio poetae

The same Metelli will make the poet Naevius pay,

and forthwith had the impertinent fellow arrested. If Naevius enjoyed the favour of the Marcelli, as he presumably did, they failed to protect him. True, he was not killed or even beaten, which casts some doubt on the view that he was punished under the old law of the Twelve Tables; but he did spend some time in prison before being released by the tribunes (Gellius 3.3.15). Plautus, who had started to write in this period, took note of what had happened (*Mil.* 211-2), and thereafter no serious attempt was made to reproduce the Aristophanic spirit in Roman comedy. Terence's complaints against his critics are confined to the prologues; even there no names are mentioned, and no very grave charges are made.

Still, the people's attitude to public figures remained, as always, ambivalent. Although disrespect was not a feature of Graeco-Roman comedies, it did appear from time to time in the popular sketches which we call, rather misleadingly, mimes. In 136 B.C. an actor made a derogatory reference to the playwright Accius, who promptly sued him for damages (*ad Herennium* 1.24). As a civil suit, the action went initially to a praetor, who appointed a *iudex*, in this case P. Mucius

---

[6] *ROL* 2, Naevius, *Unassigned Fragments*, 27.
[7] *ROL* 2, Naevius, *Comedies in Greek Dress*, 69-71.
[8] *ROL* 2, Naevius, *Various*, 2. The sources are printed and assessed by Jocelyn (3); on one or two points he seems unduly sceptical.

Scaevola. The defendant pleaded that it was permissible to mention a man whose plays were performed under his own name; but Scaevola was not persuaded and found for the plaintiff. Some years later Lucilius brought an action on similar grounds, but the *iudex*, whose name is given as C. Caelius (*ad Herennium* 2.19), dismissed the case. It is not easy to place these actions precisely within the history of *iniuria*. The first edict on *iniuria* (late third century B.C.?) was couched in very general terms and may be disregarded here. In the second, the *edictum de conuicio*, the praetor stated 'Whoever shall be said to have publicly insulted another contrary to good manners, or by whose agency it shall be said that public insult took place contrary to good manners, I shall grant an action against him' (Lenel, 400). This may well, as Plescia believes (283), have come into force in the lifetime of Lucilius. But in any case it is clear from the actions already mentioned that people were not always allowed to say what they liked. One wonders, therefore, how Lucilius got away with so much. The answer must have something to do with categories of utterance. As theatrical performances were under state control, some limits on free speech were perhaps to be expected. Again, as the Twelve Tables showed, people could not abuse each other with impunity in the street. On the other hand in the law courts, which did their business in the public square, counsel had what seems to us an astonishing freedom to traduce the opposition. While it is anachronistic to talk of 'legal privilege', there does seem to have been a convention whereby political enemies paid each other back in kind instead of going to law. The same applied to proceedings in the senate. Lucilius, however, was not a senator or a barrister; he did not go round shouting at people in the street; and he was not a writer of mimes or comedies. His satires, initially at any rate, were read to private audiences. And so, although some protests were made (1085, 1086), there was no formal means of redress. Even if there had been, many of his victims would probably have thought it more undignified and more damaging to take legal action; for that would have advertised the offensive allegations even more widely; it would also have given the impression that the fellow's scurrilous verses were to be taken seriously. A familiar dilemma.

More important was the social factor. Gaius Lucilius belonged to a wealthy landowning family. He was born in Suessa Aurunca on the borderland between Campania and Latium; and it seems that he also had estates in Bruttium and Sicily.[9] He did not follow a senatorial career, but a brother of his probably did, and his aristocratic connexions are seen in the fact that he was Pompey's great uncle. At one period Lucilius lived in a mansion in Rome,[10] and his whole career strongly suggests that he

---

[9] The supposition would explain why Lucilius said jokingly that he wrote for Tarentum, Consentia, and Sicily (after 635); why he made the journey south, described in Book 3; and why Horace said that he himself had *no* estate in Tarentum (1.6.58-9).

[10] See Asconius on Cicero, *Pis.* 12 (reading Manutius' *Lucili*).

was a Roman citizen. When he died in Naples in 102, he was given a public funeral. In the days of the free oligarchy such a man had little need to fear his fellow-citizens. He also happened to be on friendly terms with one who, for nearly twenty years, was the dominant figure in Roman politics.

Publius Cornelius Scipio Aemilianus (born 185 B.C.) was the son of Aemilius Paullus, who was consul in 182 and 168. (His first three names were the result of adoption.) After distinguished service in Macedonia, Spain, and Africa he became consul, in a highly irregular manner, in 147 B.C. and destroyed Carthage in the following year. After holding the censorship in 142, Scipio went on an embassy to the east in 140 and was away until the late summer of 139. Five years later he became consul for the second time. He laid siege to Numantia in Spain, and the town surrendered in the summer of 133. Next year Scipio was back in Rome, where he had to face the disturbances following the death of Tiberius Gracchus. Although married to Gracchus' sister Sempronia, he could not conceal his disapproval of what Tiberius had done, an attitude which not only alienated a number of his personal supporters but also destroyed his general popularity. On the other hand he was now the leading figure in the senate, where the majority was conservative. He began to work against the Gracchan agrarian commission, and he was using the grievances of the Italian allies for that purpose when he died suddenly and mysteriously in 129. Scipio was a well-educated man and a fine soldier. But he was ruthless and arrogant; and although he cannot be blamed for having serious misgivings about Tiberius Gracchus, he himself does not seem to have had any constructive policy for dealing with the terrible social and economic problems of the day.

Among Scipio's friends, a few appear in Lucilius' fragments, notably Manius Manilius (633), Gaius Laelius (201), and probably Scipio's brother Q. Fabius Maximus Aemilianus (1049). Mention of Rutilius Rufus can be inferred from Cicero, *De Fin.* 1.7 (after 635). Scores of others must also have been known to the satirist, obvious examples being L. Furius Philus, P. Rupilius, and Sp. Mummius. It has been suggested by Cichorius (55-6) that Lucilius came to know Scipio himself at an early age because the latter had an estate at Lavernium, not far from Suessa Aurunca. Certainly he was a member of the general's staff in Spain in 134 B.C. (Velleius 2.9.4), and later one of the satires recorded an incident that took place in Rome when Lucilius and many others were escorting Scipio home from the Forum (258). In the years 132-29 Scipio was Lucilius' patron in the sense that he encouraged his work and gave him social prestige. Lucilius, for his part, attacked Scipio's opponents and publicised a number of his *bons mots*. But there was no financial dependence, and although the friendship was unequal in terms of political power Lucilius was not afraid to tease the great man. He alleged that he wrote for Tarentum, Consentia, and Sicily because he failed to meet Scipio's exacting standards of Latinity (after 635), and he noted his friend's pedantic pronunciation of *pertaesum* as *pertisum: quo facetior uideare et scire plus quam ceteri* (983) 'so that you may seem more clever and more expert than the rest.' Then there is the famous story of how Laelius came into the dining-room and found Lucilius chasing Scipio around the table with a twisted napkin (Ps. Acro on Horace 2.1.72). That certainly points to a relaxed informal relationship. Other evidence is scarce, and its interpretation depends in part on one's answer to an exasperating question, namely 'When was Lucilius born?'

The problem may be summarised as follows. According to St Jerome, Lucilius was born in 148 B.C. and died in 102 at the age of forty-six. In recent times Christes has argued in favour of that date (12-23). But if, as Velleius says, he served at Numantia in 134 B.C., Lucilius then could not have been more than fourteen, which is surely incredible. In the next sentence of that passage (2.9.4) Velleius records that Jugurtha and Marius were at Numantia when they were 'still young men' – *iuuenes adhuc*. Now Jugurtha was born about 160 B.C. and Marius in 157-6; so Velleius might have been expected to mention the fact if Lucilius had been ten years younger still. Again, the anecdote about the horseplay in the dining-room would be surprising if Scipio was nearly forty years older than his pursuer. More generally, the early satires have an air of established solidity and worldly wisdom which one would not expect from a teenager, however precocious. And the later books contain material from the 140s (e.g. 424-5) which one would be reluctant to see as merely secondhand reports from an earlier generation. A way out of the difficulty was suggested by Mauritz Haupt, who pointed out that the consuls of 180 B.C., like those of 148, were called Postumius Albinus and Calpurnius Piso. Perhaps this misled Jerome or his source (Suetonius?); in which case Lucilius was born in 180 B.C., a date defended by Krenkel (3) and accepted by Charpin (vol. 1, p. 8). He was then a contemporary, not only of Scipio and Laelius but also of the playwright Terence and the philosopher Clitomachus. That in itself is entirely credible, but the assumption is not free from snags. Apart from making him a rather late beginner (which need not matter greatly) this date raises awkward questions with some of the amatory poems. Fragments from Books 29 and 30 might pass as the confessions of a susceptible gentleman just turned fifty. But what of the sexual experiences referred to in Book 8 (331-5)? They seem rather embarrassing if they represent the revelations of a man over sixty.[11] Conceivably the words should be assigned to another speaker. But then there is the collection entitled 'Collyra' which, according to Porphyrio constituted Book 16. If Porphyrio is right, that must have been written when Lucilius was nearly seventy. The only alternatives, as far as I can see, are to emend Porphyrio's figure or else

---

[11] Not an anachronistic reservation. See, e.g., Ovid, *Am.* 1.9.4: *turpe senilis amor.*

assume that the book contained reminiscences of events long gone by. That was certainly the case with some of the other books. A different approach, favoured by Munro (215), Cichorius (13), and others, is to look for a compromise by emending Jerome's numeral from XLVI to LXVI, thus producing a birthdate of 168 B.C. That, of course, might be right; but once Jerome and Haupt are abandoned there is no external evidence left, and in fact the intermediate date does not help very much.

Certain fragments in Book 26 show how the problem is connected with the relationship of Lucilius and Scipio. Someone is offering advice:

> *quid cauendum tibi censerem, quid uitandum maxime* (712)

What I thought you should beware of and avoid above all else,

> *hunc laborem sumas laudem qui tibi ac fructum ferat* (713)

here's a labour which will bring you reputation and success,

> *percrepa pugnam Popili, facta Corneli cane* (714)

noise abroad Popilius' battle, sing Cornelius' doughty deeds,

> *quare hoc colere est satius quam illa, studium omne hic consumere* (718)

This, not that, deserves attention; spend your energies on this.

It looks as if Lucilius, like Horace in 2.1, is being advised by an elderly and rather pompous man to write epic rather than satire. And, again like Horace, he seems to have declined on the grounds of incapacity:

> *ego si, qui sum et quo folliculo nunc sum indutus, non queo* (691)

If, because I'm me and wear this little envelope, I can't ...
[that should not stop someone else from doing the job.]

This reconstruction would be just acceptable if Lucilius was in his late forties and his adviser was fifteen or twenty years older. But in that case 689 must be assigned to another context:

> *tuam probatam mi spectatam maxime adulescentiam*

That young character of yours which I have tested and observed.

If Lucilius was forty-eight years old, the *adulescentia* in question could not have been his.

A rather similar situation seems to have been presented in Book 30:

> *sicubi ad aures*
> *fama tuam pugnam clarans adlata dicasset* (1009-10)

Whenever
news came to my ears reporting the fame of your battle,

*quantas quoque modo aerumnas quantosque labores
exanclaris* (1011-2)

how great the cup of your woes and hardships, and in what manner
you drank it dry.

[In due course an account will be provided by a suitably gifted
writer]

et te his uersibus interea contentus teneto (1015)

and in the meantime rest content with the verses I give you.

It is not certain that these fragments were addressed to Scipio. Cichorius
(189) believed the general in question was Sempronius Tuditanus (cos.
129) who was fighting a campaign in Illyricum. In any case the lines show
once again Lucilius' determination not to attempt a full-dress epic
encomium. No doubt there was an element of modesty here, but Lucilius
may have felt that formal tributes properly came from one's social
subordinates. After all, Ennius had been *employed* to do that sort of
thing. Whatever hints people might drop, he would not compromise his
position as a gentleman. If he was going to pay compliments, he would do
so in his own way. The *sermo* as he conceived it was quite capable of
giving praise. It could also help the great man's cause by ridiculing the
opposition.

We must now look more closely at some of the attacks Lucilius made,
starting with a reference to Q. Metellus Macedonicus. This man had
acquired his name as praetor in 148 B.C. when he recovered Macedonia
from the pretender Andriscus, and over the next decade he and Appius
Claudius Pulcher (consuls in 143) were Scipio's most powerful rivals. In
138 Metellus defended L. Aurelius Cotta against Scipio (see below); he is
mentioned as an enemy of Furius Philus, a close friend of Scipio's, in 136.
As censor in 131 he was worried by the shortage of recruits for the army,
and so he made a speech, urging Romans to marry – even though wives
were admittedly a great nuisance (Gellius 1.6). In Lucilius we find

*homines ipsi hanc sibi molestiam ultro atque aerumnam offerunt
ducunt uxores, producunt quibus haec faciant liberos* (644-5)

Men devise this tiresome nuisance freely of their own accord,
taking wives, begetting children for whose sake they do all this.

The lines were almost certainly a gibe at the course recommended by
Metellus; Lucilius himself was apparently a bachelor. Of the other
fragments from Books 26-30 one makes fun of Lentulus Lupus' procedure
as a judge (805-11, see p. 167 below); another refers to Troginus, a soldier

who had earned the nickname of *calix* 'Tankard' (1021); another, if Cichorius (207) is right, speaks of a thievish character called Q. Mutto (1067). We also hear of some shirker in the unsuccessful Spanish campaign at Palantia early in 136 B.C. (1123). There is not much evidence here of the pugnacious satirist; yet the complaints acknowledged in 1082-6 (see p. 7 above) must have had some basis. It was probably in these books that Lucilius attacked the various tribes and their leading men; and even when allowance is made for rhetorical exaggeration we cannot ignore Horace's statement that Metellus was wounded (*laesus*) by Lucilius' verses (2.1.67). One concludes, therefore, that the satirist's trenchancy is not adequately reflected in the surviving fragments of Books 26-30.

In Book 1, which, as Raschke says, was probably published about 125 B.C., a council of the gods discussed what to do about the increasing decadence and depravity of Rome. Debate centred on the character of Lucius Cornelius Lentulus Lupus (consul 156 B.C.) who had been found guilty of extortion in 154, had opposed Cato, and hence Scipio, over Carthage, had become censor in 147, and thanks to the support of Metellus and Pompeius had been appointed *princeps senatus* in 131, a post coveted by Scipio himself. While such a man held authority, clearly no improvement could be expected, and so the gods decided to remove him from the scene. His death took place after a great storm in 126 B.C. (39-41), and Lucilius, who was not noted for his tact or taste, wrote the satire soon afterwards, describing Lupus' tolerance of evil ways (12, 13), his repulsive face (37), and his death, which the gods brought about through his own gluttony (46).

Another set piece appeared a few years later in Book 2. The Stoic jurist Q. Mucius Scaevola, who was Laelius' son-in-law, had been on good terms with Scipio, but after Scipio's death he began to move in a different direction. He married his daughter to Glabrio, the pro-Gracchan tribune of 123 B.C., and though not a supporter of Gaius Gracchus he deplored his murder and the persecution of his followers. He was praetor in Asia in 120, and on his return was accused of extortion by the Epicurean T. Albucius. According to Cicero (*De Orat.* 1.72) Lucilius was somewhat displeased with Scaevola (*subiratus*); he certainly showed a characteristic zest in having him charged with assault (54-5), robbery (58-9, 60), pederasty (63), and gluttony (67-9, 70). This does not mean, however, that Lucilius took the side of the prosecution. Albucius, for his part, was pilloried as an extreme philhellene with all the attendant affectations (84-6, 87-93). It may well have been the attacks contained in these first two books that Persius had in mind when he wrote

> secuit Lucilius urbem,
> te Lupe, te Muci, et genuinum fregit in illis (1.114-5)

> Lucilius crunched the city –
> Lupus and Mucius and all their kind – and smashed his molar.

One notes, however, that the attacks were not delivered by Lucilius *in propria persona*; they came from his characters. This dramatic technique, along with his outspokenness, his exuberant style, and his interest in literary criticism, naturally reminded people of Aristophanes (Horace 1.4.6-8).

Like others, the Scipionic faction was never stable.[12] We know of several men who broke away from it in the 130s, e.g. P. Mucius Scaevola, C. Cato, and C. Fannius; and in 129 the group was deprived of its leader. Nevertheless, many of its members retained their antipathies and suffered accordingly; two of Scipio's nephews, for instance, were attacked by C. Gracchus.[13] As Gruen says (95) 'despite factional shifts and political upheaval, there is unmistakable continuity in the opposition to the Gracchi. The shadow of Scipio Aemilianus still hangs over the events of the late 120s.' The anti-Metellan stance was also retained. Lucilius mocked Macedonicus' fourth son Caecilius Metellus Caprarius, on account of his name 'Goatman', providing him with a snout and a set of hooves (233-4). He also gave warning to prevent 'Cecilius' from becoming 'rustic pretor' – *pretor rusticus* instead of *praetor urbanus* (232). Caprarius did become praetor in 118. Was he in fact rather stupid? Many years before, in 134 or 133 B.C., Scipio remarked that if Caprarius' mother had produced a fifth son he would have been an ass (Cicero, *De Orat.* 2.267).

In Book 11 we hear of a racketeer in league with a crooked judge:

> Gaius Cassius, here, the businessman, widely referred to
> as Headman the cutpurse and thief – Tullius Quintus the judge
> pronounces *him* legatee; the others' claims are rejected (445-7).

The man is identified with some plausibility by Cichorius (314) as C. Cassius Sabaco, who was expelled from the senate in 115 B.C. for giving illegal assistance to Marius. A few years after this a demagogue is described as he whips up indignation against the aristocracy:

> *peccare impune rati sunt*
> *posse et nobilitate facul propellere iniquos* (270-1)

> They thought they could sin unpunished
> and repel their opponents with ease by means of their noble birth.

The speaker may have been the fiery C. Memmius, who voiced such sentiments as tribune elect in 112 and as tribune in 111.[11] Whoever is

---

[12] See, in addition to Astin, the studies of Gruen and Briscoe.
[13] See C. Gracchus in Malcovati (2) 193-4 and Plutarch, *C. Gracchus*, 6.2.
[14] See Cichorius, 283-5 and Gruen, 140.

portrayed, his style is ridiculed:

> *haec, inquam, rudet ex rostris atque heiulitabit*
> *concursans ueluti Ancarius (?) clareque quiritans* (273-4)

These complaints, I say, he will roar and yell from the rostrum,
dashing about like Ancarius (?) and loudly bellowing 'Romans!'

This brings us into the period of the struggle with Jugurtha. In 116 B.C. L.
Opimius (consul 121) headed an embassy to Numidia. Later he was
accused of having accepted bribes on that occasion, and he was
condemned in 109. The charge may well have been fabricated in order to
ruin the killer of Gaius Gracchus (Gruen, 144), but that did not prevent
Lucilius from referring to Opimius as 'this Jugurthan' (450).

The examples given above represent contemporary, or near-contem-
porary, gibes. But Lucilius was not always so topical. In the fragment
just quoted, Q. Opimius (consul 154 B.C.), the father of 'the Jugurthan',
is said to have behaved immorally as a boy (450-2). L. Aurelius Cotta,
when tribune in 154 B.C., had tried to escape paying his debts; in 138
Scipio accused him of maladministration, but thanks to the skill of
Metellus Macedonicus and some heavy bribery he was acquitted. Lucilius
called him 'a great trickster who readily accepted bribes but was slow to
pay' (440-2). Ti. Claudius Asellus was accused of profligacy by Scipio
when the latter was censor in 142 B.C. He retaliated by prosecuting Scipio
in 140 and alleging that his censorship had been a disaster. The
allegation was referred to by Lucilius (424-5), and we may be sure he
added Scipio's rejoinder, which said, in effect, 'No wonder it was a
disaster, since it was concluded by L. Mummius, the man who reinstated
you.'[15] As Book 11 belongs to the period 115-110 B.C., these stories are all
over twenty-five years old. The same procedure can be seen in Book 14,
where someone complains about the quaestor whom he had on his staff in
Spain in the 130s or 140s: Publius Pavus Tuditanus (?) was a *lucifugus
nebulo* 'a shifty shady character' (499-500). Finally we have a fragment
(1138-9) referring to (a) Lucius Hostilius Tubulus, who was prosecuted
for bribery during Scipio's censorship and later (it is said) took poison
(Gruen, 30), (b) L. Cornelius Lentulus Lupus, the *princeps senatus* of
131 mentioned above, and (c) C. Papirius Carbo, a strong supporter of
Tiberius Gracchus, who clashed with Scipio on several occasions and was
suspected (among others) of causing his death. In 119 he too committed
suicide. The three men are linked with the son of Neptune (the lawless
Polyphemus):

> *Tubulus si Lucius umquam*
> *si Lupus aut Carbo aut Neptuni filius,*

[15] See Cicero, *De Orat*.2.268; Astin, 120 and 326.

and it is clear from the context in which the fragment is quoted (Cicero, *ND* 1.63) that Lucilius accused them of perjury and sacrilege. They were probably already dead, but, as we have seen, *de mortuis* was not a Lucilian principle.

The sparseness of the details cited above is all too plain. They do not tell us how far Lucilius dealt with political issues as distinct from personalities, or whether he ever took a line independent of Scipio's, or how his views developed in the twenty-five years after his friend's death. But they do indicate the kind of attack that he was capable of making and the social position from which he made it. That position in turn helps to explain the ease and confidence of his other pronouncements, whether on literature or the conduct of life.

(ii) Horace

Since Horace was once a *tribunus militum* in Brutus' army, then held the post of *scriba* in the treasury, and was later described as watching the games from the same part of the stadium as Maecenas (2.6.48), one infers he was a knight. So when he says he is below the *census* of Lucilius (2.1.75), he must be speaking of his general financial position. Certainly when he was writing his *Satires* in the 30s Horace came nowhere near Lucilius in wealth, whatever rewards he may have earned later. And since he was the son of a freedman and an obscure mother he had no family connexions to give him political influence. So his position *vis-à-vis* those in power was very different from his predecessor's. Nevertheless, if we consider his relations with Maecenas and Octavian (Augustus) in the periods covered by the *Satires* and *Epistles*, we will find that a complex and unusual situation developed. While it is true, of course, that Horace's role in politics was insignificant, to describe him as 'a court slave' or 'a servile spirit' is a very crude distortion indeed.[1]

Like Lucilius, Horace began to write satire after he had seen military service. The Spanish campaign which Lucilius had witnessed had been bad enough, but the double encounter at Philippi (42 B.C.) was altogether more frightful. 'Never had such warlike fury and valour been displayed as here between fellow-citizens, kinsmen, and comrades in arms. This is proved by the fact that in the two battles the number of dead was to all appearances just as great on the side of the victors' (Appian 4.137). Little wonder that Horace, still in his early twenties, should have returned home bitter and disillusioned, and that for his first poetic ventures he should have chosen the two most aggressive forms in Greek and Latin literature – iambic and satire. Yet although he might invoke Archilochus

---

[1] For the phrase 'a court slave' see Dryden, 87; to Voltaire Virgil and Horace were *des âmes serviles*, see Erskine-Hill, 265.

and Hipponax (*Epod.* 6.13-4), inveigh against a former slave who now strutted around as a military tribune (*Epod.* 4), and abuse an ageing and importunate aristocratic lady (*Epod.* 8), the absence of names suggests that he was in no position to make specific attacks. After all, the country was now controlled by his recent enemies; the property left by his father had been confiscated; and indeed he might count himself lucky to be alive. In view of all this, the audacity of 1.2 (the critique of adultery) was considerable. The names Maltinus (25) and Cupiennius (36) were perhaps chosen for etymological reasons. (*Malta* meant an effeminate fop and Cupiennius might be associated with *cupio*.) Yet as the names were real, they must have aroused comment. We hear, for instance, of a C. Cupiennius Libo who was an acquaintance of Octavian. Fufidius the greedy moneylender (12), though perhaps no longer alive, was an actual person; the absurd Tigellius (3) had been a friend of Octavian's (1.3.4). More to the point, the Sallust who was crazy over freedwomen (48) may well have been the celebrated historian and the admirer of Julius Caesar. The immodest Catia (95) was probably a Roman matron, like Sulla's daughter Fausta (64). Fausta's lovers have real names (64 and 67), and the Galba who took such a suspiciously lenient view of adultery (46) belonged to the aristocratic *gens Sulpicia*. Not surprisingly the poem gave offence in certain quarters. In 1.4.92 Horace tried to play it down by recalling a relatively harmless gibe: 'Surely you don't think me vicious just because I had a laugh at Rufillus and Gargonius.' These two, whoever they were, had been contrasted in 1.2.27; one was supposed to chew breath-sweeteners whereas the other smelt like a goat. *Satire* 1.7 may also belong to this early period; for the joke about Caesar's assassination, which provides the rather feeble climax, would have been less likely after Horace had become an *amicus* of Octavian's minister. The piece, however, was not thought objectionable enough to be excluded from the collection of 35 B.C.

In these years C. Maecenas, a rich Etruscan noble, had been an active supporter of Octavian. He had fought at Philippi; then he had helped to arrange the marriage with Scribonia; and he had played a part in the negotiations at Brundisium in 40 B.C. In 38 fighting broke out between Octavian and Pompey's son Sextus, who by the treaty of Misenum in the previous year had been given control of Sardinia, Corsica, Sicily, and the Peloponnese. In these engagements Octavian suffered some serious reverses, and as a result Maecenas was sent to Greece to obtain naval reinforcements from Antony. In the spring of 37 B.C. Maecenas helped to patch up the alliance between Octavian and Antony at Tarentum. Then he returned to Rome, and he was in charge of affairs in 36 when Octavian was campaigning against Sextus Pompey in Sicily. Sextus also had supporters in the capital, and on two occasions Maecenas had to suppress them (Appian 5.99 and 112). Maecenas was again in charge in

35 B.C., when Octavian was in Illyricum.[2]

Yet there was another side to Maecenas' personality. He refused to follow the senatorial cursus and insisted on remaining a knight. He enjoyed ease and luxury, and his clothes were both casual and expensive. Most important, he loved literature and was himself a writer of sorts. The two sides of his life – the political and the artistic – came together in his activities as a patron. Octavian was aware that, like Pompey and Caesar, he should have writers among his supporters. For various reasons (time, temperament, diplomacy?) he left most of these cultural relations to Maecenas. How far Maecenas actually took the initiative cannot be determined. One assumes he was on the look-out for genuine talent, but he may well have had more 'approaches' than he wanted. The pest on the Sacred Way (1.9) sounds like a recognisable type. Horace himself says (*E.* 2.2.51-2)

> *paupertas impulit audax*
> *ut uersus facerem*
>
> Lady Poverty, daring as ever, impelled me
> to turn out verses –

a statement which, for all its playful exaggeration, implies that the poet had been hoping for patronage. At any rate, in the late spring of 38 B.C., acting on recommendations from Varius and Virgil, Maecenas invited to an interview the man who had fought against him at Philippi.[3] Nine months later, after his mission to Antony, he admitted Horace to his circle of *amici*. Possibly 1.4 belongs to those intervening months. While it contains about a dozen satirical references, half of those mentioned are known to have been unimportant; we have no information about the rest, but the same may well apply to them. The lines about Horace's loyalty and discretion (80-5) might have been intended to reassure his prospective patron. The theory would also explain the absence of any reference to Maecenas: such familiarity would have been presumptuous before Horace had been invited to join the group. Whether or not this guess is right, once Horace became an *amicus* of Maecenas his use of names grew less abrasive.

---

[2] See *Elegiae in Maecenatem* 1.43 in *Minor Latin Poets*, trans. J.W. and A.M. Duff (Loeb); Pliny, *NH* 7.148 (Philippi); Appian 5. 53 (Scribonia); Appian 5.64 (Brundisium); Appian 5.92 (mission to Antony). A good account of his career is provided by Reckford.

[3] *Septimus octauo propior iam fugerit annus* (2.6.40) is a hard line. It probably means, in effect, 'Nearly seven years have passed'. *octauo propior* adds little to the sense, merely indicating that the present point is nearer to the eighth year than to the sixth. (So Kiessling-Heinze *ad. loc.* and Shackleton Bailey 37, n. 13. In the Penguin translation I was probably wrong to follow the other view, i.e. 'Seven, nearly eight years'.) If we date 2.6 to the end of 31 B.C. and move back nearly seven years, we reach January or February of 37. To judge from 1.6.61 the first interview will then have been in April or May of 38.

At first, relations between patron and client were rather tentative (1.3.63-5, 2.6.42-3), but the friendship ripened. In the spring of 37 B.C. Horace accompanied Maecenas and the other negotiators to Brundisium on the way to the conference which eventually took place at Tarentum. Shortly after, he composed a light-hearted and studiously non-political account of the trip (1.5). In that year and in 36 Horace could presumably have written attacks on Sextus Pompey and his supporters. Hints of what might have been done are found in *Epod.* 4.19 – *contra latrones atque seruilem manum* 'against brigands and a band of slaves' – and in *Epod.* 9.10 – *seruis amicus perfidis* 'the friend of treacherous slaves'. But no such attacks were made. In September of 36 Sextus Pompey was defeated at Naulochus. That left Octavian and Antony. During the winter of 36/35 the pact made at Tarentum still held. So there was no question of attacking Antony's supporters. On the contrary, at the end of 1.10 Horace boasts of his friendship with Asinius Pollio and Valerius Messalla, who had been adherents of Antony; he also refers to L. Gellius Poplicola (Messalla's half-brother), Calpurnius Bibulus, and C. Fannius, who were still working on Antony's behalf.

Leaving aside 1.2, 1.7, and 1.4, we may classify the names in Book 1 as follows. (The numbers refer to the satires.)

Living people: 1. Crispinus, Fannius, Tanais (?), Visellius' father-in-law (?). 3. Labeo (?), Ruso, Alfenus (?), Hermogenes, Crispinus. 5. Aufidius Luscus, Sarmentus, Cicirrus. 6. Tillius, Novius the younger. 7. Persius, Rex. 8. Iulius, Voranus, Canidia (?), Sagana (?). 9. Hermogenes. 10. Hermogenes, Demetrius, Fannius.

Dead people: 3. Tigellius, Sisyphus. 6. Laevinus. 10. Laberius, Cassius.

Type-names: (including figures from literature and folklore and people who have survived on account of their notoriety): 1. Ummidius, Naevius, Nomentanus. 3. Maenius, Novius, Balbinus, Hagna. 5. Apella. 6. Barrus, Syrus, Dama, Dionysius, Natta. 7. Sisenna, Barrus. 8. Pantolabus, Nomentanus. 9. Bolanus (?).

Nicknames: 8. Pediatia. 10. Pitholeon, Alpinus, Pantilius. *simius* in v. 18 is an insult rather than a nickname.

Figures from myth: 1. Tantalus, the daughters of Tyndareus. 3. Helen.

If we except Labeo and Alfenus, whose identity is problematical, Tillius seems to have been the only person of any importance in public life. But even he was a man without family connexions, and his career had been decidedly checkered.

Yet if Horace did not attack Maecenas' political opponents, there were other, more subtle, ways of contributing to his friend's prestige.[4] He

---

[4] These compliments are examined very fully by Du Quesnay, 41-53. But like other elements in 1 they can only be called 'political' in a rather extended sense of the word.

could compliment him indirectly, as in the reference to the landscaping on the Esquiline (1.8). He could praise the integrity of the group as a whole (1.9). More important, Horace could make Maecenas part of a moral *sermo*, as he did in 1.6, showing how the great man had offered his patronage without objecting to the poet's humble birth. The qualities ascribed to Maecenas are, of course, suited to the theme of the poem in which they occur, e.g. tolerance (1.3), lack of social prejudice (1.6), absence of back-biting (1.9). But although the qualities are selected, they should not be regarded as fictitious.

About 34 B.C. Maecenas presented Horace with what is traditionally known as 'the Sabine farm'.[5] In fact it was a sizeable country house with eight servants (2.7.118); and the estate supported five local families (*E*. 1.14.2-3), all of whom presumably paid Horace rent. This generous gift might have been expected to strengthen the patron's claims on his client's services – services which could have been used with telling effect in the next three years. For it was then that the working agreement between Octavian and Antony finally broke down. As war approached, the air became thick with propaganda, ranging from political complaints to vulgar sexual abuse.[6] A few verses of *Epod.* 9 show the kind of contribution Horace might have made:

> *Romanus, eheu – posteri negabitis –*
> *emancipatus feminae*
> *fert uallum et arma miles et spadonibus*
> *seruire rugosis potest,*
> *interque signa turpe militaria*
> *sol aspicit conopium* (11-16)

A Roman soldier as a woman's slave –
  for shame! our grandsons will deny it –
carries his stake and weapons and can bear
  to serve her shrivelled eunuchs' will.
Amid the standards of the camp, the sun
  beholds the vile mosquito-net.

But again there is nothing of that kind in the *Satires*. This raises the question of how much pressure was actually exerted by Maecenas in the period of the *Epodes* and *Satires*. Two over-simple answers can be avoided: first the sentimental view that Maecenas provided an income out of sheer benevolence without expecting anything in return (that overlooks his career as a politician), and secondly the cynical view that he kept badgering his client to write political propaganda whether in the form of satire or panegyric (that underrates his artistic and diplomatic

---

[5] Approximate dating is supplied by 2.3, which is set on the farm and alludes in v. 185 to the aedileship of Agrippa (33 B.C.).

[6] The exchanges are studied by Scott and Hallett.

sensitivity). Between these positions there is room for several shades of opinion. My own impression is that Octavian would have welcomed some form of eulogy; that on one or two occasions Maecenas tactfully conveyed this wish to Horace and equally tactfully cushioned his refusal. But in the end all we have is the poetry itself, and that tells us what Horace's powerful friends accepted, not necessarily what they desired. As for satire, there is no evidence that Horace was urged to attack the enemies of Maecenas and Octavian. If he was, he refused, partly perhaps out of loyalty to some of his former comrades, but mainly because, unlike Lucilius, he thought of satire not as a vehicle of political attack but as a kind of entertainment in which individuals and their private faults were mentioned chiefly as illustrations of a moral argument.

Given such an attitude, and given too his position in the establishment, Horace had little reason to worry about libel. But that did not prevent him from staging a scene in which the old lawyer Trebatius Testa warned him about its dangers:

> si male condiderit in quem quis carmina, ius est
> iudiciumque (2.1.82-3)

If a party compose foul verses to another's hurt,
a hearing and trial ensue.

The phrase *ius iudiciumque* refers to the two stages of the civil process. The first stage (*in iure*) took place before a praetor, who clarified the claims and counter-claims, decided what the question at issue actually was, and then appointed a *iudex* to try the case. What law had Horace in mind? R.E. Smith thought it was Sulla's law *de iniuriis*. But that does not seem to have dealt with defamation, though it may have been extended later so as to do so. Perhaps we should think rather of the fourth edict, which was certainly in existence by that time:[7] *ne quid defamandi causa fiat. si quis aduersus ea fecerit, prout quisque res erit animaduertam* (Lenel, 401), 'Let nothing be done with the intent to defame. If anyone breaks this rule I shall take action against him in accordance with the facts of the case.' But while Horace's phrase *ius est iudiciumque* implies the existence of a current law, the words *si condiderit quis carmina* were doubtless intended to recall in a playfully portentous way the ancient legislation against slanderous abuse in the Twelve Tables. As for the adjective *mala*, that prepared the way for the pun on *mala carmina* (libellous verses / rotten poetry); it was not meant to raise the question of magical incantations. In the same way, centuries later, Arnobius could speak of a *carmen malum quo fama alterius coinquinetur* (*Adv. Nat.* 4.34) 'a malicious poem designed to besmirch another person's good name'.

[7] See Watson, 39.

Whatever the terms of the law in 30 B.C., Horace knew he was in little danger of infringing it. The names which he used satirically in Book 2 may be listed as follows (the numbers refer to the poems):

Living people: 1. Trebatius, Caesar (Octavian), Milonius (?), Canidia (?). 2. Avidienus (?), Trausius (?). 3. Damasippus (?), the son of Aesopus, the sons of Arrius, Turbo. 5. Furius, Nasica, Coranus. 6. Lepos (?). 7. Mulvius, Crispinus. 8. Vibidius, Balatro, Canidia (?).
Dead people: 3. Fufius, Staberius, Aristippus, Oppidius, Polemon, Marius. 4. Catius, Aufidius. 7. Priscus (?), Volanerius.
Type-names: 1. Pantolabus, Nomentanus, Cervius, Turius, Scaeva. 2. Gallonius, Albucius, Naevius. 3. Nerius, Cicuta, Proteus, Perellius, Opimius, Nomentanus, Menenius. 5. Dama, Davus. 7. Davus. 8. Nasidienus (?), Hydaspes (?), Nomentanus, Porcius.
Figures from myth: 1. Castor, (Pollux). 3. Orestes, the son of Atreus (Agamemnon), Ajax, Agave. 5. Ulysses, Tiresias, Penelope.

Apart from Octavian, the only important man in the first category is Trebatius, if indeed he was still alive. But the wit directed at him is a kind of playful teasing which is quite compatible with respect. The book, then, was unlikely to cause trouble. But Horace could not disavow the practice of ridiculing people without renouncing the Lucilian tradition. So he concluded the piece with an amusing quibble:

> *esto, si quis mala; sed bona si quis*
> *iudice condiderit laudatus Caesare? si quis*
> *opprobriis dignum latrauerit, integer ipse?*
> *'soluentur risu tabulae, tu missus abibis.'*

> *Foul* verses, yes; but what if a party compose
> *fine* verses which win a favourable verdict from Caesar?
> Or snarl at a public menace when he himself is blameless?
> 'The charge will dissolve in laughter; you will get off scot free.'

We have followed in summary the career of Maecenas down to 31 B.C. The ninth epode, quoted a short while ago, was set at Actium, and it may be that both Maecenas and Horace were present at the battle. But if so, they returned soon after, for Maecenas was needed in Rome, the most urgent task being the suppression of the younger Lepidus' conspiracy.[8] In this period Maecenas, along with Agrippa, saw all the official correspondence and had the authority to alter and seal Octavian's letters (Dio 51.3.5-6). Since Horace was known to be on such close terms, people would ask him to use his influence with Maecenas on their behalf (2.6.38). Though he enjoyed the reflected glory, Horace found the

---

[8] For Lepidus see Velleius 2.88, Appian 4.50, Dio 54.15.4.

quasi-official life and its duties rather a strain, and he treasured the Sabine farm as a refuge.

After 29 B.C. Maecenas is no longer found in charge of affairs. He continued busy in politics for several years (*Odes* 3.8.17-28 and 3.29.25-8) and the friendship between poet and patron continued to flourish, as can be seen from the first collection of *Odes* which was published in 23 B.C. Nor was the dependence all on one side. Maecenas, who tended to be rather neurotic, needed the support of his friend; one thinks, for example, of 2.17 (*cur me querellis*). But soon after the appearance of *Odes* 1-3 came the conspiracy of Murena and Caepio against Augustus. Maecenas got early news of its detection and told his wife Terentia, who was Murena's sister.[9] This humane and understandable indiscretion, which did not succeed in saving Murena, angered Augustus and damaged Maecenas' position. Still, it seems that their relations were not completely severed. According to Dio (54.6.5) there was a discussion in 21 B.C. about the future of Agrippa, in which Maecenas is supposed to have remarked drily 'You've made him so important that he must either become your son-in-law or be put to death.'

By now Horace was writing his first book of *Epistles*, which appeared in late 20 or 19 B.C. The most revealing piece is no. 7, which will be discussed in Chapter Five. While it is wrong to talk of a rift, one does sense a certain degree of tension, which is also reflected, perhaps, in *E* 1.17 and 18. Nevertheless, the friendship survived, and (as with *Odes* 1-3) the first and penultimate pieces were addressed to Maecenas. By now the great man's career was virtually over. As Seneca says in Tacitus, *Ann.* 14.53, he might as well have been in retirement abroad. He was not appointed deputy in 16 B.C. when Augustus went to Gaul. Dio (54.19.6) thinks this was because of the strain caused by the emperor's liaison with Terentia. More probably Maecenas no longer felt equal to such duties. Whatever the reason for his political decline, the last testimonia are free from bitterness. In 12 B.C. Augustus intervened in a trial and instructed the prosecuting counsel not to abuse his friends Apuleius and Maecenas, who were assisting the defendant (Dio 54.30.4). And there is a respectful and affectionate reference in *Odes* 4.11.17-20. Maecenas died at the end of September, 8 B.C. In his will he made Augustus his heir and urged him not to forget Horace: *Horati Flacci ut mei esto memor* (Suetonius, *Life of Horace*).

Except for a passing reference (1.3.4) and a discreet allusion (1.5.29) Horace does not mention Octavian until the time of Actium. *Epod.* 9 celebrates the victory, but the language is by no means fulsome, and anyway the poem is addressed to Maecenas. Later, because of his proximity to the almighty (*deos*), Horace is supposed to have news of Dacia and to know Octavian's intentions about settling his veterans

[9] Suetonius, *Aug.* 66.3. See Nisbet-Hubbard on *Odes* 2.10.

(2.6.51-8). He jokingly disclaims all such knowledge, thus affirming his acquaintance with Octavian and yet at the same time protesting the negligible extent of his influence. In 2.5 there are some pompous words about the victor, anticipating a new campaign against Parthia:

> *tempore quo iuuenis Parthis horrendus, ab alto*
> *demissum genus Aenea, tellure marique*
> *magnus erit* (62-4)

In the days when a youthful hero, scourge of the Parthian race,
born of Aeneas' noble line, shall rule over land
and sea ...

That sounds highly flattering. But the speaker is the rascally Tiresias, who is giving advice on legacy-hunting. And the oracle goes on to tell how the improvident Nasica tried to restore his fortunes by marrying his daughter to a rich old fogey. So again an extravagantly deferential tone is established, only to be undermined by humour. The final example comes in 2.1, where Trebatius urges Horace to praise Octavian's military victories. Horace sidesteps in Lucilian style – he lacks the power to describe such epic scenes. Trebatius then tries again:

> *attamen et iustum poteras et scribere fortem,*
> *Scipiadam ut sapiens Lucilius* (16-17)

But you could depict his fairness and courage, as the wise Lucilius
did with Scipio.

Horace answers:

> *haud mihi deero*
> *cum res ipsa feret: nisi dextro tempore Flacci*
> *uerba per attentam non ibunt Caesaris aurem,*
> *cui male si palpere recalcitrat undique tutus* (17-20)

> I shan't be found wanting when the chance occurs.
> If the moment isn't right, then Floppy's words won't penetrate
> Caesar's pricked-up ear. Rub him the wrong way
> and he'll lash out right and left with his hooves in self-defence.

So we have the same pattern: deliberately over-pitched eulogy, followed by satirical deflation. One *hopes* the image is that of a horse.

In the next seven years Octavian, who took the name 'Augustus' in 27 B.C., came to occupy a more significant place in Horace's poetry. He is mentioned in nearly one in five of the odes in Books 1-3, and plays a prominent part in 1.2, 1.12, 1.37, 3.4, and 3.25. But before talking too readily of adulation we must remember what Augustus had achieved in the way of peaceful reconstruction, and what he meant to the vast majority of Roman citizens who did not belong to senatorial families.

Again, Horace himself had been treated with consideration during his period of political disenchantment, and by the late 30s he had come to believe that any hope of survival and regeneration rested with the future Augustus. Finally, those laudatory passages have to be assessed in terms of ancient panegyric. When compared with the *Panegyricus Messallae* or the *Laus Pisonis*,[10] or with later effusions like Statius' poem on the equestrian statue of Domitian (*Silv.* 1.1), even the most enthusiastic odes appear restrained.

As well as profiting from Horace's skill as a *uates*, Augustus would have liked to employ him on a more personal basis, perhaps because of his experience in the civil service. In a letter to Maecenas (about 25 B.C.?) he said: 'As I am over-worked and unwell, I would like to deprive you of our friend Horace. So he will give up spongeing at your table and come to mine here in the palace to help me with my correspondence' (Suetonius, *Life*). It was a unique opportunity for power and enrichment, which most people would have seized with alacrity. But not Horace. No doubt he spent a good deal of time constructing his *recusatio* ('Greatly honoured' ... 'in ordinary circumstances would have been delighted' ... 'health very uncertain' ... 'the greatest regret'.) And to his credit Augustus, who was not used to being turned down, acquiesced. He even wrote inviting Horace to use the official residence as his own. This does not mean, of course, that Horace enjoyed, or sought, a position of equality. One cannot imagine him replying in kind when the emperor called him 'a charming mannikin' or 'an unsullied cock' (Suetonius, *Life*). Nor did he risk addressing Augustus in any of his epistles. Instead of accepting this as a sign of his pre-eminence, Augustus was slightly piqued and wrote saying: 'I want you to know I'm cross with you for not talking to me rather than anybody else in most of those pieces. Are you afraid that if you are seen to be a friend of mine it will blight your reputation with posterity?' (Suetonius, *Life*). That could not be ignored, and so, probably between 14 and 12 B.C., Horace wrote the *Epistle to Augustus* (*E.* 2.1). Coming as it does after the *Carmen Saeculare* and the official odes of Book 4, the epistle shows that imperial patronage is no longer being managed by a tactful intermediary.

The main problem was one of tone. The recipient of a Horatian epistle was not accorded any superior status; he was expected to listen politely to what the poet had to say; and sometimes he was chided for his shortcomings. That would hardly do for Augustus. Yet a protracted eulogy would be equally out of place. What Horace did was to write a general literary essay of nearly 200 lines. To this he added a formal preface and a more relaxed conclusion, in both of which he addressed the emperor. The essay, written in a lively and often satirical vein, does not

---

[10] For the *Panegyricus Messallae* see Tibullus, Loeb translation, 306-22; for the *Laus Pisonis* see *Minor Latin Poets*, Loeb translation, 294-314.

mention Augustus, but it reminds him indirectly of his obligations to poetry (118-38), and more than once it challenges his tastes (23-92, 182-207).[11] The concluding section (from 214 on) is very dextrous, incorporating Augustus in the poem both as reader and as patron. The Palatine library is mentioned as his donation; he is likened to Alexander, and then by a deft distortion the comparison is turned to Augustus' advantage;[12] his military exploits are celebrated by one who protests his inability to do so. The final joke, in which the subject and recipient of a bad poem is carried to oblivion, represents the satirical corollary of *uixere fortes* (*Odes* 4.9.25-8). As such, it ties the potentially pompous material to the light-hearted framework of an epistle.

It is less easy to come to terms with the introduction, which reaches a climax of deferential enthusiasm in vv. 16-7:

> *iurandasque tuum per numen ponimus aras,*
> *nil oriturum alias nil ortum tale fatentes*

> We build altars on which to swear by your divinity,
> declaring your like has never been and never will be.

Closer examination shows that the unusual degree of flattery is connected with the subsequent critique of the public's literary conservatism. The argument seems to run thus: 'Since the superiority of your political genius is acknowledged today, in your lifetime, the same should be true of our poetic genius.' If this is right, the emperor is not just being flattered; nor is he just being educated; he is being used.

As Reuben Brower remarked (183), 'An age in which the leading poet could honour the chief of state with a piece of literary criticism seems to us fairly agreeable.' True, but no age remains constant. After Horace's death in 8 B.C. there were still 25 years of the Augustan age left to run. The last six years or so brought increasing gloom and apprehension. The emperor was now an ailing seventy; his programme of moral reform had been defied by his own family; his dynastic plans had gone awry; the Pannonian revolt was still unchecked; there was plague in Rome and famine in the country at large. According to the elder Pliny (*NH* 7.149) these and other troubles brought him to the verge of suicide. In A.D. 8 the younger Julia was banished and Ovid relegated to Tomis. About the same time further disturbance was caused by 'the outrageous behaviour

---

[11] Augustus was keen on boxing (Suetonius, *Aug.* 45.2), a sport dismissed by Horace in v. 186 as 'the entertainment of the lower classes' (*plebecula*). For some of his traditional ideas see Suetonius, *Aug.* 31, 40, and 64. What Suetonius means by saying that he liked the *comoedia uetus* (*Aug.* 89.1) is uncertain. The problem calls for proper discussion, as distinct from brief dogmatic assertions.

[12] Because Alexander gave Choerilus a gold coin for every good line, Horace alleges that he had no taste in poetry (232-4, 237-8); but Ps. Acro says Choerilus received only seven coins in all.

of Cassius Severus, who denigrated distinguished men and women in his scandalous writings' (Tacitus, *Ann.* 1.72). Augustus, who throughout most of his reign had been fairly tolerant of verbal attack,[13] reacted in a novel way: he held an inquiry into libellous books under the law of treason – the *Lex Maiestatis*.[14] Cassius was found guilty and relegated to Crete in A.D. 8 or 12. The gentle Maecenas was no longer there to restrain his chief's anger.[15] By now the implications of autocracy were frighteningly clear.

(iii) Persius

'Born at Volaterrae in Etruria, he was a Roman knight but was connected by blood and marriage with men of the senatorial order.' These words from the *Life* make it clear that in his social background Persius had more in common with Lucilius than with Horace. But he was unlike both his predecessors in that he lived the whole of his life under a despot and his friends ended up in opposition. Before relating this last fact to Persius' *Satires* we must first give a brief account of who these people were and what happened to them.

1. Verginius Flavus, who taught Persius rhetoric (*Life*), was exiled with Musonius Rufus (no. 16) after the failure of Piso's conspiracy in A.D. 65. According to Tacitus (*Ann.* 15.71) it was because he was 'encouraging his students' enthusiasm by his eloquence' – *studia iuuenum eloquentia ... fouebat*. In other words the charge was one of subversion.

2. Annaeus Cornutus from Leptis in N. Africa was a freedman in the household of one of the Annaei.[1] He wrote on logic and rhetoric and produced a commentary on Virgil, but Persius speaks of him primarily as a teacher of Stoic philosophy (5.63-4). His only extant work is an allegorical interpretation of Greek myths in which he adopts a more moderate standpoint than that of Cleanthes and Chrysippus (Tate, 53). In 62.29.3 Dio tells how, when Nero was projecting a major epic on Roman history, some thought he should write 400 books. 'That's rather a

---

[13] See Suetonius, *Aug.* 51, 55, 56; Seneca, *De Ben.* 3.27; Tacitus, *Ann.* 4.34.8; Macrobius, *Sat.* 2.4.19.

[14] The *Lex Iulia Maiestatis* was a law of Caesar's. The phrase used by Tacitus is *specie legis eius*, which means that 'what should have been handled as *iniuriae* was dressed up as *maiestas*' (Goodyear, 151). According to Seneca, *Contr.* 10, *praef.* 7-8, Titus Labienus was the first writer whose books were burnt by a decree of the senate. For a discussion of the chronology see Bauman, ch. 12 and the article by Hennig.

[15] 'Maecenas would always release him from the grip of his anger and put him in a gentle mood' (Dio 55.7.1). In Dio 52.31.5-6 he is represented as advising Augustus to ignore slander. According to Seneca (*De Ben.* 6.32.2) Augustus acknowledged that the scandal of his daughter would have been handled differently had Maecenas and Agrippa been alive.

[1] Perhaps we should think of Annaeus Mela rather than his brother Seneca. The *Life* says it was many years before Persius came to know Seneca. This would be odd if he had attended Cornutus' classes in Seneca's house.

lot,' said Cornutus, 'no one will read them.' 'But look at Chrysippus,'
said someone, 'you praise and emulate him, and yet *he* wrote far more.'
'Yes,' replied Cornutus, 'but those books were of some practical value.'
For this he narrowly escaped execution and was banished to an island.

3. Servilius Nonianus (consul A.D. 35) was a distinguished historian
(Syme 3.91-109). His daughter probably married Barea Soranus (no. 12).
Persius looked upon him as a father (*Life*).

4. Annaeus Lucanus (b. A.D. 39) studied with Persius under Cornutus
and greeted his *Satires* with enthusiasm (*Life of Persius*). In A.D. 60 he
won first prize at the Neronia for an encomium of the emperor. Four
years later he gave recitations from *The Civil War*; but by now his
success was resented by Nero, who walked out of one of the sessions and
put a ban on publication (Tacitus, *Ann.* 15.49). As mutual hostility
continued to develop, Lucan composed a poem which contained a libel
on the emperor (Suetonius, *Life of Lucan*). Not long after, he joined
Piso's conspiracy and perished in consequence.[2]

5, 6, 7. Persius was related to Arria, daughter of the elder Arria whose
husband Caecina Paetus had plotted against Claudius in A.D. 42. When
he was sentenced, his wife showed him how to die by stabbing herself and
then handing him the dagger, saying 'It doesn't hurt, Paetus' (Pliny, *Ep.*
3.16). As a boy, Persius wrote verses in her honour.

8. The younger Arria's husband was the Stoic Thrasea, whom Persius
knew for ten years and occasionally accompanied on journeys. Thrasea
belonged to a senatorial family from Padua, an area with a strong sense
of the past. He had adopted the name of his father-in-law, Paetus, and in
due course he would write a book on Cato. At first Thrasea co-operated
with the new regime. He held the consulship in A.D. 56, but thereafter
became more and more disenchanted. In A.D. 59, following the murder of
Nero's mother, the senate was giving thanks for the emperor's lucky
escape when Thrasea walked out in disgust. He deplored the growing
frivolity and licentiousness of court life, and did not conceal his contempt
for Nero's musical performances. In A.D. 62 he opposed the death penalty
in the case of a man who had written abusive verses about Nero, and he
further annoyed the emperor by securing the abolition of automatic votes
of thanks to provincial governors. All this happened before Persius' death
in November 62. Soon after, Thrasea withdrew from public life, but this
did not save him from being executed in 66 as an accomplice of Piso.[3]

9, 10. Fannia, the daughter of Arria and Thrasea, married the Stoic
Helvidius Priscus about A.D. 55. He derived from Thrasea the habit of
speaking his mind (*libertas*), and like Thrasea he is said to have
celebrated the birthdays of Brutus and Cassius (Juvenal 5.36-7). He was

[2] See Ahl, 35-47 and 333-53.
[3] See Tacitus, *Ann.* 16.21-35; Syme (2) 558-61; Wirszubski, 138-43; M. Griffin, index
under Thrasea Paetus.

banished in A.D. 66. This did not mean the end of his career, but his later activities do not concern us at the moment.

11. Seneca was born between 4 and 1 B.C. Persius came to know him rather late, perhaps in the mid 50s, but the acquaintance did not lead him to admire Seneca's *ingenium* (*Life*). Since Persius would already have been familiar with Seneca's written works, *ingenium* here probably means something like our 'personality'. In A.D. 49 Seneca was appointed Nero's tutor, and continued to advise him after he became emperor in 54. This position brought a painful dilemma; for if Seneca was to guide Nero towards the ideal of a just ruler, he had to retain his good will. But to retain his good will he had to ignore, or even defend, Nero's increasingly outrageous behaviour. He persevered until A.D. 62, by which time his own reputation was badly tarnished and his influence gone. He lived three years in retirement, but was forced to commit suicide for alleged complicity in Piso's plot.

To these can be added a number of people who belonged to the same network of friends and relatives, and whom Persius may well have known.

12. Barea Soranus (consul suff. 52) came to no harm in Nero's early years. But as proconsul of Asia in 61/2 he refused to punish the city of Pergamum when it forcibly prevented Nero's freedman Acratus from plundering its statues and paintings (Tacitus, *Ann.* 16.23). This 'popularity-hunting' told against him, as did his friendship with Rubellius Plautus (no. 15). His commitment to Stoicism is proved by the combination of his name with that of Thrasea (no. 8). Together they symbolised 'virtue incarnate' (*uirtus ipsa* in Tacitus *Ann.* 16.21); and together they were condemned.

13. Linked with Thrasea and Helvidius in Tacitus *Ann.* 16.28 is Paconius Agrippinus. His Stoicism is further attested in two passages of Epictetus (1.1.28-30 and 1.2.12), where his conduct wins the philosopher's commendation. His father had been executed for plotting against Tiberius (Suetonius, *Tib.* 61.6); he himself was banished in 66.

14. Curtius Montanus was attacked in the same series of prosecutions for writing detestable verses (*detestanda carmina* in Tacitus, *Ann.* 16.28). It is not clear, however, that he was a Stoic.

15. Rubellius Plautus was the son of Julia, Tiberius' granddaughter. In birth he was therefore as close as Nero to Augustus (Tacitus, *Ann* 13.19). This made him a natural target for Nero's suspicion (*Ann.* 14.22 and 57). He was obliged to leave Rome in A.D. 60, and was later murdered. He was a pupil of the Stoic Musonius (no. 16), and his 'Stoic arrogance' was held against him by his accuser Tigellinus.

16. Musonius Rufus, the Stoic preacher, came from Volsinii in Etruria.[4] He accompanied Rubellius Plautus (no. 15) to Asia in A.D. 60, and helped him to face death calmly when Nero's henchmen arrived in

---

[4] For Musonius see the study by Van Geytenbeek.

62. Musonius subsequently returned to Rome, but was banished after Piso's conspiracy 'for encouraging his students' enthusiasm by his philosophical teaching' (Tacitus, *Ann.* 15.71). Under Vespasian he succeeded in securing the condemnation of Publius Egnatius Celer, the Stoic who had betrayed Barea Soranus (no. 12). This is related by Tacitus (*Hist.* 4.40).

17, 18. Annius Pollio was exiled for his part in Piso's conspiracy (Tacitus, *Ann* 15.71). The link with the Stoics is provided by his wife Servilia, who, as we know from Tacitus, *Ann.* 16.30, was the daughter of Barea Soranus (no. 12).

19. In A.D. 66 Annius Pollio's brother, Annius Vinicianus, son-in-law of the general Corbulo, was executed for another plot against Nero (Suetonius, *Nero* 36).

20. L. Antistius Vetus (consul 55) urged his son-in-law Rubellius Plautus (no. 15) to resist Nero's plan to have him murdered (Tacitus, *Ann.* 14.58). Antistius himself later committed suicide (Tacitus, *Ann.* 16.11).

The common features in most of these cases are plain enough: Stoicism, a growing hostility to the regime, and a punishment of death or exile. Now there is no need to discuss what form of government the Stoics thought best in principle. In the tradition of the school some had admired the mixed constitution, while others had written in praise of monarchy (M. Griffin, 202-6). In practice they were content to live under an autocrat and to participate in his government as long as it seemed tolerable to do so. In A.D. 54 Seneca did not feel that his position as Nero's adviser was incompatible with Stoic doctrine, and Thrasea accepted the consulship in 56. But what were the indispensable conditions of co-operation? And how should the Stoic behave when those conditions ceased to obtain? Thrasea, with his background, held that one should co-operate as long as the senate retained its liberty and status. In republican times those privileges had been guaranteed by the senate's constitutional position; under Augustus their erosion had been tactfully disguised; by now it was clear that what was left depended on the good will of the emperor. So there was always the possibility of conflict.

One relevant factor was the attitude of Thrasea and others to Brutus, Cassius, and Cato. In Augustus' time Brutus and Cassius were treated respectfully by Livy, Pollio, and Messalla; but under Tiberius their images were omitted from the funeral procession of Junia, who was related to them both (Tacitus, *Ann.* 3.76). Worse, the historian Cremutius Cordus was prosecuted for praising Brutus and calling Cassius 'the last of the Romans' (Tacitus, *Ann.* 4.34). Under Nero it counted against Cassius Longinus that he had a bust of his ancestor with the inscription 'to the leader of the cause' (Tacitus, *Ann.* 16.7). Thrasea and Helvidius, as mentioned earlier, observed the tyrannicides' birthdays; and Lucan, in his final desperate phase, extolled what they had done (*Life of Lucan*). Under Vespasian, Helvidius' opponent said let Helvidius be put on the same level as Cato and Brutus for his *constantia* and *fortitudo*; he himself continued his humble service (Tacitus, *Hist.* 4.8). The remark implies that such qualities went with a resistance to dictatorship. Under Nerva, the knight Titinius Capito had images of Brutus and Cassius in his house; he was not allowed to set them up anywhere else (Pliny *Ep.* 1.17). The same pattern is visible with Cato. It was not just for his philosophical opinions that he was copied by M. Favonius; Cicero's *Cato* was a political document, as is shown by Caesar's counterblast. Augustus had 'restored the republic'; so he prudently tolerated the praise of Cato. But a more clumsy and nervous emperor might resent it. The long passage in Book 9 of Lucan's *Civil War* (544-603) presents Cato not just as a virtuous man but as an upholder of law and freedom against despotism. It is hard to believe that Thrasea's study of Cato eschewed politics. There were certainly strong political implications in the comparison of Thrasea to Cato in the prosecution's speech (Tacitus, *Ann.* 16.22). Finally, under Vespasian, offence was caused to 'certain powerful persons' by the *Cato* of Curiatius Maternus (Tacitus, *Dial.* 2 and 3).

Now few would maintain with Rogers (290) that Thrasea, along with his friends, was 'advocating the overthrow of the government by force and violence'. But this does not oblige us to believe that their admiration of Brutus and Cato was purely moral or just a matter of sentimental hero-worship. The truth is, surely, that those republican figures represented the senate's self-respect. When things were quiet they were harmless enough, but as Nero's contempt of the senate increased they became symbols of disaffection. This blended with other types of objection – moral objections to Nero's cruelty and licentiousness, and social/cultural objections to his artistic exhibitionism. No wonder Thrasea wore an expression of severe disapproval – like a schoolmaster (Suetonius, *Nero* 37.1, cf. Tacitus, *Ann.* 16.22). What, then, was Nero's reaction? We may be sure he was aware of this mounting disgust, but he did not need to draw any false inferences about republican aspirations. All he had to do was to realise that these Stoic senators hated him and would have preferred another master. To a suspicious mind that carried disturbing implications; for there was no question of abdicating and living quietly at Baiae. Roman emperors did not abdicate; nor were they peacefully deposed. As in other, more modern, polities the constitution was now one of 'absolutism moderated by assassination'. As a result, when Piso's conspiracy was discovered Nero panicked. Instead of holding an inquiry to establish the degree of everyone's involvement, he simply instituted a purge. Had Persius been alive he would have suffered exile at least for his association with the accused, even if he had never written a line.

But of course he had written six satires, and we must now ask whether these poems contained material which was likely to cause offence in the period between, say, A.D. 59 and 62. In 2 the shrewd Nerius (14) comes from Horace (2.3.69). Staius (22) is a judge with a slightly dubious reputation. He must have been a well-known figure, but we cannot be sure that he was still alive. The aristocrat M. Aurelius Cotta Messallinus (72) was much hated for his numerous prosecutions (Tacitus, *Ann.* 6.5). There is also corroboration for Persius' charges of extravagance and debauchery (Tacitus, *Ann.* 6.7). Why did Persius mention him? Perhaps his victims included some relatives of Macrinus, the addressee, or of the poet. He was consul in A.D. 20 and subsequently proconsul of Asia. In 4 Alcibiades is lectured by Socrates; then a landowner, Vettidius, is mocked for being mean; Cerdo (51) is a collective name for the masses. *Satire* 6 starts with a joke about Ennius (10-11); Bestius (37) comes from Horace (*E.* 1.15.37); Caligula (43) and his wife Caesonia (47) are ridiculed in connexion with a bogus triumph. Caligula had died in 41, nearly twenty years before. In 3 the sloppy Natta (31) and Dr Craterus (65) come from Horace (1.6.124 and 2.3.161), and Orestes from mythology (118). In 5 the stupid Glycon (9) was a contemporary actor; Publius (74) and Dama (76) are type-names; Bathyllus (123) was a dancer in the time of Augustus; Chaerestratus (162) and Chrysis (165) are taken from Menander; Pulfenius (190) is any hulking centurion. Attius Labeo in 1.4 and 50 is a popular translator of the *Iliad*; Pedius (85) comes from Horace's courtroom (1.10.28), but as a Pedius Blaesus was expelled from the senate for extortion in A.D. 59 (Tacitus, *Ann.* 14.18) there is a strong possibility of a double allusion; the loutish philistine in vv. 127-33 is not given a name. So far fairly innocuous stuff.

Is there nothing, then, in the warning given to Persius in 1.108-9:

> *uide sis ne maiorum tibi forte*
> *limina frigescant*

> Better watch it; you may get a chilly reception
> from those baronial porches.

The words could, I suppose, be largely conventional, deriving as they do from Horace 2.1.60-2:

> *o puer, ut sis*
> *uitalis metuo, et maiorum ne quis amicus*
> *frigore te feriat*
> My lad, I'm afraid
> you may not be long for this world. One of your powerful friends
> may freeze you stiff.

Certainly, as Kenney (1) has pointed out, the satirist's apologia *was* by now something of a convention – a convention which Juvenal would continue. But even if the aristocracy as a whole was not affected by Persius' satire, perhaps those closest to the emperor were. And what of Nero himself?

Satire 4, as already observed, begins with Socrates admonishing Alcibiades. Britannicus in the fifteenth century suggested that this represented Seneca addressing the young Nero, and a number of respectable scholars (most recently D.Bo) have found this plausible. Against this theory is the fact that the references to Socrates and Alcibiades are specific; that in tone and content the philosopher's admonition sounds quite unlike anything that Seneca would or could have said to Nero (think of the *De Clementia*); and that the picture of the young Greek politician manipulating the *demos* does not correspond to anything in Nero's Rome. But what of those lines from 3?

> O mighty father of the gods, when sadistic lust, with its dagger
> dipped in fiery poison, incites dictators to crime,
> may it please thee to punish their cruelty in this and no other way:
> let them see Goodness and waste with remorse at having betrayed her
>
> (35-8).

There is no proof that Persius intended any allusion here; the instances he gives are the stock examples of Phalaris and Dionysius. Still, if we bear in mind the increasingly oppressive atmosphere of the years 59-62, any attack on tyranny could have been applied to Nero. Thirty years later, in A.D. 91, Maternus was put to death for saying 'something about tyrants' in a practice speech (Dio 67.12.5).

We come, finally, to 1, the condemnation of Rome's taste and morals. In v. 121 Persius probably wrote *auriculas asini quis non habet?* 'Who does not have ass's ears?' This completes the question in v. 8: *nam Romae quis non –?* 'For in Rome who does not have –?' And it is in line with the very general scope of Persius' condemnation: *no* one has any taste. It seems that later someone wrote *Mida rex* 'King Midas' either in the margin or above *quis non* so as to remind the reader of the fable in question. This double tradition was known to the scholiast and to the writer of the *Life*. They reversed the process described above, maintaining that the original reading *Mida rex* was altered either by Persius himself or by Cornutus after the poet's death to prevent Nero from taking personal offence. But even if, as we have argued, Persius wrote *quis non*, he was still taking a risk; for *any* reference to the Midas fable was capable of causing trouble.

The satire contains other passages which were even more dangerous. Before considering what they were we should recall that among the various kinds of poetry being written at the time were versions of the *Iliad* (Attius Labeo), tragedy (Seneca), pastoral (Calpurnius Siculus), elegy (Cocceius Nerva), and miscellaneous compositions by Lucan.

Other writers known to Nero were the future emperors Vitellius and Titus, and the epic poet Silius Italicus. Tacitus says that some of the promising younger talents would dine with the emperor and then spend the evening reading poetry and improvising verses together (*Ann.* 14.16). Suetonius says that Nero gave recitals of his poetry at home (*Nero* 10), not only to Romans but also to delegations of Greeks (*Nero* 22). Among his compositions were an epic on Troy in more than one book, a piece on Attis or the Bacchanals (Dio 62.20.2), and various other poems, some erotic, some satirical. He was insatiable in his desire for applause and could be sensitive to adverse criticism (Suetonius, *Nero* 25). Now in the first satire we find unfavourable comment on Attius' *Iliad* (50-1), on tragedy (67-8), on elegy (51-2), and on epyllion or romantic epic (34, 93-5, 99-102); scorn is directed at recitations and improvisations of wealthy Romans around the dinner-table (51-2); and particular reference is made to drivel written about Attis and the Bacchanals (93, 101,105). It therefore seems perverse to deny that the emperor and his friends were included in Persius' ridicule. Admittedly it is going too far to maintain that Nero was singled out for criticism and that the entire satire focusses on him. We cannot be sure that the verses quoted in vv. 93ff. and 99ff. were written by Nero himself, and even if they were it would not alter the fact that the satire as a whole was meant to have a general application. Nevertheless, such refinements are of no interest to a tyrant. If he had seen reason to take offence, nothing else would have mattered.

Although none of Persius' satires actually appeared in his lifetime, one assumes that he hoped eventually to publish them. In the meantime Macrinus and Cornutus doubtless heard or received the pieces addressed to them; the other satires were presumably read to small private audiences; and as the poet's reputation started to grow, copies would have been requested. If 1 had fallen into the wrong hands, the results might have been fatal. Certainly in the witch-hunt following Piso's conspiracy the satires could not have remained secret. In the event Persius died before any of these things happened. But the risks were real enough; and so the poet must be regarded as a courageous and highly imprudent young man.

In A.D. 69 many of the exiles returned, including Helvidius Priscus, who was appointed praetor for the following year. Helvidius' first thought was to bring to justice those responsible for the deaths of Thrasea Paetus and Barea Soranus. With the help of Musonius he secured the condemnation of Egnatius Celer. He then tried to open an inquiry into the activities of powerful senatorial *delatores*, like Eprius Marcellus; but the attempt failed owing to the intervention of Vespasian's son, Domitian, and his lieutenant Mucianus. Helvidius' larger aims are a matter of debate.[5] Did he want to increase the power and dignity of the

---

[5] For discussion of Helvidius see Toynbee, 54-7; Dudley, 132-6; and Wirszubski, 147-50.

senate by belittling Vespasian? Surely yes. Did he also oppose
Vespasian's dynastic policy by advocating that the next emperor should
be appointed by the senate? Possibly, but the evidence is weak. Did he,
as Dio says (65.12.2), incite the people to overthrow the principate and
restore the free republic? Most unlikely, since he had no military
backing, and anyhow the plebs had no wish to see the return of the old
senatorial oligarchy. Or was he essentially an anarchist? Hardly, for he is
mentioned with respect by Tacitus (*Hist.* 4.5-6) and Marcus Aurelius
(1.14.2). Nevertheless, his denunciations of monarchy and his praise of
libertas were readily misrepresented; and his rudeness to Mucianus,
Marcellus, and above all to the tolerant Vespasian gave the impression
that, unlike Thrasea, he was actually seeking martyrdom. Eventually he
was banished and subsequently put to death. Other philosophers were
expelled. About three years later, in A.D. 75, a Cynic was flogged for
criticising the marriage of Titus and Berenice, and another was beheaded
for giving vent to abuse (Dio 65.15.5). Vespasian died in A.D. 79. His
successor, Titus, lived only two years more, and Domitian became
emperor in 81.

(iv) Juvenal

Lucilius took part zestfully in the aristocratic free-for-all of the
second-century republic. Horace implicitly joined Octavian's faction by
accepting Maecenas' patronage, yet refrained from attacking the
Antonian opposition and gave his satire a general, more moral,
orientation. Persius belonged to a group which displayed its disapproval
of the emperor and suffered accordingly. Juvenal was much further away
from the centre of power. He was neither a senator, nor a famous
preacher, nor a member of the palace staff. He made no heroic gesture of
defiance; like the great majority of the educated public, he survived the
new regime in a spirit of sullen acquiescence. Declaimers were safe
enough; in fact they were encouraged to show their talents in a public
competition every four years (Suetonius, *Dom* 4.4). The subject-matter
of their rhetorical embroidery involved little risk. Written attacks were
another matter. In virtue of his censorial power, which he held in
perpetuity from A.D. 85, Domitian 'forbade the publication of lampoons
directed at prominent men and women, and made sure that the authors
were disgraced' (Suetonius, *Dom.* 8.3). This alone would have inhibited a
budding satirist. But there was also the far graver danger of offending the
emperor himself.

Now in some fourth-century scholia, in Sidonius Apollinaris (fifth
century) and in a *Life* which may be later still there is a confused report
which says that Juvenal was exiled to Egypt by Domitian for writing or
speaking some verses on a favourite actor (Courtney, 5-8). The kernel of
this tradition was accepted by Highet (22-7) and used in his

reconstruction of the poet's biography. Green (18-22) takes a similar line, and Ferguson (XVIII) is inclined to agree. It would, of course, be a colourful series of events if true. But when the different forms of the theory are fully set out, they reveal so many improbabilities and so many inconsistencies that it seems wiser to side with the sceptics, like Coffey and Courtney, and to assume that the whole story has been constructed on the basis of the satire about the Egyptians (especially *quantum ipse notaui* in v. 45)[1] and the lines about Paris in 7:

> What the patricians fail to provide, an actor will.
> Why haunt the halls of nobles like Barea or Camerinus?
> It's *Pelopea* who appoints our prefects, *Philomela* our tribunes (90-2).

If the exile is a fabrication, we may think of Juvenal as living a shabby-genteel existence in Rome, and gaining some kind of fulfilment by delivering declamations. A verse of Martial's published in A.D. 92 calls him *facundus* 'eloquent' (7.91). His career as a satirist did not begin until later. Other writers of the period, by choosing inoffensive subjects and plying the emperor with judicious flattery, managed to survive unharmed; but many of them, like Martial and Statius, found that the career offered by the Muse was financially precarious.

Domitian's reign was not without positive features. He was moderately successful in war and quite popular with the army. (He increased their pay.) He was shrewd in financial affairs and notably fair in his administration of the provinces (Pleket, 296-315); he was not disliked by the general public. But as time passed he had to contend with a mounting hatred on the part of the senate. Various reasons have been suggested, e.g. his restraint of greedy governors, his habit of choosing non-senatorial executives (perhaps because of the patricians' inexperience); and in general his tendency to by-pass the senate as an organ of government. These irritations were aggravated by a number of measures designed to increase his own monarchical power, e.g. his retention of the consulship and censorship, his alteration of October to 'Domitianus', and his acceptance of the title *dominus et deus*. Such behaviour inevitably caused resentment; resentment produced conspiracies; conspiracies led to fear, which prompted acts of cruel repression. A horribly familiar cycle.

One would like to know how far the number and severity of Domitian's punishments have been exaggerated by a hostile tradition. Unfortunately one can only draw inferences from the unsatisfactory data supplied by Suetonius (*Dom.* 14ff.) and Dio (67). By way of illustration, here is a list of charges, followed by the names of people executed.

---

[1] As there is no satisfactory evidence for *quantum* = *ut* in Juvenal's time, it is better to translate 'as far as I myself have observed'. This does not corroborate, but rather qualifies, the statement about the Egyptian rabble.

Armed revolt: Antonius Saturninus.

Conspiracy: Vettulenus Civica Cerealis.

Treasonable remarks: Maternus.

Subversive writing: Hermogenes of Tarsus (for certain allusions in his histories); Junius Arulenus Rusticus (for eulogies of Thrasea and Helvidius); Helvidius the younger (for criticising Domitian's divorce of his wife in a play ostensibly about Paris and Oenone).

Sexual immorality: three Vestals and one of the men involved; Paris the actor (for seducing the emperor's wife).

Impiety: Domitian's cousin, Flavius Clemens.

In some cases the grounds alleged are incredible; e.g. Sallustius Lucullus is supposed to have been killed for giving his name to a new type of lance, Aelius Lamia for a couple of harmless witticisms at his own expense, Flavius Sabinus because a herald had inadvertently announced him as 'emperor designate', Salvius Cocceianus because he had celebrated the birthday of his uncle Otho. One wonders why Domitian felt threatened or insulted by these men. Others were sent into exile, and of these some were later killed, like Salvidienus Orfitus, Mettius Pompusianus, and the freedman Epaphroditus. Others again had to endure exile as relatives or friends of the condemned, e.g. Arria, Fannia, Verulana Gratilla, and Domatilla, the widows of Thrasea, Helvidius, Arulenus Rusticus, and Flavius Clemens respectively. In addition to these named individuals (and a handful of others) we hear of a few anonymous victims, like the pupil of Paris who resembled his master, the *paterfamilias* who made a disastrous joke at a gladiatorial show, and the woman who undressed in front of Domitian's portrait. Others too were tortured and killed, like Hermogenes' copyists and those who mourned for Paris. Finally there are general statements like 'No one could discover the total number of those put to death by Domitian' (Dio 67.11.3).

How is this material to be interpreted? One way is to accept everything Suetonius and Dio say. The opposite approach is to reject every allegation unless names are supplied, to place a favourable construction on Domitian's actions wherever possible,[2] and to assume that all the accused were guilty. My own inclination would be to accept the named cases, to assume that many others also perished, and to keep an open mind about guilt except in the obvious instances like the widows mentioned above. Whether all this amounted to a 'reign of terror' is a matter of semantics. (How many deaths constitute a reign of terror?) The important point for our purpose is that even the mildest satirical

---

[2] Waters (1), who presents a detailed and ingenious defence of Domitian, suggests (wholly seriously?) that the emperor's fly-catching (Suetonius, *Dom.* 3.1) was connected with his archery: 'he was keeping his eye in.' Alternatively he disliked flies as 'dirty, disorderly, and promiscuous' (52, n. 9).

comment was out of the question, to say nothing of grossly insulting allegations like those made by Juvenal in 2.29-33.

Eventually, in A.D. 96, the assassin struck, and the cloud of dread began to lift. M. Cocceius Nerva, the new emperor, guaranteed that no senator would be put to death, forbade any more prosecutions for impiety, and recalled exiles. An inscription to *Libertas* was erected by the senate and people, and *Libertas publica* and *Roma renascens* appeared on the coinage. The pendulum, however, could not swing back too far. In the first place, Nerva, whose record under Domitian had been rather ambiguous, was not appointed by the senate but by the praetorian prefects along with certain palace officials and a group of individual senators. Reprisals were taken only against minor figures, while powerful Domitianic prosecutors like Regulus and Veiento were left unharmed. More significant still, Nerva was forced by the prefect Aelianus to execute Petronius and Parthenius, two of the men who had killed Domitian. It was already clear that this ageing and essentially peaceful man did not wield the necessary power to hold the empire together. Fortunately there was a way out, and (whether voluntarily or under pressure) Nerva took it. At the end of October A.D. 97, three months before his death, he adopted as his son the 44-year-old Spaniard M. Ulpius Traianus, commander of the army in Upper Germany, and had him acclaimed emperor. A short but dangerous transition had been accomplished.

Before Trajan returned to Rome in the middle of A.D. 99 he executed Aelianus and the praetorians who had forced Nerva to order the death of Petronius and Parthenius. On his return he continued Nerva's efforts to get rid of Domitian's informers (Pliny, *Pan.* 34-5); he paid very little attention to slanders (Dio 68.6.4); he did his best to restrain the senate's flattery, even if he failed to check the enthusiasm of Pliny (*Pan.* 54.3-5); though no intellectual, he allowed the liberal arts to recover (perhaps encouraged by his wife); and instead of being remote and suspicious he was friendly and accessible to all (Dio 68.7.3). 'Now at last our spirits are reviving,' says Tacitus. 'Nerva has harmonised the old discord between the principate and liberty, and every day Trajan is increasing the happiness of our times' (*Ag.* 3.1). Later he speaks of 'the rare good fortune of this age in which we can feel what we like and say what we feel' (*Hist.* 1.1). New writing began to appear. Several minor figures are mentioned by Pliny;[3] more significantly, Tacitus, now in his early forties, published his *Agricola* and *Germania*; and Plutarch, who had written relatively little before this, began to produce major works when nearly sixty.[4] The new spirit is attested by Pliny in his *Panegyric*. Addressing Trajan, he says 'You urge us to be free: we shall be. You urge us to

[3] See Pliny *Ep.* 1.13, 1.16, 4.27, and 6.15. And one must not forget Pliny himself.
[4] See C.P. Jones (1) 73-4.

express our feelings openly: so we shall' (66.4). Such liberty was still, of course, a privilege rather than a right, and no doubt it fell short of what we would regard as adequate. Nevertheless, it brought a real easing of tension, and it meant that Domitian's reign could now be openly criticised. In a speech which may well have been delivered in Trajan's presence Dio Chrysostom speaks of the 'many acts of injustice' committed by Domitian, and he praises Trajan as a good ruler who, like Hercules, has chosen to follow Royalty rather than Tyranny (*On Kingship* 1.67-84). More frankly, Pliny could now refer to Domitian as a 'most appalling beast' (*immanissima belua* in *Pan.* 48.3); Tacitus writes movingly of a fifteen-year period in which all the most energetic men have been destroyed by 'the emperor's savagery' (*saeuitia principis* in *Ag.* 3.2); and Juvenal towards the end of 4 has some lines of bitter regret:

> atque utinam his potius nugis tota illa dedisset
> tempora saeuitiae, claras quibus abstulit urbi
> inlustresque animas inpune et uindice nullo (150-2)

Yes, and how much better if he'd spent on such frivolities
all those savage years when he plundered Rome of her noblest
and most distinguished souls with none to avenge or punish.[5]

Now this kind of retrospective criticism was not new. Nero, who treated the memory of Claudius with contempt (Suetonius, *Nero* 33.1), had taken no exception to the travesty ascribed to Seneca and entitled *Apocolocyntosis Diui Claudii* 'The Pumpkinification of the Blessed Claudius'. More surprising, perhaps, is the fact that Domitian allowed adverse comment on Nero. Martial deplored his cruelty in killing Lucan (7.21); Statius called him a *rabidus tyrannus* for the same reason (*Silv.* 2.7.100) and went on to mention his murder of Agrippina (118-19); the satirist Turnus recalled the poisoning of Britannicus by Nero's agent Lucusta: *ex quo Caesareas suboles Lucusta cecidit.*[6] Why Juvenal did not avail himself of the same licence is something of a mystery. Perhaps he felt his position was not strong enough to justify the risk. Another mystery is why, if he was bursting with indignation and just waiting for Domitian's end, Juvenal should have delayed something like fifteen years before publishing his first book of satires. Rather than speculating about such questions, however, we will survey Juvenal's treatment of

---

[5] This passage illustrates Juvenal's abrupt changes of tone. The previous lines, describing the frantic assembly of the council, are comic-satirical. The following lines are sardonic: Domitian was finished as soon as he offended Smith (see Ferguson on v. 153). Whether the words *uindice nullo* contain a punning allusion to C. Julius Vindex, who led a revolt against Nero in A.D. 68 (8.222), cannot, of course, be decided. The reader's view will depend on whether he thinks it more effective to postpone the change of manner until *sed periit*, as I do.

[6] For Turnus see the scholiast on Juvenal 1.71 and Coffey (2).

important men and women and then offer a general comment on his response to Trajan's regime.

Book 1 may well have appeared before Trajan left for the Parthian war in A.D. 113. If he read it, he will have noticed Juvenal's indignant remark about the lenient sentence passed on Marius Priscus, the cruel and dishonest governor of Africa (1.49-50). Trajan himself had presided at the trial, but we do not know how far he endorsed the senate's verdict on his fellow-countryman; anyhow the affair had finished in A.D. 100. In vv. 33-6 there is an unfair suggestion that powerful informers are still operating; and in a more repressive period exception might have been taken to the lines about the (unnamed) praetor who rises early to pay his respects to rich and childless ladies (3.126-30). In 6.292 Rome's corruption is attributed to the evil effects of a long peace. This seems at first sight a strange assertion in view of Trajan's arduous campaigns in Dacia and Parthia; but the context shows that Juvenal is thinking, not of the empire, but of the city itself. When had *that* last been in danger? *Satire* 7.90 contained the notorious words about Paris. Malicious readers might have thought of Trajan's friend Pylades (Dio 68.10.2), but there is no evidence that Pylades abused his position, and anyhow the satire appeared a year or two after Trajan's death. If we leave aside what is said about Greeks in 3 and 6 (see Chapter Five), there was little to annoy Hadrian. The satirist commends the new emperor as a potential patron (7.1-3, 17-21), and he can safely reflect on the sad folly of a general's ambition (10.133-46) now that Trajan's assertive policy has been abandoned. It is true, however, that some of Hadrian's army-regulations may be criticised in 16 (Highet, 287 n.1).

In surveying Juvenal's victims it is remarkably difficult to identify contemporary characters. This is partly because of our general lack of evidence. In 11.2-23, for instance, we hear of a Rutilus who was once comfortably off but has ruined himself by his expenditure on food. As he is contrasted with Ti. Claudius Atticus, we assume he is real; but we know nothing else about him. Again, a single name is often unspecific. Cossus in 3.184 is an arrogant noble. The name attaches him to the *gens Cornelia*, but does not pin him down. Worse still, he is coupled with a Veiento who is naturally equated with A. Fabricius Veiento. But Veiento had been dead several years; so the same could be true of Cossus. Or consider the Lentulus whose wife has been seduced by a gladiator (6.78-81). He is not even imagined as an individual; he simply represents any member of that family, which in turn represents the aristocracy. Another kind of problem is posed by Hispo, the versatile homosexual in 2.50. According to Syme, the name is rare; he adduces only a handful of examples, including Ti. Caepio Hispo who was consul in A.D. 101 and proconsul of Asia in 117-18.[7] How should this be interpreted? The main

[7] See Syme (3) 72 and Highet, 291-2.

possibilities are (a) that Juvenal's description would have been applied
unhesitatingly to the senator. That would certainly have been dangerous,
since presumably he enjoyed the emperor's favour. In that case the
reference is very exceptional. (b) That the description was patently
unsuited to the senator. This might have reduced the danger, but it
provides no positive explanation for the choice of name. (c) That
prosopography has not unearthed all the Hispones that were living in the
first decade of the second century; one of them might have had an
appropriately malodorous reputation. We would also have to assume he
was not influential enough to cause trouble. (d) That if Juvenal had a
specific man in mind he was dead. (e) That the name was chosen to evoke
hispidus 'hairy', and was meant to recall the hypocrisy of the
pseudo-Stoics described at the beginning. This last idea must surely
represent part of the truth, but it would hardly have been enough to
protect the satirist if (a) had been the case. Hypothesis (b) offers little
help. Of (c) and (d) the latter seems slightly the more probable. If to
etymology one adds the unpleasant associations attached to a man like
Roman(i)us Hispo, who was an informer under Tiberius (Tacitus, *Ann.*
1.74), that might be enough to account for the use of the name. Whatever
view one adopts, Hispo, along with Hispulla (6.74 and 12.11) and Gillo
(1.40), belongs to a very small group.[8] The general conclusion, which will
be modified slightly in Chapter Five, is that when a contemporary is
satirised he usually turns out to be someone who has fallen into disgrace
and is therefore less dangerous, or else a person of no consequence in
society, like an actor, a whore, or an academic. Perhaps we should not be
over-impressed by those initial expressions of euphoria on the part of
Tacitus and Pliny. After all, Trajan accepted Domitian's decisions as
valid precedents and shared no less than thirty-five of his *amici*.[9]
Circumspection was still advisable.

As remarked before, however, the reign of Domitian was no longer

---

[8] 'A bull as fat as Hispulla' (12.11) is a comic inversion of the usual human/animal
comparison. It was a rude thing to say, but if Hispulla was notorious for having an affair
with an actor (6.74) perhaps it was not dangerous. Gillo (1.40) sleeps with a rich old lady in
the hope of a legacy. The name is 'very uncommon', according to Syme (2), 777. Fulvius
Gillo was proconsul of Asia in 115-16. So the same question arises as with Hispo. But there
seems to be no etymological play. Horsfall, 422, pointed out that *gillo* was used for a
wine-container; but the Latin passages adduced, e.g. Plautus, *Truc.* 585 and *Poen.* 863,
indicate that the ribald joke about containers (*uasa*) has reference to *testiculi* rather than
penis. It was remarked by Highet (292-3) that Fulvius Gillo and Calpurnia Hispulla were
related to Pliny by marriage, and that Corellia Hispulla was his friend (*Ep.* 3.3). Syme
(3.72) notes a couple of links between the name Hispo and Comum. Tantalising details, but
hardly enough to establish a specific animosity towards Pliny and his circle.

[9] The continuity of advisers is stressed by Crook. See his prosopographical index on pp.
148ff. Waters (2) argues against the traditional contrast between Domitian and Trajan.
One can, I think, accept many of his arguments and still believe that Trajan represented a
fairly light, and Domitian a pretty dark, shade of grey. For a detailed study of Domitian and
the senate see B.W. Jones.

tabu. Early in 1 we come across Domitian's favourite Crispinus (27), the showy barrister Matho (32), and the unnamed informer (Regulus?) with his sinister colleagues Massa and Carus (35-6). In 2 there is a direct attack on Domitian himself. Its Juvenalian pungency may be seen by comparing it with a corresponding passage in Pliny (*Ep.* 4.11.6): '[He condemned a Vestal to death for sexual impiety] although he himself had not only polluted his niece with incest but had killed her; for she died as the result of an abortion (her husband was already dead).' Juvenal too uses the episode to high-light Domitian's hypocrisy:

> Lately we saw such a man – an adulterer stained by a union
> worthy of the tragic stage – reviving harsh legislation
> which brought alarm to all, even to Mars and Venus,
> at the very time when Julia was relieving her fertile womb
> of so many a foetus, with every lump the image of Uncle (29-33).

The whole of 4 is Domitianic. Parodying a loyal poem by Statius,[10] the main section describes an emergency meeting of the emperor's cabinet to decide how to deal with the present of an enormous turbot. Crispinus is there again; so are Pegasus the jurist, the mild and compliant Crispus, Acilius and his son (the latter doomed to die in exile), the lecherous and hypocritical Rubrius, the glutton Montanus with his huge belly, and the deadly informers Fuscus, Veiento, and Catullus. Behind these farcical deliberations lies the grim actuality of dread – a dread that is visible on every face (74-5). Here, then, is a poem which does attack important people, but they are all dead. There is also another point, which was spotted by the eagle-eyed Syme (2.6, n.2). One figure belonging to Domitian's council is significantly absent from Juvenal's spoof, namely M. Cocceius Nerva, the emperor-to-be, who adopted Trajan and paved the way for his accession.

In view of 4, and of many other references to Domitianic figures, it is sometimes said that Juvenal's vision of Rome, instead of moving in time, had as it were been arrested, and that the horrors of that age recurred to him again and again like a nightmare (e.g. Highet, 9). A parallel is found in the *Discourses* of Epictetus, in which the figure of the tyrant is thought to have been modelled on Domitian (Starr, 20). There is then a temptation to take the comparison further: as Epictetus had been banished by Domitian in A.D. 95, surely Juvenal had suffered the same fate and been scarred by the experience? Now one readily concedes that the events of the 90s must have made a lasting impression on the poet. While there is no proof that he came to any harm, and while, unlike Tacitus (*Ag.* 45.1), he had no need to feel any guilt for collaborating in acts of oppression, it is clear from his satires that, given his social outlook and his well-to-do acquaintances (attested by Martial 12.18.4), he shared

[10] See Griffith, 137-50.

the senate's hatred of the princeps. That much is reasonable inference. Nevertheless, when we survey the first three books as a whole (i.e. *Satires* 1-9), there does not seem to be a disproportionate emphasis on Domitian's reign. Many illustrations of wickedness are drawn from the age of Nero (and earlier), and there is a powerful attack on Nero himself:

> Give the people a free vote: without hesitation
> every decent man would prefer Seneca to Nero.
> To punish that creature in a fitting manner, a single ape,
> a single snake, and a single bag would not have sufficed.
> His crime was that of Agamemnon's son, but cases are altered
> by motives. The latter, at the instigation of heaven itself,
> was avenging a father murdered over his wine; he never
> defiled himself by strangling Electra or shedding the blood
> of his Spartan wife; he never mixed a poisoned cocktail
> for his own relations; never sang the part of Orestes
> or wrote a Trojan epic. What crime cried louder for vengeance
> on the part of Verginius' men or those of Vindex and Galba
> of all that Nero committed in his savage and bloody reign? (8.211-23)

Here, too, tales heard in boyhood could have played a part. But a further question arises: would such memories still have been relevant to young, or even middle-aged, readers in A.D. 120? And what of passing allusions to men like Q. Sulpicius Camerinus (7.90-1) and Rubellius Blandus (8.39-40)? Here, as Syme and Townend have shown,[11] a different kind of factor must be borne in mind, namely the publication of other literary works, some of them specifically historical. First of all, Juvenal's older friend, Martial, continued to be read in the first decade of the century, and his twelfth book, written after his return to Spain in A.D. 100, still contained reminiscences of the 80s and 90s. Pliny's *Letters*, which appeared in instalments between about 105 and 109, revived memories of the recent past. (One thinks, for example, of the account of the Vestal's execution in *Ep.* 4.11 and the trial of Marius Priscus in *Ep.* 2.11.) Suetonius' biographical studies *De Viris Illustribus* contributed to the same effect, as did the *Dialogus* of Tacitus, which was set in the mid 70s and seems to have prompted certain lines in Juvenal 7 (see p. 124). The *Histories*, which are probably referred to in 2.102-3, were published about A.D. 110. They dealt with events between A.D. 69 and the death of Domitian in 96. (Unfortunately the text breaks off in Book 5, before the end of 70.) Finally, the *Annals*, which covered events from A.D. 14-68, were completed in 120 or soon after. They might, therefore, have influenced Juvenal's eighth satire and could certainly have influenced his tenth. In particular, 10.56-107 could owe something to Tacitus' account of the fall of Sejanus in the latter part of Book 5, which is no longer extant.

[11] See Syme (2), 776-7; Townend, 148-60.

These works secured a kind of secondary topicality for the people and events described. At the same time they provided a rich store of *exempla* for the satirist. Such evidence, however, should not be pressed too far. While it is true that any reference to the period A.D. 69-96 could have been prompted by the *Histories*, it seems unlikely (*pace* Syme 5, 272-4) that any reference to the period A.D. 14-68 in *Satires* 1-6 could have been suggested by the *Annals*. Yet in 1 there is mention of Lucusta, Corvinus, and Tigellinus from the reign of Nero; 3 speaks of Publius Egnatius Celer, who betrayed Barea Soranus in A.D. 66, and also of the dozing Claudius. In 5 Claudius appears again, and we hear of Nero's long-nosed courtier, the ex-cobbler Vatinius; *Satire* 6 brings in Agrippina (Nero's mother), Caesonia (Caligula's wife), Messalina (Claudius' wife), and the Augustan dancer Bathyllus; in 7, which could have been influenced by any of Tacitus' works, the wide-ranging method of reference is much the same, taking in contemporary poets, music-teachers, and barristers; Domitian's Paris, and the poets Serranus, Saleius, and Statius; Camerinus and Barea, who perished under Nero; Secundus Carrinas who was exiled by Caligula; Theodorus, Tiberius' tutor; and the Augustans Virgil and Horace.

Again, in the important article referred to above, Townend suggests that after 8 'Juvenal has exhausted his most fruitful vein of literary exploitation' and that in Books 4 and 5 'satire becomes a routine' (159). It is quite true that after 8 the method of attack used hitherto is abandoned – at least until Book 5, where Juvenal shows signs of reverting to his earlier manner. Whether this change of technique should be explained just negatively, as due to exhaustion, is less certain. Juvenal was trying several new approaches, and it is a common experience that, when a successful mode is abandoned, readers and listeners are disappointed with what takes its place. Yet it would be unfair to lump, say, 9, 10, and 15 together simply because none of them resembles *Satires* 1-8. Even readers who are revolted by 9 can appreciate it as a *tour de force*; but clearly it was unrepeatable. After a conversation with a single figure, Juvenal widened his viewpoint so as to embrace the whole of the civilised world. *Satire* 10 is a declamation on the vanity of human, not just Roman, wishes; and therefore the *exempla* are drawn not only from Roman history (both republican and imperial) but also from Greek history, and, beyond that, from the world of legend. In 15 (on a case of cannibalism in Egypt) the scope narrows again; the satire concentrates on a specific instance of human depravity, but it is not a Roman instance. So perhaps the differences of satirical method displayed in these poems arise in part from their different themes. In any case we can hardly talk of a routine. As for the other late pieces, the smaller number of named victims may have something to do with the literary form. *Satires* 11 and 14 are more akin to didactic epistles, and a large part of 12, like 15, is devoted to satirical narrative.

It is, however, the first eight satires, with their aggressive personal technique, which pose the original question most starkly: if the days of fear had gone, why did Juvenal attack so few prominent contemporaries? Perhaps he was reluctant to give offence. But while that may be allowed as a factor in the case of the aimiable Horace, who *could* have attacked anti-Caesarian figures from a position of security, it is much less convincing with regard to the unplaced and censorious Juvenal. One must surely conclude that the chief cause of his restraint was prudence, or caution, or apprehension – at any rate some gradation on the scale of fear. Thanks to a favourable tradition Trajan enjoys unshakeable esteem as a good emperor. Fair enough; but Fronto says 'he sometimes enjoyed the company of actors and was a pretty hard drinker' (Loeb, vol. 2, p. 8); according to Dio 'he was keen on boys and wine' (68.7.4), and the same report is found in other writers.[12] One hardly needs to transpose this idea into Juvenalian hyperbole to see how impossible it would have been. In 1.155 the threatening figure is not Nero but Tigellinus. But right-hand men were also beyond criticism. No sane writer of the day would have ridiculed Augustus' Agrippa or Tiberius' Sejanus, or Vespasian's Mucianus; and although Trajan's Licinius Sura had died a few years before the (assumed) date of Book 1, his shortcomings (e.g. the homosexuality hinted at in Epictetus 3.17.4) were still not open to public censure.

Juvenal was therefore in a dilemma. To be 'willing to wound and yet afraid to strike' was an undignified condition and clearly incompatible with the function of a satirist. Yet there was no credit or satisfaction to be had from merely attacking the dead. We do not know how long he deliberated; and it is futile to speculate about drafts and revisions. In the end he hit on a way of escape: he would simply ignore the passage of time. The last eighty years, or more, of Roman history would be treated as 'now'. Any example of crime, vice, or misfortune would be given a contemporary relevance; anything shocking would be made topical. Inevitably there would be one or two anachronisms. Informing had ceased, castration had been forbidden, and condemned persons were no longer being burnt. Still, as conditions depended so much on the character of a single man, one never knew when such things might recur. Informers, after all, had been banned before by Titus (Suetonius, *Titus* 8.5); castration had more than once been declared illegal;[13] and astrologers, philosophers, and other undesirables had been banished and restored. And what of the long series of well-meaning regulations about gluttony, adultery, jerry-building, and much else besides, which had never been revoked but were merely ignored? If one took the period from

---

[12] See *Hist. Aug.*, Hadrian 3.3, 2.7, 4.5; Julian, *Caesars* 327c, 333a.
[13] Castration was forbidden by Domitian (Suetonius, *Dom.* 7), Nerva (Dio 68.2.4), and Hadrian (Ulpian, *Dig.* 48.8.4.2).

Tiberius to Trajan as a whole, perhaps a dark picture was also the most authentic.

The results of Juvenal's decision are well known. Satire 8, for example, begins with an address to Ponticus, a contemporary figure. At v. 39 Juvenal says he is talking to Rubellius Blandus; yet Rubellius lived under Nero, and his conduct was by now a matter of hearsay (71-2). Then in v. 74 Juvenal turns again to Ponticus. Later Plautius Lateranus, who was executed after Piso's conspiracy in A.D. 65, is described in the present tense as he hurtles past in his light car (147). This, to be sure, is not Juvenal's only way of handling time,[14] but it is the most striking and characteristic, and it had far-reaching effects on his reputation. For in the seventeenth and eighteenth centuries, when readers were less particular about the niceties of chronology, it looked as if many of his victims, including Domitian, were contemporary.[15] And so he came to be regarded as the 'opposition satirist' *par excellence* and was praised for being 'a zealous vindicator of Roman liberty'.[16]

---

[14] Another way is not to ignore but to diminish the lapse of time, as when *nuper* 'lately' is used to refer to an event over twenty years old (8.120); yet another is to stress the *difference* between former and present times, as in 8.98ff.

[15] 'There was more need of a Brutus in Domitian's days, to redeem or mend, than of a Horace, if he had then been living, to laugh at a fly catcher. This reflection at the same time excuses Horace, but exalts Juvenal', Dryden, 87. This implies that the fly-catcher (Domitian) was living when Juvenal wrote.

[16] For Juvenal as the 'opposition satirist' see Weinbrot, 154-81; 'A zealous vindicator of Roman liberty' is Dryden's phrase (87).

CHAPTER THREE

Style and Public

STYLE

(i) Lucilius

In antiquity, the standard edition of Lucilius, which dated from republican times, consisted of three rolls, arranged according to metre. The first roll (Books 1-21) contained hexameters; and so, although these were not the earliest verses Lucilius wrote, they were the first which an ancient reader would have encountered. Near the beginning came the dignified line

> *consilium summis hominum de rebus habebant* (5)

> They were holding debate on human affairs of the greatest moment.

Since there is a very similar line in *Aen.* 9, namely

> *consilium summis regni de rebus habebant* (227),

one infers that both Virgil and Lucilius were drawing on Ennius, and in fact we know that in the *Annals* the gods discussed Rome as it was in the period of Romulus. Other fragments, too, have a serious ring, like the formula which marks the end of a speech:

> *haec ubi dicta dedit, pausam dedit ore loquendi* (18)

> Once he had uttered these words he made a pause in his speaking.

If we did not know the context we would not guess that the following lines came from a satire:

> *nam si tu fluctus undasque e gurgite salso*
> *tollere decreris, uenti prius Emathii uim,*
> *uentum, inquam, tollas, tum cuncta quieta iacebunt*
> *litora* (42-5)

> For, if thou shouldst resolve to remove the waves and billows
> from the salty sea, first remove the Emathian wind's
> violent blast – the wind, I say – then every shore
> will lie at rest.

Other instances occur throughout the collection, e.g.

> *omnia tum endo muco uideas feruente micare* (1024)
>
> Then in the seething depths of the house all was confusion.

If the editors are right, this scene of feverish activity was observed from a dilapidated dining room with furniture fit only for a junk-shop. Again, at 1181, we read:

> *uicimus o socii et magnam pugauimus pugnam*
>
> O comrades I have prevailed and fought a mighty fight.

According to Donatus (on Terence, *Eun.* 899), the deity who presided over this encounter was not Mars but Venus. In such cases (as distinct from the tragic parodies quoted in Chapter One), Lucilius is not so much ridiculing the high style in itself as using the high style to create a comic effect. Aristophanes had done the same sort of thing, but there was a more immediate precedent available in Plautus. One thinks, for example, of Sosia's lines in *Amphitruo*, 188ff:

> *uictores uictis hostibus legiones reueniunt domum,*
> *duello exstincto maximo atque internecatis hostibus,* etc.
>
> The foe is vanquished and the legions march back home victoriously;
> a major war has been extinguished, and our foes have been laid low,

or of Chrysalus' grandiloquent speech in *Bacchides*, beginning

> *Atridae duo fratres cluent fecisse facinus maxumum* (925)
>
> The sons of Atreus, brothers twain, are famed for doing a mighty deed.

Again, rhetoricians of all periods recognised that the censure of vice (*uituperatio*) called for an emotional style which would rouse the listener's indignation. In describing this type of orator, Cicero called him 'weighty, vehement and fiery' – *grauis, acer, ardens* (*Orat.* 99). Similar terms were used by later writers when describing Lucilius. According to Juvenal:

> *ense uelut stricto ... Lucilius ardens*
> *infremuit* (1.165-6)
>
> as though with sword at the ready ... the hot Lucilius
> roars in wrath.

Later still, Macrobius calls him an *acer et uiolentus poeta* (*Sat.* 3.16.17) – 'a vehement and violent poet'. As we noted earlier, these writers exaggerated the proportion of angry denunciation in Lucilius' satires; in doing so, they over-stressed the frequency of passionate rhetoric. Nevertheless, the same sort of testimony comes from Gaius Trebonius, who was very much closer to Lucilius in time.[1] In May 44 B.C., he wrote to Cicero (*Fam.* 12.16.3), enclosing some angry and obscene verses against Antony. 'If,' he says (in summary), 'I am a little outspoken in some of my words, the vileness of the person concerned will justify my attack. Also, why should Lucilius be allowed such *libertas* any more than I? He hated the men he wounded just as heartily, but his victims did not deserve to be attacked with such verbal *libertas* any more richly than mine.' So although the fragments do not include any continuous passage like Cicero's elaborate castigation of Verres or Catiline, it would be unwise to reject *in toto* what those witnesses say. Hints of what we have lost are contained in

> *inpuratum hunc in fauces inuasse animamque*
> *elisisse illi* (54-5)

that this filthy creature then laid hold on his gullet
squeezing his life away,

> *homo inpuratus, et est inpune rapister* (57)

He's a filthy fellow, a thief who has never been punished,

and

> *uultus item ut facies: mors, icterus morbus, uenenum* (37)

His expression is just like his face: death, jaundice and poison.

One would also like to know more about the attacks which Lucilius made on the various tribes. *Prima Papiria Tusculidarum* (1132) sounds like an impressive beginning.

We have rather more evidence of another kind of writing which is also beyond the register of ordinary conversation and which brings us back again to the comic inventiveness of Plautus. Here are a couple of examples from the earliest collection (Books 26-30):

> *depoclassere aliqua sperans me ac deargentassere*
> *decalauticare, eburno speculo despeculassere* (640-1)

[a woman]
looking forward to decupping and desilverplating me,
to destoling and deglassing of an ivory looking-glass,

---

[1] Trebonius cannot be assigned to any political pigeon-hole. He opposed Clodius in 60 B.C., then changed sides and assisted the triumvirs in 55, served as consul under Caesar in 45, abetted his murder in 44, protected Antony, and then turned against him. He was murdered by Dolabella in Smyrna in 43.

uiginti domi an triginta an centum cibicidas alas (760)

[whether] you maintain
twenty, thirty, or a hundred food-destroyers in your house.[2]

There the comic diction is supported by the metre (the trochaic septenarius). The same is true of the following scene in iambic senarii:

nemo hos ancipites ferro effringat cardines (941)

No man will break these double hinges with an axe

uecte atque ancipiti ferro effringam cardines (942)

With bar and double axe I'll break the hinges down

*uas ex fenestris in caput
deiciam qui prope ad ostium aspirauerint* (943-4)

From the window I'll throw down a pot
upon the head of any who have struggled to the door

'Gnatho, quid actum est?' 'depilati omnes sumus' (945)

'Gnatho, what's happened?' 'We've been taken for a ride.'

'caede ostium, Gnatho, urgue.' 'restant, periimus.' (946)

'Push, Gnatho, smash the door in.' 'They won't shift; we're done.'

The comic tone also makes itself felt in hexameters. Here, from Book 7, is a call-girl describing how she must labour to be beautiful:

*rador subuellor desquamor pumicor ornor
expolior pingor* (296-7)

Then I am shaved and plucked, scaled pumiced adorned
smoothed and painted.

A great deal of Lucilius' work, however, was composed at the level of what we might call heightened talk. This was a conscious decision, as we see from his remarks about tragedy (pp. 4-5 above) and his refusal to attempt anything in the way of epic (pp. 46-7 above). His unassuming attitude is reflected in the terms which he uses to describe his own writing. He calls it *ludus* (1039) 'amusement', *sermones* (1039, 1085, 1086) 'talks', *poemata* (1091) 'short poems', and *schedium* (1131) 'an improvised construction'. The most general term for miscellaneous work of this kind was, of course, *saturae*; and although the word does not

---

[2] Marx lists Lucilius' comic coinages in vol. 1, p. 162.

happen to occur in the fragments, he may well have used it in his title.[3]

Ennius had set the precedent with his *saturae*, which were written in iambic senarii, trochaic septenarii, and hexameters. They included some elevated lines:

> *contemplor*
> *inde loci liquidas pilatasque aetheris oras* (3-4)

> From that position
> I gaze at the clear expanse of the sky on its aery pillars,

and also some comic jingles:

> *restitant occurrunt obstant obstringillant obagitant* (5)[4]

> Men who loiter to accost you and obtrude obstruct upset.

But it seems that the base from which they moved and to which they returned was much closer to everyday speech. There was a version of Aesop's fable about the farmer who tried to persuade his friends, and then his kinsmen, to help him mow a field. A mother lark, who was familiar with human behaviour, did not bother to move her chicks to safety until she heard that the farmer and his son were about to do the job on their own. The moral was:

> *ne quid expectes amicos quod tute agere possies*

> Don't expect your friends to tackle what you can perform yourself.[5]

The same feet-on-the-ground approach is suggested by a line on awkward, over-fussy people who

> *quaerunt in scirpo soliti quod dicere nodum* (27)

> 'look for a knot in a bulrush' to quote the usual saying (cf. Lucilius, 34),

and by the animal comparison in 23, with the etymological play:

> *simia quam similis turpissima bestia nobis*

> The ape's appearance is very like ours; and it's very ugly.

In a more serious vein, one assumes, was the debate between Death

---

[3] The plural *saturae* would have referred to the books of the collection. Unfortunately, as Gratwick points out (168), Nonius Marcellus, to whom we owe the preservation of nearly all the fragments of the first collection, chose to cite them simply by their book-number. The later fragments, however, are cited in the form *Lucilius in sexto satyrarum*. Aulus Gellius sometimes uses *saturae* or *satirae* in his citations.

[4] Compare Ennius' play on *frustra* (28-31) with Lucilius' play on *satis* (208-10).

[5] The fable is summarised by Aulus Gellius, 2.29.1.

and Life,[6] but that was balanced by amusing attacks on objectionable types like the glutton (1), the slanderer (8-9), and the parasite (14-19). A significant feature of the *saturae* was the part played by Ennius himself. At one point he is hailed in (mock?) elevated language:

> *Enni poeta salue, qui mortalibus*
> *uersus propinas flammeos medullitus* (6-7)

Good fortune, poet Ennius, who dost pledge
mankind with fiery verses marrow-deep!

In 22 he seems to be priding himself on his equability:

> *non est meum ac si me canis memorderit*

I don't, as if a dog had bitten me ...

And in 21 he shows he does not always take himself too seriously:

> *numquam poetor nisi si podager*

I never poetise without the gout.

Finally, we should not forget the other Ennian pieces which Lucilius had available: his panegyric on Scipio Africanus, his sepulchral epigrams, his coarse imitation of Sotades, and his comic poem on delicatessen.

Lucilius developed what Ennius had started. His habit of self-projection – his way of talking about his health, his estates, his travels, his love-affairs and so on – has been mentioned in Chapter One. Here we shall illustrate two opposite features of his style, namely his earthiness and his rhetorical sophistication. The first quality often emerges from his treatment of animals. There are fragments of a version of Aesop's fable about the fox and the sick lion (1111ff.). The lion is very decrepit indeed – covered with mange and eczema:

> *inluuies scabies oculos huic deque petigo*
> *conscendere* (1113-14)

In a gentle whisper he invites the fox to enter his den:

> *deducta tunc uoce leo 'cur tu ipsa uenire*
> *non uis huc?'* (1116-17)

but the fox notices the one-way footprints of other animals and is not so easily tricked:

---

[6] The piece is mentioned by Quintilian 9.2.36.

'quid sibi uult, quare fit ut introuorsus et ad te
spectent atque ferant uestigia se omnia prorsus?' (1119-20)[7]

As we have noted already (p. 9) there are several fragments about
horses. At other times the connection between man and animals is
established by Chaucerian similes: one fellow has a jaw and tooth like a
rhinoceros (109-10); another resembles a huge butcher's dog (1175);
another has one eye and two feet like half a pig's carcass (112-13); a girl is
free and frisky like a Thessalian filly, and some man is eager to break her
in (1041-2). Sex, food and money are dealt with in vivid metaphors: he
grinds, she winnows (302; cf. 361); at a banquet beccaficos flutter about
(1109); ground barley is a poultice which relieves a grieving stomach
(966-7); gluttons are bellies – *uiuite uentres* (70); a miser gets his hooks
on the cash – *nummos inuncat* (530); a rascal will carry off the lot with
his sticky fingers – *uiscatis manibus* (846); a swindler sells the goods by
public auction and you have to lick up the remains – *extrema ligurris*
(555). Various kinds of coarse behaviour are described: we hear of men
belching (130), bellowing with laughter (131), and snorting with anger
(608); and someone else scratches himself like a pig against a tree (356).

This interest in lowly detail was not inhibited by any views about
poetic and unpoetic words. To be sure, Lucilius might laugh at Ennius
for using phrases which fell short of epic or tragic dignity (Horace,
1.10.54). But as he had no lofty pretensions himself, he was free of such
restrictions. Fronto noticed this in the second century A.D., and remarked
that Lucilius used the appropriate vocabulary for whatever skill and
business he was describing (Loeb, vol. 1, p. 4). When talking of hunting
he spoke of *spara, rumices* and *tragula* (156) – different types of spear;
the good infantryman (*ueles*) is said to thrust his weapon under the vine
(*uitem*) – i.e. the shelter (*uinea*) which protected troops when they were
attacking fortifications (1263; cf. 994); in a storm at sea, a wave overtops
the *carchesia* (620) – the holes at the masthead – and the halyard
(*anquina*) has to be slackened off (618). Other examples could be quoted
from medicine, cookery, and horsemanship. Nor was there any barrier
against imports. Some words came from Gaul (*bulga* 'bag', *bracae*
'trousers'); others were Oscan (*pipas* 'you cheep'), Umbrian (*gumiae*
'gluttons'), Etruscan (*mantisa* 'makeweight'), Syrian (*mamphula* 'loaf'),
and possibly Sardinian (*musimo* 'wild sheep'). Such hospitality reflected
the poet's generous conception of the genre.

Lucilius' sophistication reveals itself in many ways – in his wit, his use
of Greek, his range of literary ideas. Here we shall confine ourselves to his
grasp of rhetoric. Not only does he talk about rhetorical figures – e.g.
bonum schema 'a good figure' in 416, and the effect of rhyme in 191-2 – he

---

[7] Horace renders the same idea thus: *me uestigia terrent / omnia te aduersum spectantia,*
nulla retrorsum (*E.* 1.1.74-5) 'Those footprints scare me; / all of them face in your direction,
none of them back.'

also uses them with great freedom. Exclamations and rhetorical questions need no illustration, but one notes the zeugma in 132:

uertitur oenophori fundus, sententia nobis

The wine-jar was turned upside down, just like our intentions,

the abusive alliteration in 111:

non peperit, uerum postica parte profudit

She never bore him as a baby but blew him out of her bottom,

the euphemism for death in 455:

si quid pueris nobis me et fratre fuisset

If in our boyhood aught had become of me and my brother,

the increasing tricolon in 1105:

non datur; admittit nemo; nec uiuere ducunt

No admittance; none opens the door; they doubt if she's living,

and antiphrasis (i.e. denying you will mention something and thereby mentioning it) with chiasmus (the sequence a-b-b-a) in 1174:

non tango quod auarus homo est, quodque improbus mitto

I do not touch on the fellow's greed; his vice – I ignore it,

and the play on words in 1193:

nequam aurum est; auris quouis uehementius ambit

Naughty notes! Nothing's so strong in soliciting votes.

A glance at the fragment on *uirtus* (p. 6 above) will show more than one instance of anaphora (e.g. the repetition of *uirtus*), homoeoteleuton (rhyme), asyndeton (the absence of connectives), tricolon-arrangement (phrases grouped in triads), and alliteration. Clearly, Lucilius was not a naive writer, if by that one means a writer unaware of artistic techniques.

(ii) Horace

Various kinds of theory – rhetorical, moral and poetic – can be used to orient oneself to Horace's *sermones*. Describing the plain style of oratory (the *genus subtile*), Cicero says it is restrained and unpretentious, with a deceptive appearance of simplicity; the structure is loose, but not rambling; the language scrupulously correct. When employing this style, the orator will be sparing in his use of metaphors, archaisms and new words; his wit will be revealed in the elegance of his narrative and in his use of ridicule. Buffoonery, obscenity and cruelty are all to be avoided (*Orat.* 79-90). Whereas the grand style moves the listener, and the middle style gives pleasure, the plain style is particularly helpful in proving a case. For moral and social theory we turn to the first book of Cicero's *De Officiis*, which was based on Panaetius' *Peri tou kathêkontos* (*On Propriety*). In paragraphs 130-1 Cicero mentions the manners, appearance and walk that are characteristic of a gentleman. The humour of such a man is refined, polite, clever, and witty – *elegans, urbanum, ingeniosum, facetum* (104). His conversation (*sermo*) is lively, but at the same time relaxed and free from dogmatism; it is grave or gay, according to the subject; and except when reproof is called for, it avoids any show of anger (134-7).

Moving now to poetic theory, we must take account of two of Callimachus' pronouncements, both of which he attributes to Apollo. The first comes in the *Hymn to Apollo*. Envy has just expressed her contempt for the poet who does not produce large quantities of verse. Apollo answers:

> Great is the stream of Assyria's river, and yet on its water
> it carries a great deal of dirt from the land and a great deal of rubbish
>
> (108-9).

Then, in the prologue of the *Aetia* (*Origins*), Callimachus describes a divine intervention:

> When, you see, for the very first time I placed a tablet
>   upon my knees, Apollo of Lycia said:
>   [I charge you], my poet, make your victim as fat as possible;
>   as for the Muse, be sure to keep her slender.
> This, too, I command you: tread a way which the waggons
>   do not pound; and never drive your chariot
> along the common ruts of the highway; follow a path
>   which no one has trodden, though your route will be more narrow
>
> (1.21-8).

We have already mentioned Horace's reference to Lucilius as a muddy river (1.4.11; 1.10.50); in 1.10.31-5, Callimachus' vision of a deity is cleverly adapted to Horace's argument (see p. 172 below); the joke about fat victim and slender Muse reappears in 2.6.14-15 *pingue pecus domino facias et cetera praeter / ingenium*; later, in *E.* 2.1.76-7, Horace complains that a work is censured, not because it is crudely or clumsily made (*crasse compositum illepideue*), but because it is new; and in *E.* 2.2.80 he alleges that the noise of Rome prevents him and others from following the poets' narrow path (*contracta ... uestigia uatum*). So

Callimachus clearly had some influence on Horace's style. He also provided a respectable Greek precedent for avoiding the major genres.[1]

The poet of the *sermones* comes into sharper focus when he is contrasted with the bard (*uates* in the special sense).[2] From birth the latter is under the protection of the gods; in a countryside permeated with the spirit of religion, he experiences the inspiration which enables him to sing of gods, heroes and men – not ordinary men, but leaders and rulers. His song teaches the community by celebrating and immortalising glorious achievements and by reminding the people of the beautiful and historic land in which they live. Such a song is sonorous and melodious, with a splendour of diction that is independent of the metre. The forms in which this poetry is embodied are epic, choral lyric, and (less centrally) tragedy. Personal lyrics on wine, love and death are also granted a certain merit (see, for example, *Odes* 2.13 and 4.9), but they are usually placed, at least by implication, on a lower level, because they do not have the same moral and patriotic dimension. The *uates*, therefore, is a revered, almost holy, figure; yet on occasions he becomes an object of laughter, as in the picture of the intoxicated devotee of Bacchus (*E.* 1.19) and the crazy babbler of the *Ars Poetica* (453ff.). The satirist is at the other end of the poetic scale. On one occasion, indeed, for tactical reasons, he is even denied the name of poet:

> *neque enim concludere uersum*
> *dixeris esse satis; neque si qui scribat uti nos*
> *sermoni propiora, putes hunc esse poetam.*
> *ingenium cui sit, cui mens diuinior atque os*
> *magna sonaturum, des nominis huius honorem* (1.4.40-4)

> You would not think it enough simply to fashion
> a metrical line. Nor, if a man composed, as I do,
> in a style rather near to prose, would you count him as a poet.
> The honour of that name should be kept for someone with natural
> gifts, an inspired soul, and a voice of mighty music.

Yet the two writers are not totally different species. The satirist, too, has his duty to the community; and although he claims little in the way of *ingenium* (genius), he is subject to many of the same rules. Several of the precepts in the *Ars Poetica* which are meant primarily for the *uates* apply also to the writer of *sermones*. Organic unity is important; so is the craft of choosing and combining words:

> The writer pledged to produce a poem must also be subtle
> and careful in linking words, preferring this to that.
> When a skilful collocation renews a familiar word,
> that is distinguished writing (45-8).

---

[1] For the Callimachean element in Horace see Cody and Wimmel, sections C and E.
[2] For a discussion of the concept *uates* see Newman.

All poets have similar aims:

> The aim of a poet is either to benefit or to please
> or to say what is both enjoyable and of service (333-4).

Care must be taken (292-4); criticism is essential (385-90); and such criticism must be candid:

> An honest and sensible man will fault lines that are feeble,
> condemn the clumsy, proscribe with a black stroke of the pen
> those which haven't been trimmed, prune pretentious adornment,
> where a thought is rather obscure, insist on clarification,
> detect ambiguous phrases, and mark what ought to be changed (445-9).

The most compendious, and also one of the finest, statements of classical theory comes in *E.* 2.2:

> But the man who wants to achieve a poem of genuine quality
> will take, along with his notebook, the mind of a rigorous censor.
> Any words deficient in lustre or lacking solidity
> or those which he deems unworthy of honour, he will have the courage
> to expel from their place, although they may be reluctant to leave
> and still hang back, seeking refuge in Vesta's temple.
> He will do well to unearth words which have long been hidden
> from the people's view, bringing to light some splendid terms
> employed in earlier days by Cato, Cethegus and others,
> which now lie buried by grimy dust and the years' neglect.
> He will also admit some new ones, raised by their father Usage.
> Flowing strong and clear like an unpolluted river,
> he will spread prosperity, enriching the land with the wealth of his language.
> He will show his skill and care by pruning the over dense,
> stripping untidy pieces, and taking out the feeble.
> In spite of the strain he will make it seem like fun, as a dancer
> switches with ease from nimble satyr to blundering Cyclops (109-25).

When Horace differentiates his hexameters from higher forms of poetry, he stresses their kinship with conversation. They are *sermoni propiora* (1.4.42); unlike the soaring lyrics of Pindar, they represent the *Musa pedestris* (2.6.17); they crawl along the ground (*E.* 2.1.251). To gain some notion of what is meant by this, we may turn to scholarly compilations like those of Ruckdeschel, Hofmann, and Bo (1.335-50). There, listed in various ways, we will find words, forms, usages, constructions and expressions which, because of their frequent occurrence in comedy, Cicero's letters, or Petronius, and their rarity in Lucretius, Cicero's speeches and the *Aeneid*, are classified as colloquial Latin. Here are a few examples:

(1) Words: 'low' or 'familiar' words (*buccae* instead of *genae* for

'cheeks', *caballus* instead of *equus* for 'horse', *moechus* instead of *adulter*; nouns ending in *-o*, like *agaso* (lackey) and *popino* (greedy-guts); verbs like *ambulo* (stroll), *blatero* (chatter), and *garrio* (jabber); grossly vulgar words, like *caco* (shit), *mingo* (piss) and *futuo* (fuck); interjections like *heus* (hey!), *ohe* (whoah!) and *pol* (by golly!).

(2) Forms: diminutives like *agellus* (bit of ground), *asellus* (ass), *auricula* (ear); adjectives ending in *-osus*, like *annosus* (old) and *cerebrosus* (hot-tempered); frequentative verbs like *calefacto* (heat), *cursito* (dash about), *factito* (do).

(3) Usages: animal names for insults – *simius* (ape), *cimex* (bug); *hic homo* (yours truly) for *ego*; *belle* (nicely) and *pulchre* (beautifully) for *bene* (well); *misere* (desperately) for *magnopere* (greatly); *crepo* (rattle on about) for *dico* (say); *clamo* (shout) for *uoco* (call); *uiuo* (live) for *sum* (am).

(4) Constructions: co-ordination instead of subordination; *ut* introducing a direct question; *i* followed by another imperative; *ocius* in an impatient question in the sense of 'hurry up'.

(5) Expressions: formulas of request – *si me amas, si uis, sodes*; asseverations – *inteream si* (I'll be blowed if), *dispeream ni* (damn me if ... not); proverbs – *hac urget lupus hac canis* (here the wolf snarls, here the dog).

That is one approach. It reveals the pithiness and colour of colloquial speech-units, and offers interesting parallels to modern usage. But such a method is perhaps most congenial to the student of language. Those whose main concern is literary may prefer to work from an actual poem, trying to *sense* the colloquial quality of words and phrases, and observing how they function in a living context. Kiessling-Heinze's edition or the *Oxford Latin Dictionary* can be used as a control. Thus at the opening of 1.9, *nescio quid nugarum* (some piece of nonsense) and *totus in illis* (quite wrapped up in it) show the poet happily engrossed in a world of his own. He is interrupted by the pest's over-familiar greeting: *quid agis, dulcissime rerum?* (My dear chap! How are things?). He replies in phrases of conventional politeness: *suauiter ut nunc est ... cupio omnia quae uis* (Fine at the moment ... all the best!); he then makes it even clearer that he does not intend to prolong the conversation – *numquid uis?* (Was there anything else?). By v.8 he is becoming desperate (*misere discedere quaerens*) and he envies Bolanus his hot temper – a slang use of *cerebrum*. But he cannot get rid of the pest, who continues to jabber on – *garriret*. The tone of the passage can be confirmed by consulting the lexicographical works mentioned above.

Satires 1.9 is the most continuously colloquial of the satires. What it represents, however, is the conversation of educated people; the pest, as he says himself, is *doctus* (7). Horace seldom records working-class speech. In 1.5 we are *told* of abusive interchanges between slaves and bargees, but all we actually hear is

> *'huc appelle!' 'trecentos inseris.' 'ohe,*
> *iam satis est!'* (12-13)

'Bring her in here!' 'How many hundred do you want to pack in?'
'Whoah, that's enough!'

From the altercation of Sarmentus and Cicirrus (56-60) only two insults
are recorded; and in 1.7 all we hear is the *coup de grâce*, which is not
notably demotic. Again, in Book 2 Ofellus does not talk like a peasant
(2.116-36), and Davus' language is rarely servile (*meiat* in 2.7.52). It may
well be that Lucilius operated more freely at this end of the spectrum.

When we move on to the *Epistles* we sense a difference. According to
Ps. Acro on *E.* 1.1, the only change is the fact that the addressees are
thought of as absent instead of present. But there is more to it than that.
The moral emphasis moves from censure to affirmation; while there are
still occasional passages of ridicule, Horace offers more discussion and
advice; names are much less frequent. Again, since the *Epistles* contain
less dialogue, Horace is less concerned to reproduce the effect of fluid
conversation. So the thought ends more often at the end of a line. Elisions
are less numerous; and the diction is more restrained, containing fewer
plebeian words, fewer metaphors and (apart from some innuendo in *E.*
1.20) no obscenity. As an example of colloquial writing in the context of
an epistle, we may take the speaker's words in *E.* 2.2.3-14:

> Here's an attractive lad
> with a fair skin, beautifully built from head to toe.
> Eight thousand and he's yours, signed sealed and delivered.
> He's home-bred, quick to obey his master's orders;
> he has had a touch of basic Greek, and will soon pick up
> any skill that's required; wet clay can be moulded;
> he'll even sing you a simple song to go with your wine.
> Too many claims arouse misgivings. Only a salesman
> who wants to get rid of his goods will praise them above their worth.
> I'm not obliged to sell; I'm poor but not in the red.
> None of the dealers would make you this offer. I'll do it for you, sir –
> but no one else (3-14).

The lines cleverly *indicate* the man's patter, but can hardly be said to
reproduce it. Metre aside, grammar, diction and dialect have all been
tidied up so as to meet Augustan standards.

Even at their most informal level, therefore, the *sermones* are a great
deal more than unprocessed conversation. And in fact, when we look
back at what was said earlier about their humble and prosaic nature we
find, as so often with Horace, that the expressions used are not
straightforward. In 1.4.41ff., he is trying to avoid unpopularity by
playing down his status as a poet; in *E.* 2.1.251 he is protesting his utter
inability to honour Augustus with a formal poem; and in 2.6.17 he is
humorously contrasting his lowland Muse with the high location of his

castle in the hills. The very phrase *Musa pedestris* is paradoxical.[3] But
even if the *sermones* are thought of as normally low-key, we must
remember that they do not remain constantly on the same level. They
rise and fall according to the speaker's emotional tone. Let us look at *E.*
2.1.250ff.:

> For my part, rather than writing talks
> that creep on the ground, I'd sooner celebrate mighty deeds,
> describing the lie of the land, the course of rivers, the setting
> of forts on mountain summits, barbarous kingdoms, and then
> the ending of strife throughout the world by your command,
> Janus guardian of peace, locked behind his bars,
> and the Parthian overawed by your imperial might –
> if only my powers matched my yearning.

There, with just a hint of irony (for such grandeur is not for him), Horace
respectfully alludes to the style which he is declining. Elsewhere the
irony is quite explicit, as in the mock-Homeric introduction to the verbal
brawl in 1.7 and the similar passage in 1.5.51-6. Amusing, too, in their
various ways are the gipsy's warning in 1.9.31-4, the oracular obscurity of
Tiresias (2.5.55-65), the lofty Lucretian affirmations in 1.5.101-3 and
2.4.93-5, the legalistic phraseology of Trebatius in 2.1 (especially 7-9 and
80-3), Catius' gastronomic pedantry (2.4 *passim*), and the sen-
tentiousness of Balatro (so patently insincere) as he comforts Nasidienus
in 2.8.65-74.

Heightened effects, however, are not invariably humorous. In 1.3
Horace says:

> *iura inuenta metu iniusti fateare necesse est,*
> *tempora si fastosque uelis euoluere mundi.*
> *nec natura potest iusto secernere iniquum,*
> *diuidit ut bona diuersis, fugienda petendis* (111-14)

If you're willing to read your way through the records of human history,
you will have to admit that justice arose from the fear of its opposite.
Nature cannot distinguish right and wrong as she does
in the case of desirable and undesirable, wholesome and harmful.

That is a piece of serious exposition written, without parody, in
Lucretius' manner. From time to time the preaching in the diatribes
takes on a sharper tone:

> *non uxor saluum te uult, non filius; omnes*
> *uicini oderunt, noti, pueri atque puellae.*
> *miraris, cum tu argento post omnia ponas,*
> *si nemo praestet quem non merearis amorem?* (1.1.84-7)

---

[3] Cf. Callimachus, *Aetia* 112.9 (Loeb p. 86) *Mouseôn pezon epeimi nomon.*

Your wife and son don't want you to recover.
Friends and neighbours, young and old, they all detest you.
Since you put money before all else, small wonder that no one
offers you any affection; what do you do to earn it?

Once, in an exceptional passage, a spendthrift is reminded of his larger
obligations:

> *ergo*
> *quod superat non est melius quo insumere possis?*
> *cur eget indignus quisquam, te diuite? quare*
> *templa ruunt antiqua deum? cur, improbe, carae*
> *non aliquid patriae tanto emetiris aceruo?* (2.2.101-5)

> So can't you think of a better way
> to spend your surplus? Why should any respectable man
> be in need when you are rich? Why are the ancient temples
> of the gods collapsing? You selfish creature, why don't you offer
> something from that enormous pile to the land of your birth?

More sombre themes, like the transience of life, are largely confined to
the *Epistles*. One thinks especially of the moving comparison between
words and men in *AP* 60-72 and of the lines near the end of *E*. 2.2:

> Therefore, as no one is granted use in perpetuity,
> and one heir follows another as wave on wave, what advantage
> are barns and tenants' houses or those Lucanian pastures
> stretching into Calabria, if large and small alike
> fall to the scythe of Orcus who cannot be coaxed by money? (175-9)

It is significant that when the same truth was touched on in 2.2, Horace
purposely lightened the effect by concluding on a note of gentle parody:

> *quocirca uiuite fortes,*
> *fortiaque aduersis opponite pectora rebus.*

> So be brave, then,
> and bravely throw out your chest to meet adversity's challenge.

This alternation of high and low, grave and gay, was a feature of the
genre as Horace conceived it:

> *et sermone opus est modo tristi, saepe iocoso,*
> *defendente uicem modo rhetoris atque poetae,*
> *interdum urbani, parcentis uiribus atque*
> *extenuantis eas consulto. ridiculum acri*
> *fortius et melius magnas plerumque secat res* (1.10.11-15)

> You need a style which is sometimes severe,
> sometimes gay, now suiting the role of statesman or poet,
> now that of a clever talker who keeps his strength in reserve
> and carefully rations it out. Humour is often stronger
> and more effective than sharpness in cutting knotty issues.

That is very clearly stated, but one should perhaps add that apart from the obvious cases of heroic parody, there are several instances where grave and gay co-exist in the same passage. Here is a glimpse of the Stoic sage in 2.7:

> *quisnam igitur liber? sapiens sibi qui imperiosus,*
> *quem neque pauperies neque mors neque uincula terrent,*
> *responsare cupidinibus, contemnere honores*
> *fortis, et in se ipso totus teres atque rotundus,*
> *externi ne quid ualeat per leue morari,*
> *in quem manca ruit semper fortuna* (2.7.83-8)

> Who then is free? The wise man who is master of himself,
> who remains undaunted in the face of poverty, chains and death,
> stoutly defies his passions and despises positions of power,
> a man complete in himself, smooth and round, who is such that
> when Fortune attacks him she maims only herself.

What nobility! We almost forget that the speaker is a slave who is repeating things which he heard from his friend the doorman. Or think of the old women's yarn told by Horace's Sabine neighbour and of the advice which is soon to be so drastically discredited:

> *terrestria quando*
> *mortalis animas uiuunt sortita, neque ulla est*
> *aut magno aut paruo leti fuga: quo, bone, circa,*
> *dum licet, in rebus iucundis uiue beatus;*
> *uiue memor quam sis aeui breuis* (2.6.93-7)

> All creatures on earth have been given mortal souls;
> large or small, none has the means of escaping death.
> So my dear chap, while there's still time, enjoy the good things
> of life, and never forget your days are numbered.

Shallow nonsense from a *ridiculus mus*? And yet ... does it not anticipate another kind of music:

> *huc uina et unguenta et nimium breues*
> *flores amoenae ferre iube rosae,*
> *   dum res et aetas et sororum*
> *   fila trium patiuntur atra* (*Odes* 2.3.13-10)

Bring wine, and perfume, and the rose
whose lovely blooms too soon are dead,
while age and circumstance allow,
and the dark sisters spin their thread.

So far we have been discussing the range of Horace's language in the *sermones*. Something must now be added on the more general topic of structure. When we take the first three diatribes together, we find that in each case we are presented with some oddity of human behaviour (discontent, a tendency to run to extremes, inconsistent conduct) which is illustrated in sets of antitheses over about twenty lines. A second theme then emerges (greed, unwise sexual behaviour, unfairness in judging one's fellows); this is treated more thoroughly and at much greater length. In two cases there is a short final section recalling earlier motifs, and all three end with a gibe at some contemporary figure.

At first hearing, it must have sounded as if Horace was wandering casually from one argument to another; perhaps the main theme only occurred to him as he was talking? Yet, on inspection, it emerges not only that the transitions are carefully contrived, but that there is a firm connection in thought between the introduction and the main theme. Thus discontent is based on greed, extreme behaviour is illustrated by certain kinds of sexual folly (especially adultery), and both inconsistency and unfairness are seen to spring from a lack of balance. In the opening scene of 2.7, Davus condemns inconsistency, first in general terms and then with particular reference to Horace. At v.46 he makes a fresh beginning, accusing Horace this time of being a slave to adulterous desires. When that accusation misses the mark, he still maintains that Horace falls hopelessly short of the Stoic sage; the sage is truly free, whereas Horace is a slave to a courtesan, to his love of expensive art-works and to his belly. Finally, at v.116, the master loses his temper and drives Davus out of the room. How are the major and minor themes related? Gluttony is mentioned in vv.29-42 as the last of Horace's inconsistencies. (After eagerly looking forward to a simple meal at home, he dashes off to a dinner-party at the house of Maecenas.) The same vice is mentioned again as the last major instance of his moral slavery (102-11). More generally, the inconsistent man resembles the one who is dominated by his desires in that both lack rational control. Finally, it turns out that the motif of slavery runs through the whole poem, starting from the fact that Davus, the slave, is taking advantage of the Saturnalia to speak freely to his master.

Described in these terms, the poems may sound bland and uninteresting. But the kind of unity summarised above only becomes apparent after study. It is not obvious, and in one or two satires the details are open to dispute. The same technique is also seen in the *Epistles*. In *E* 2.2, for instance, we have to wait for over twenty verses before understanding the relevance of the slave-owner's speech, and another twenty-five to grasp the parallel between Horace and Lucullus' soldier. This subtlety of structure is one of the delights of the *sermones*. None of the poet's successors could reproduce it, and if it appeared tomorrow in a Lucilian papyrus we should all be mightily surprised.

(iii) Persius

Because of its Greek features, Persius' Prologue will be discussed in Chapter Five. Here it is enough to note that while Persius disclaims the title of 'true poet', and ridicules the tradition of dream and consecration as found in Ennius and others, he nevertheless appears to be *some* kind of poet (*poeta* in v.3); and though only a half clansman (*semipaganus* in v.6), he does bring *some* kind of *carmen* to the holy rites of the bards.

In 1 *passim* and 5.10-13 we are told emphatically what that *carmen* is not. A hint of a more positive sort comes in 5.14-15:

> *uerba togae sequeris iunctura callidus acri*
> *ore teres modico*

> You keep to the dress of citizens' speech, skilled at the clever
> juxtaposition, smooth with a moderate utterance.

The metaphor of speech as dress is not new,[1] but the phrase *uerba togae* almost certainly is. The next expression – *iunctura callidus acri* – is even more striking, since it both describes and represents Persius' most distinctive feature. Varro (first century B.C.) had used *iunctura* in the simple sense of 'combination' or 'linking' – 'a verse is a combination of words (*uersus est uerborum iunctura*).[2] Horace carried the word a stage further when he admired the effect produced by a *callida iunctura*: a clever collocation could make a familiar word new (*AP* 47-8).[3] Here also, in Persius 5.14, the speaker refers with approval to the startling effect of an original juxtaposition. He has kept Horace's *callidus*, transferring it from the collocation to the poet; but he has brought in another adjective (*acer*), applying it to *iunctura*. This adjective means 'sharp' – literally, as opposed to 'smooth' or 'even', metaphorically, as opposed to 'dull' or 'insensitive'. Normally the two types of meaning might have been given equal weight, but before we allow that to happen, we must consider the third expression: *ore teres modico*.

In *De Orat.* 3.199, Cicero says the grand style of oratory is 'full but well rounded' (*plena ... sed tamen teres*); the plain style is 'slender but not

---

[1] See, e.g. Diogenes Laertius 4.52, who records the remark, attributed to Eratosthenes, that Bion dressed philosophy in flowery clothes.

[2] Marius Victorinus, *GL* 6.55.11.

[3] A couple of modern examples that come to mind are the last two words in each of the following quotations from Eliot: 'And daughters ride away on casual pillions' (*The Rock*, section 2), and 'Uncorseted, her friendly bust gives promise of pneumatic bliss' (*Whispers of Immortality*).

without sinew and power'; in between is a style which partakes of both and is distinguished by a certain 'intermediate quality' (*mediocritate*). The word *teres*, as applied to rhetorical style, seems to mean having well-rounded periods as opposed to choppy and irregular sense-units; it is not readily distinguished from *rotundus*.[4] Both words are used by Horace to describe the character of the sage: he is 'complete in himself, smooth and round' – *in se ipso totus teres atque rotundus* (2.7.86). Persius too applied *teres* to a man (viz. himself), but in connection with his style, not his character. And instead of talking about a rounded diction, as Horace did in *AP* 323 (*ore rotundo*), he says *ore modico*, thus placing himself in Cicero's intermediate category. If, then, he allows himself to be called 'smooth with a moderate utterance' he can hardly have wanted *acri* in the previous phrase to mean 'rough to the ear'. So we had better take it as 'sharp' in the sense of 'clever', the cleverness consisting in the unexpected, and yet strikingly perceptive, nature of the collocation.

When we read the *Satires* with these remarks about diction and juxtaposition in mind, we find that there are few lines in the high style of epic or tragedy; even parody of that style is not common. But there are numerous passages where the preacher's urgent tone and the dignity of his subject raise the style above the level of everyday speech. (Several instances were quoted in Chapter One.) Again, while we can readily point to colloquial words and phrases, it is less than accurate to say that Persius *follows*, or restricts himself to, current usage. Some of his words are rarely encountered elsewhere (e.g. *canthus, obba,* and *tucceta*); others are given extended meanings (e.g. *aqualiculus* is properly a pig's belly rather than a man's; *aristae* normally denotes cereals, not bristling hairs; *pulpa* usually means just 'flesh', not 'flesh as the seat of carnal desire'); others he made up himself (e.g. *Pegaseius, semipaganus,* and *poetrides*); grammatical forms are given odd functions (e.g. infinitives are used as nouns, and nouns as adjectives); and (most important) the 'combinations' which he refers to are often strikingly original.

To illustrate these points we turn to one of the shorter satires, viz. no. 2, which is an attack on foolish and immoral prayers. The liveliness of style comes partly from the varied syntax in which statement, question, prayer and command follow each other in quick succession, and partly from the shifts of tone produced by different levels of diction. Thus a worshipper murmurs: 'If only my uncle would pop off (*ebulliat*)', and 'O that I might rub out (*expungam*) that ward of mine ... he's mangy (*scabiosus*) and suffering from jaundice (9-14).' At the other end of the scale we have some lines worthy of a Hebrew prophet:

---

[4] Cf. Cicero, *Orat.* 40, where in Isocrates' view Theodorus is *praefractior* (rather too broken up) *nec satis rotundus* (and not sufficiently well-rounded).

o curuae in terris animae et caelestium inanes,
quid iuuat hoc, templis nostros inmittere mores
et bona dis ex hac scelerata ducere pulpa? (61-3)

Souls bent on earth, devoid of the things of heaven!
What profit is there in carrying our ways into the churches,
using this sinful flesh to decide what is good for the gods?

And sometimes the two effects come together, as when the sordid or stupid nature of a prayer is heightened by the solemn formulae of supplication, e.g. *o si ... o si* (9-10), *da ... da* (45-6), *sunto sitque* (58).

Another satirical technique (which goes back as far as Plautus but is employed by Persius in typically drastic ways) is that of presenting things as human agents. Thus the wrong sort of prayer is *emax* 'eager to buy' (3), the censer is a silent accomplice (5), a coin sighs in despair (51). Conversely, a human body is a *spes macra* 'a skinny hope' (35), and a dead man is a *bidental* – a piece of ground which has been railed off after being struck by lightning (27). The gods are treated similarly. They are taken aside as if their statues were alive (4), Jupiter's stupidity supposedly extends to his beard (28), and he is prevented from 'answering the call' by too many plates of stew – *morantur* (43) includes the idea of constipation.

It is a well-known fact that in ancient poetry originality was achieved by making innovations within a traditional genre. When Horace took over phrases and ideas from Lucilius, he modified them so as to meet the requirements of classical theory. Virgil did the same with Ennius. In each case, repetitions were removed, excessive rhyme and alliteration were modified, metrical harshness was reduced, and so on. The result was something new and modern. It also possessed that kind of finality which one associates with a 'classic'. This achievement posed an intractable problem for the writers of the Neronian age. However, poetry must move in some direction if it is not to stagnate, and Persius saw the possibility of using the Augustans, especially Horace, to help him produce a range of highly individual effects. So when in 2 he came to write about discreditable prayers, he thought first of the hypocrite in Horace *E.* 1.16, who

when he offers a pig or an ox to appease the wrath of the gods,
utters aloud 'Father Janus' or 'Apollo', and then
mutters in a furtive inaudible whisper 'Lovely Laverna,
grant I may cheat ...' (58-61)

Then he turned to another kind of supplication at the beginning of 2.6, where Horace, in thanking Mercury for his farm, refuses to offer foolish prayers like

'Please could I stumble on a pot of silver and be like the fellow
who finding some treasure bought and ploughed the very field
in which he had worked as a hired hand; it was Hercules' favour
that made him rich' (10-13).

By conflating these two passages and 'processing' them in his own
peculiar way, Persius produced:

'Good sense, good name, good character' – these words ring out for
                                                                    strangers
to hear; under his breath he privately mutters 'If only
uncle would pop off, what a splendid funeral we'd have!' 'If only
Hercules would let my spade thump on a crock of silver!' (8-12)

The new element is the prayer for someone else's death. Could this too be
derived from Horace? One thinks of the satire about legacy-hunting
(2.5), but as yet there is nothing significant. Then comes the following
prayer:

'Although I'm his guardian, I'd like to rub that youngster out.
I'm next in line and he's mangy and swollen
with jaundice' (12-14).

That must surely have been prompted by Horace 2.5.45-6, where the
captator hopes for the death of 'a delicate son /reared in splendid
surroundings' (*ualidus male filius in re /praeclara sublatus*). Certainly
the expansion of 'delicate' into 'mangy and swollen with jaundice' is very
much in Persius' manner. Possibly, too, that is where he found
praeclarus, a word which he transferred from the boy's background to the
uncle's death. Persius then concludes the prayers with 'That's his third
wife that Nerius is burying.' Why Nerius? The context implies someone
who, to say the least, is astute in money-matters. And there is a financier
called Nerius in Horace 2.3.69. What makes the reminiscence almost
certain is the fact that Horace's Nerius is mentioned immediately after 'a
bonus so kindly offered by the Lord of Luck' (*Mercurius*). We already
know from Horace's prayer to Mercury in 2.6 (quoted above) that
Mercury must be in the back of Persius' mind. He eventually comes
forward in vv.44-6:

You hope to build up your assets by killing a bullock; its liver
is used to summon Mercury: 'Grant that my house may prosper;
grant growth to my flocks and herds!'

So in the few lines we have quoted, Persius' memory had encompassed
four Horatian passages. In *his* prayer to Mercury Horace had made a
Callimachean joke:

> Make fat the flocks I own and everything else
> except my head (2.6.14-15).

Persius does not repeat the joke and, in v.46, he omits the adjective; but (as we shall see in a moment), he makes fatness an important motif in the satire. He even speaks of 'fat gold' (*pingui auro* in vv.52-3).

All this is remarkable enough, but there remains an even more surprising possibility. Could it be that a frame for the whole satire was provided by two lines of Ovid? In a passage about prayers in *Pont.* 4.8.39-40, he says:

> *nec quae de parua pauper dis libat acerra*
> *tura minus grandi quam data lance ualent*

> Incense offered to the gods by the poor from a tiny casket
> is worth no less than what comes from a lordly dish.

In Persius, after the opening address, we have

> *at bona pars procerum tacita libabit acerra* (5)

> But most of the nobles offer incense from a silent casket,

and just before the end we find:

> *quin damus id superis, de magna quod dare lance*
> *non possit magni Messalae lippa propago* (71-72)

> Instead let's give to the gods what mighty Messala's descendant
> with his bloodshot eyes is unable to give from his mighty dish.

I make the suggestion with considerable diffidence; but Persius' mind worked in strange ways, and he may even have had another kind of interest in Ovid's poem.[5]

I turn now to a different feature of Persius 2. As the focus of attention moves from hypocrisy (5ff.) to superstition (31ff.), and then to sheer stupidity (41ff.), two motifs are developed. One has to do with man's greed and his attempt to bribe the gods with gold. There are about a dozen references in all, with a cluster between vv.52 and 60. More interesting, and more characteristic, is the motif of food, whether

---

[5] Nisbet points out in a letter that Ovid, *Pont.* 4.8 is addressed to P. Suillius Rufus, the husband of Ovid's step-daughter. Suillius, who had served under Germanicus, was banished in A.D. 24. He returned after the death of Tiberius and survived into the reign of Nero. He was exiled again in 58, close to the probable date of Persius 2. Could his earlier banishment have been engineered by Cotta Messallinus, who in A.D. 24 was hostile to supporters of Germanicus (Syme, 4.130)? If so, then Persius 2 might possibly contain a compliment to Suillius as well as an insult to Cotta. One wonders whether there could have been any link between Suillius and Macrinus, the recipient of the poem.

consumed by gluttons or offered to the gods. The images seem to be
deliberately chosen for their grossness: offal and greasy guts (30), huge
platefuls of thick goulash (42), tripe which melts on the fire (47), piles of
innards and cakes (48-9), sinful flesh (63), a great dish of offerings (71).
Even the spiritual qualities at the end of the satire, which recall those of
Macrinus at the beginning, are presented in culinary terms: *ius* and *fas*
(human and divine commands) are blended in the soul,[6] and, still more
astonishing, the heart is to be cooked in high-quality honour (*incoctum
generoso honesto*). Such spiritual food-offerings *are* acceptable to the
gods.

The misuse of food and drink is a recurrent theme in Persius. To the
Stoic, it signified not just a foolish disregard of one's health but a disorder
of the soul. In 3, Persius elaborates, as so often, a few lines taken from a
different context in Horace. In *E.* 1.16.21-3, Horace had warned
Quinctius not to confuse reputation with the actual truth:

> or, if people constantly say you're sound and healthy, [don't]
> conceal and disguise your fever as dinner approaches, until
> your hands, which are smeared with grease, suddenly start to tremble.

Persius works that up into a vivid account which ends as follows:

> Bloated with food and queasy in the stomach our friend goes off
> to his bath, with long sulphurous belches coming from his throat.
> As he drinks his wine, a fit of the shakes comes over him, knocking
> the warm tumbler from his fingers; his bared teeth chatter;
> suddenly greasy savouries slither from his slackened lips.
> The sequel is funeral march and candles. The late lamented,
> plastered with heavy odours, reclines on a lofty bed
> stiffly pointing his heels to the door (3.98-105).

That is undeniably strong and, in its ghastly way, funny. But with its
graphic power goes a certain coarseness. Horace would not have given us
a close-up of a fatal seizure.

In 3, as in 2, food represents a strand in the poem's fabric. Other kinds
of imagery, too, can carry the argument along. In 3 the companion,
scolding the lazy student, says *effluis amens* – 'you're oozing mindlessly
away' (20). This is immediately followed by *contemnere* – 'You'll be
rejected'. Then the underlying metaphor comes into full view:

> When a half-baked jar is tapped
> the greenish clay gives a dull answer betraying its quality.

Finally the speaker goes back to an earlier stage in the potting process:

---

[6] *Compositum ius* on its own would have meant a compound sauce; cf. the *duplex ius* in
Horace 2.4.63.

You are soft, damp, earth; away and have yourself moulded
on the whirling wheel till you're properly finished.

In 5, speaking of procrastination, Persius says tomorrow is always 'a little
ahead' – *paulum erit ultra* (69). He then continues the argument by
extending that idea:

Although you are under the same carriage and close to the rim
of the wheel that revolves in front, it's futile trying to catch it,
for you are running in the rear position on the back axle.

In 6 the satirist remonstrates with an over-eager heir:

You're in front, why shout for the baton before I've finished? (61)

This leads by implication to a picture in which A holds out B to C – a
grouping taken up by the new image in the following line:

I'm your Mercury, proffering a purse like the god in the picture.

Persius' imagery, then, is more peculiar and more arresting than
anything in Lucilius or Horace. In several other respects, however, the
comparison works to Persius' disadvantage. I shall mention one here, as
it is broadly connected with style. Reading 2, one observes that although
the address continually changes direction, moving from Macrinus (1) to
the suppliant (15) to Jupiter (40) and so on, yet Persius' presence is not
acknowledged in return (except, perhaps, at v.19), and hence no dialogue
develops. In satires where there *is* an interlocutor, Persius has taken little
trouble to give him an identity. *Satires* 3 and 5 look at first as if they
might prove exceptions, but in 3 the student seems to be left behind after
v.62 and the voice of the companion blends into that of Persius himself;
in 5 the speaker in vv.5-18 may be Cornutus, but no really clear
indication is given, and after v.73 even Cornutus disappears as the
diatribe on slavery gets under way. A different, and interesting, idea is
tried in 4 where Socrates harangues Alcibiades; but again, this scene is
abandoned after v.22, and it is not satisfactorily related to the Roman
section that follows.[7] Finally, in 1, Persius unconcernedly admits that his
interlocutor is a mere shadow:

---

[7] In the Greek section Socrates takes the young Alcibiades to task (1-22). In the Roman
section (23-52) Persius reflects on the fact that no one ponders on his own character, but
instead finds malicious fault with his neighbours. Perhaps we should infer that Alcibiades
fails to practise introspection, but that is not made clear. Again, the sunbather is abused by
a stranger for showing his posterior to the public (35-6). Clearly we are meant to condemn
this foul attack. But the insulting words recall what Socrates had previously said to
Alcibiades: 'What's your idea of the highest good? To ... pamper your skin with regular
sunshine?' (17-18), and 'Stop wagging your tail at the flattering rabble' (15).

You, whoever you are, my fictitious debating opponent (44).

Although past centuries took a different view, admiring Persius primarily for his moral sentiments, today he is studied mainly for his language. Vocabulary, constructions, tonal contrasts – all these repay attention; but the hallmark of his style is provided by those strange metaphorical expressions which so often represent an ingenious blend and transformation of Horatian elements. His didactic intention was surely genuine, but more orthodox Stoics would have insisted that the message could have been conveyed – and indeed *should* have been – in a simpler, more straightforward manner. So one concludes that Persius wrote in that compressed idiosyncratic way because it gave him a particular kind of pleasure. Some of that same pleasure was transmitted to those readers who 'snapped up' copies of the collection when it first appeared.[8] And it is still available to us. Granted, the poetry is 'a concentrated brew' (1.125), but those who persevere usually find the taste worth acquiring.

(iv) Juvenal

In *AP* 73-92, Horace develops the typically Roman idea that each poetic form is governed by a set of rules related to subject, metre, and style – rules which together make up the *lex operis* or 'law of the genre' (135). The law of satire is nowhere formulated, but in 2.1.1-2 Horace implies that a satirist is expected to be morally responsible and to operate within the law of libel. Beyond that, we can deduce a set of regulations which define satire as hexameter poetry ridiculing vice and folly in a style based on educated conversation, but rising to higher levels when required. In Persius' case one might amend the law slightly by saying 'in a style which rejects the inflated rhetoric of tragedy and obtains its most arresting effects by original combinations of familiar words'.

The kind of utterance that Persius rejects is described in the opening of 5. The phrase *fabula ... maesto ... hianda tragoedo* (5.3) – 'a play to be mouthed by a dismal tragedian' – is of particular interest, for it anticipates some well-known lines of Juvenal. At the climax of his long tirade against women in 6, Juvenal speaks of empresses who have poisoned their husbands and of women who are willing to murder their stepsons. He then continues:

> *fingimus haec altum satura sumente coturnum*
> *scilicet, et finem egressi legemque priorum*
> *grande Sophocleo carmen bacchamur hiatu*
> *montibus ignotum Rutulis caeloque Latino?* (634-7)

---

[8] *Diripere coeperunt* in the *Life*.

You think this is fiction? That my satire has donned theatrical boots,
that going beyond the bounds and law of earlier writers
I am raving in Sophocles' gaping style a lofty song
of things unknown to Rutulian hills and Latin skies?

The language is appropriately elevated. One notes the personification of
satire, the synecdoche of *coturnus* for tragedy, the internal accusative
with *bacchari*, the use of *hiatus* to characterise tragic diction, and those
phrases which evoke old Italy – Italy as she was before Greece took her
captive. In plain terms, Juvenal's main point is clear enough: 'I suppose
you think I am presenting fiction, and that the things I describe are
unheard of in Italy.' This is categorically denied: 'I only wish the
material *were* unreal – *nos utinam uani* (638); but it isn't. Such crimes
are not only committed, they are acknowledged with pride.' Then a
further opportunity for amplification occurs to him: 'Let us grant,' he
says, 'that Medea, Procne and the rest are *not* fantasies but historical
figures, even then these Roman women are worse; for whereas the Greeks
acted from passion, the Romans' motives are squalid and mercenary'
(643-52).

What, then, has happened to the law of the genre? Has Juvenal
transgressed it or not? In one sense, arguably, no, because *satura* has
always been a true reflection of social reality, and his own brand (he
assures us) is no exception. But that is only part of the story. Roman vice,
we are told, has now become so appalling as to challenge and surpass that
of Greek tragedy. Mention is made of Caesonia, who is said to have
driven Caligula mad with a love philtre (616-17), and of Agrippina, who
poisoned Claudius with a mushroom (620-1). Nor were male *exempla*
lacking. As 8 shows, the enormities of Nero and his court were vividly
present to Juvenal's mind. 'His crime,' he says, 'was the same as that of
Agamemnon's son' (215). Juvenal himself had observed the horrors of
Domitian 'the adulterer who defiled himself by a copulation of the tragic
type' (2.29-30). Later he would describe an episode which was even more
abominable than anything contained in tragedy (15.28-31). If such things
were to be treated in satire, the law of the genre would have to be
extended. True, the swollen diction parodied by Lucilius and Persius
would be avoided, or (to put it another way) the extreme implications of
the witty phrase *Sophocleo carmen bacchamur hiatu* would not be
followed up. Nevertheless, the gentlemanly conventions of the *sermo*
were now no longer adequate. One thinks of what Quintilian said in his
discussion of *ethos* and *pathos*. 'The latter,' he wrote, 'is almost wholly
concerned with anger, hatred, fear, resentment and pity' (6.2.20), all of
which, except pity, are Juvenal's stock-in-trade. And so, Quintilian
adds, while *ethos* is more like comedy, *pathos* is more like tragedy.

To develop this a little further, we must start again from Juvenal's
subject-matter, or rather the subject-matter as Juvenal saw it. He is

living in a world where humane and civilised conditions no longer obtain. The capital city, which should represent the summit of human achievement, is a savage place – *saeuae Urbis* (3.8-9); a Roman woman is 'a most savage viper' – *saeuissima uipera* (6.641); an emperor's regime has been a period of savagery – *tempora saeuitiae* (4.151). Vice has reached monstrous proportions: rather than a censor, a haruspex is needed to expiate the sins of pseudo men (2.121); the behaviour of women is equally unnatural (*monstra* in 6.286). And the capital is part of a wider world in which atrocities take place, like the case of *feritas* recently attested in Egypt (15.32). The vices and follies ridiculed by Horace, though sometimes extremely serious, were contained within the world of nature, and his stylistic range was perfectly adequate to deal with them. But perversion, sadism, incest, cannibalism – these evils called for a style which transcended the norm.[1] Juvenal was already aware of this in 1, when he spoke of 'charging across the plain' – *decurrere campo* (19) – and 'crowding on full sail' – *utere uelis, totos pande sinus* (149-50). As Bramble says, 'open plain and full canvas, symbols for the higher genres, replace the untrodden path and small boat of the temperate' (164).[2]

This quotation will remind us that tragedy is not the only kind of literature that represents power and vehemence. Another, and a more satisfactory, approach to Juvenal is offered by accounts of the grand style in oratory. According to Cicero (*Orat.* 97), the exponent of this style was *amplus, copiosus, grauis, ornatus* – 'elaborate, abundant, impressive, ornate'; and such a man commanded the greatest power (*uis*). One feature of this power was *indignatio* – a technique for arousing 'great hatred against a person or deep dislike of a thing' (*De Invent.* 1.100). The same term was applied to the corresponding feelings, which were naturally aroused by certain topics. Cicero mentions fifteen of these topics, of which numbers seven and eight are the most relevant here. 'The seventh topic is when we express our indignation, claiming that some horrible, cruel, outrageous, tyrannical deed has been perpetrated by force, violence, and by means of wealth. The eighth topic is when we show that the crime in question is no ordinary one, nor is it characteristic even of the most audacious men; that it is something beyond the range of savage people and barbarous tribes and brute beasts' (*De Invent.* 1.102-3). When indignation makes verse, as Juvenal claims it does (1.79),

[1] In his brilliant appreciation of Senecan tragedy, Herington distinguishes three characteristic movements: The Cloud of Evil, The Defeat of Reason by Passion, The Explosion of Evil. Such enormities call for a commensurate style. See in particular pp. 178, 182, and 197. The problem is that to sustain this level of excited horror a writer must have very substantial resources. There is a fatal temptation to issue dud cheques after one's credit has been exhausted. In Juvenal's case irony helps to keep him solvent.

[2] Bramble adduces parallels on p. 166 n.5, 167 n.1, and 168. He has a somewhat different view, however, of 6.634-7, taking the lines as explicitly embracing the style of tragedy (165).

the result is bound to be declamatory, and that again entails an extension of the *lex operis*.

As with Horace, however, rhetorical theory can only take us so far. In Juvenal's case it fails to show how the impassioned or stately or (occasionally) romantic hexameters, with all their technical devices, are made to serve a satirical purpose. A few examples will show how the dignified is employed to intensify the squalid:

> *sed uatem egregium, cui non sit publica uena,*
> *qui nihil expositum soleat deducere, nec qui*
> *communi feriat carmen triuiale moneta,*
> *hunc, qualem nequeo monstrare et sentio tantum,*
> *anxietate carens animus facit, omnis acerbi*
> *impatiens, cupidus siluarum aptusque bibendis*
> *fontibus Aonidum (7.53-9)*

But the peerless bard, whose vein is not of the common sort,
who is not prepared to fashion material sold in the market
or to strike from the public mint a song for mass circulation –
the type of man I cannot point to but only feel –
is formed by a mind that knows no worry and is wholly free
from bitterness, yearning for woodland haunts and worthy to drink
from the Muses' fountain.

That is the ideal. But as Juvenal turns to reality the familiar sardonic note reappears:

> *neque enim cantare sub antro*
> *Pierio thyrsumque potest contingere maesta*
> *paupertas atque aeris inops, quo nocte dieque*
> *corpus eget: satur est cum dicit Horatius 'euhoe!' (59-62)*

Dismal poverty cannot hope
to seize the thyrsis and sing within a Pierian cave
when it doesn't possess the cash that is needed night and day
by the body. Horace's belly is full when he cries 'o rapture!'

At the beginning of the same satire, high and low are more closely interwoven. Caesar alone has had regard for the plight of the Latin Muses:

> *cum iam celebres notique poetae*
> *balneolum Gabiis, Romae conducere furnos*
> *temptarent, nec foedum alii nec turpe putarent*
> *praecones fieri, cum desertis Aganippes*
> *uallibus esuriens migraret in atria Clio (3-7)*

when distinguished and famous poets
were trying to take a lease on Gabii's dingy bath-house
or a city bakery, and others considered it no disgrace

or shame to become auctioneers, when Clio bade farewell
to the vales of Aganippe and made for the sale-rooms in search of a meal.

A familiar instance of this procedure is parody, in which grand and mean
are made to co-exist within the same phrase. In 2, Juvenal attacks an
effeminate aristocrat who wears diaphanous clothes in court even when
he is prosecuting someone for adultery:

> *acer et indomitus libertatisque magister,*
> *Cretice, perluces* (77-8)

The phrase *acer et indomitus* is taken from *The Civil War* 1.146, where
Lucan is describing the ruthless violence of Julius Caesar on the
battlefield. The result is:

> Creticus, fiery and headstrong, master of fearless expression,
> we can all see through you.

The transparent quality of the immodest clothes is suddenly ascribed to
the wearer, and irony is rounded off with bathos.

Another kind of combination (noticed already in Persius) is that in
which a thing is substituted for a person, or vice versa. Here is an
interesting case in 8, where Juvenal is exploiting the comic ambiguity of
portraits and statues, which are, and are not, people. What point is there,
he asks, in family pride:

> *pictos ostendere uultus*
> *maiorum et stantis in curribus Aemilianos*
> *et Curios iam dimidios umeroque minorem*
> *Coruinum et Galbam auriculis nasoque carentem?* (2-5)

> displaying the painted faces
> of forebears – an Aemilianus standing there in his chariot,
> a Curius of whom only half survives, and here a Corvinus
> minus his arms, a Galba deprived of his nose and ears?

Such personification sometimes takes the form of an epigram, e.g.:

> *rara in tenui facundia panno* (7.145)

> Eloquence seldom appears in threadbare rags.

The most memorable of Juvenal's epigrams are of this binary sort, where
two opposing elements are brought together, as in

> *probitas laudatur et alget* (1.74)

> Integrity's praised and shivers

(where the elements are left side by side), or

> *orandum est ut sit mens sana in corpore sano* (10.356)
> Pray for the boon of a healthy mind in a healthy body

(where the elements reinforce each other), or

> *ille crucem sceleris pretium tulit, hic diadema* (13.105)
> One wins a cross as a prize for his crime, another a crown

(where the elements balance each other), or

> *maxima debetur puero reuerentia* (14.47)
> The utmost respect is due to a child

(where one element is surprisingly applied to the other, respect being normally due to the old). It is artificial, however, to take such epigrams by themselves. In their context they are carefully prepared for, and in many cases clinch the satirist's argument.

In the same way, instead of listing rhetorical tropes, as De Decker does very fully in his third chapter, it is more to our purpose to see how they operate in their setting. Here, for instance, is a rather ordinary passage from 3:

> *hic tunc Umbricius 'quando artibus' inquit 'honestis*
> *nullus in Urbe locus, nulla emolumenta laborum,*
> *res hodie minor est here quam fuit atque eadem cras*
> *deteret exiguis aliquid, proponimus illuc*
> *ire fatigatas ubi Daedalus exuit alas,*
> *dum noua canities, dum prima et recta senectus,*
> *dum superest Lachesi quod torqueat et pedibus me*
> *porto meis nullo dextram subeunte bacillo'* (21-8)

Here Umbricius began. 'There is no room in the city,'
he said, 'for decent professions, no reward for effort.
Today my assets are smaller than yesterday, tomorrow will see
what little is left still further eroded. I therefore intend
to go where Daedalus laid aside his weary wings,
while grayness is recent, while my old age is early and straight,
while something remains on Lachesis' spindle and I still can manage
to walk on my own two feet without the help of a stick.'

We are aware of *nullus ... nulla, hodie ... here ... cras, dum ... dum ... dum* (increasing), the hypallage *fatigatas alas*, and the periphrases for Cumae (25) and life (27) – features which, like the first gray hairs and the straight back, contribute to Umbricius' dignity and corroborate his honourable reasons for leaving. In consequence, before we even hear of

Artorius, Catulus, and the rest, we are disposed to regard those who stay behind as criminals.

Or take these lines from 13:

> *nunc si depositum non infitietur amicus,*
> *si reddat ueterem cum tota aerugine follem,*
> *prodigiosa fides et Tuscis digna libellis,*
> *quaeque coronata lustrari debeat agna* (60-3)

Now if a friend does *not* disavow a sum entrusted,
if he duly returns the battered purse with its rust intact,
his honesty's seen as a portent; the Tuscan books are consulted,
and atonement must be sought by killing a garlanded lamb.

This illustrates the new satirical stance adopted in 13: it is sheet naivety on the part of Calvinus to be surprised at his friend's dishonesty; for the straight dealing which used to be normal has now become a monstrous exception. The hyperbole is then embroidered in the lines that follow.

Because of the variations in Juvenal's attitude, we cannot make a simple comprehensive statement about his tone and style. 'Indignation enlivened, and sometimes undercut, by a pungent wit' will serve for the moment to describe 1-8. In 9 the indignation comes from Naevolus, who is the satirist's main target; the vanity of human wishes (10) is too vast a subject for indignation; in 13, Juvenal adopts the position of one who has gone beyond indignation and now regards dishonesty as the norm; yet to some extent at least, indignation returns in 15 and 16. So much is generally agreed. It is less often remarked that there are changes of style within individual poems. The lecture on integrity addressed to Ponticus in 8.74-145 differs in tone both from the exordium and from the condemnation of the degenerate nobles in 146-268. In 4, Juvenal opens with ten lines of censorious abuse, without much wit, directed at Crispinus, a prominent eques and a member of the vile Domitian's privy-council. Then, passing to something more frivolous, he castigates Crispinus' greed in buying and eating an expensive fish (11-33). This leads up to a longer and more elaborate fish story, preceded by a comic invocation of the Muses:

> *incipe, Calliope. licet et considere: non est*
> *cantandum, res uera agitur. narrate, puellae*
> *Pierides, prosit mihi uos dixisse puellas* (34-6)

Begin, Calliope! Oh, and sitting down is in order –
this is no lay; we're dealing with truth. Start your account, then,
Pierian girls, (may it tell in my favour to have called you 'girls').

After that, the setting is established in an oracular *cum*-clause, which contains a bitter sneer at Domitian:

cum iam semianimum laceraret Flauius orbem
ultimus et caluo seruiret Roma Neroni ...

In the days when the last of the Flavian line was tearing to pieces
a half-dead world, and Rome was slave to a bald-headed Nero ...

Then, with sarcastic allusions to Statius' poem on the German war, the
satire goes on to ridicule Domitian's courtiers in mock-heroic style; but
every now and then (e.g. at 74-5, 80, 84-8, 95-8) we are reminded of the
stifling atmosphere of dread.

This brings us to the matter of structure, in which again we find
considerable diversity. Sometimes the arrangement is fairly straightforward; thus 5 is based on the constituents of a dinner-party (wine,
cups, service, food), 7 on intellectual occupations, 10 on human wishes
(power, eloquence, glory, longevity, beauty), 16 on the advantages of
being a soldier. The first satire is more complex. There we have the
following scheme: 1-18, why write? 19-80, why write satire? (There are
five sections here, presented in the form 'when a, b and c are happening,
how can one *not* write satire?') 81-6, new introduction; 87-146, the
extravagance (gambling) and meanness of the rich patron, the greed of
the upstart freedman, the meanness and extravagance (gluttony) of the
rich patron; 147-71, the hazards of treating such material in satire.

In the long satire on Roman wives (6) the more detailed divisions are
open to debate, and I do not intend to canvass any proposals here. But
since everyone agrees that a new departure takes place in v.286, let us
postulate, for the sake of argument, two very long sections – namely 1-285
and 286-661 – calling them 'the absence of chastity' and 'the
consequences of wealth and idleness'. Now, since adultery is a major
consequence of wealth and idleness, it is no surprise to find that the first
theme reappears in 286-661. Conversely, within the first 285 lines, we
hear of women's extravagance (73, 137) and avarice (36, 149, 232) – vices
which foreshadow the development of the second theme. Again, in each
of the main sections we are told of unfeminine activities, e.g. litigation
and gladiatorial exercises in the first (242-67) and fraternising with
generals in uniform and becoming sick from too much wine in the second
(400-1, 425-33). In both sections, mention is made of cowed husbands and
terrified slaves (206-18 and 508-11, 218-23 and 479-93). Finally, the
love-potions and poisons of 133-5 anticipate the crimes described in
610-61.

In 13, Juvenal seems to be trying something new. The structure is set
out by Highet thus: (a) 1-12: introduction. (b) 13-173: *de crimine* – (i)
usitatum, 13-70 (ii) *necessarium*, 71-119 (iii) *leue*, 120-73. (c) 174-249: *de
ultione* (i) *noglogonda*, 174-92 (ii) *certa ex conscientia*, 192-239 (iii)
certa ex natura, 239-49. I do not want to challenge these line-divisions,
but the way the material is summarised tends to conceal the frequency
with which a handful of motifs recur. Keeping those line-divisions, we

114   *3. Style and Public*

can construct another summary, somewhat like this. *1-12*: conscience is a form of punishment, loss is small, dishonesty is prevalent, protest is silly. *13-173*: protest is silly (13-22) dishonesty is prevalent (23-30), protest is silly (31-7), though virtue once existed, dishonesty is now prevalent (38-70); loss is small (71-4), dishonesty is easy for those who do not believe in divine punishment, even those who do believe in it argue away the voice of conscience (75-111), protest is silly (112-19), [consolation begins (120-5)], if dishonesty is not prevalent, protest is not silly (126-34), but dishonesty *is* prevalent (135-9) and so protest is silly (140-2), loss is small (143-4), dishonesty is prevalent (144-58), protest is silly (159-73). *174-249*: is crime to go unpunished? (174-5), protest is silly (175-9), revenge is sweet only to those ignorant of philosophy (180-92), the criminal has a guilty conscience (192-239), he will commit another crime and will then be punished (239-49). This rather stark X-ray summary serves to show how slender the dialectical element in the satire is, and how little that matters for Juvenal's purpose. Rhetorical power is all-important.

I have devoted some space to Juvenal's structure to avoid the over-easy antithesis: 'Horace restrained and tidy, Juvenal impassioned and chaotic.' There is, of course, something in that, but the more important difference is that in Horace the structural divisions usually represent phases in a progressive argument. That is rarely true in Juvenal. In his satires we apprehend the main thought quite early; the pleasure comes from the illustrations, which are immensely varied and vivid. This last point will bear a little more elaboration. Horace was a master of anecdote, often interspersing his narrative with lively dialogue. One thinks of Opimius (2.3.142-47), the two mice (2.6.79-117), and the cautionary tale of Philippus and Volteius (*E* 1.7.46-95). Persius has no anecdotes, but his short dramatic exchanges are frequently accompanied by graphic descriptions, e.g. the recitation in 1.13-21, the waking of the student in 3.1-22 and the contrary counsels of *Avaritia* and *Luxuria* in 5.132-53.

In Juvenal dialogue is of minor importance and the anecdotes negligible. In scene-painting, however, he has no equal. He may have learned something from Persius, but in any case he will have found the importance of *enargeia* acknowledged in orthodox rhetorical theory. Quintilian devoted several sections to it (8.3.61ff.), quoting two excellent examples from Cicero. The second says 'I pictured to myself some entering, others leaving; some were staggering from the effects of wine, some were yawning from yesterday's debauch. The floor was a mess – covered with puddles of wine and wilting garlands, and littered with fish-bones.' That would have appealed to Juvenal. One thinks of the scene in 8.158-62:

sed cum peruigiles placet instaurare popinas,
obuius adsiduo Syrophoenix udus amomo
currit, Idymaeae Syrophoenix incola portae
hospitis adfectu dominum regemque salutat,
et cum uenali Cyane succincta lagona.

But when he decides to visit again the all-night tavern,
a Syrian Jew, wet with the perfume he has plastered on,
comes bustling up, a Syrian Jew from Palestine Gate,
playing 'mine host', calling him 'sir' and 'your honour'; behind him
comes barmaid Cýane, dress tucked up and flagon at the ready.

Examples abound.[3] Here I recall just two of the most poetic. The turbot
which will soon be the centre-piece of Domitian's council-meeting is as
huge as those

quos operit glacies Maeotica ruptaque tandem
solibus effundit torrentis ad ostia Ponti
desidia tardos et longo frigore pingues (4.42-4)

which the ice of Maeotis covers and then, when broken at last
by the sun, releases to be swept to the mouth of the Pontic flood
torpid with sloth and fattened by the long cold of the winter.

More impressive still is 14.74-85, where Juvenal is expanding on the
theme that character results from upbringing:

serpente ciconia pullos
nutrit et inuenta per deuia rura lacerta:
illi eadem sumptis quaerunt animalia pinnis.
uoltur iumento et canibus crucibusque relictis
ad fetus properat partemque cadaueris adfert:
hic est ergo cibus magni quoque uolturis et se
pascentis, propria cum iam facit arbore nidos.
sed leporem aut capream famulae Iouis et generosae
in saltu uenantur aues, hinc praeda cubili
ponitur: inde autem cum se matura leuauit
progenies stimulante fame festinat ad illam
quam primum praedam rupto gustauerat ouo.

The mother stork
feeds her young on the snakes and lizards found in the wilds;
they, when their wings are grown, look for the self-same creatures.
The vulture hurries home from cattle, dogs, or the gibbet,
carrying bits of the rotting carcase to give to her chicks;
this becomes the food of the full-grown vulture, when he
hunts for himself and makes a nest in a tree of his own.
The noble birds that attend on Jupiter scour the glades
searching for hare and hind; that is the prey which is laid

---

[3] Several of the more striking passages are sensitively handled by Jenkyns.

on the edge of the bed; and so, when the brood are fully grown
and rise aloft, at the jab of hunger they suddenly swoop
on the very prey that they tasted on first breaking the shell.

In that passage, which is worthy of Lucretius and recalls one of Horace's
most elaborate odes (4.4), we *almost* forget that vultures are 'obscene'
birds and correspond to repulsive human beings.

PUBLIC

In Rome, as elsewhere, methods of composition varied. Short pieces were
frequently improvised and then dictated or written down at once. One
thinks of the evening's amusement described by Catullus (50), the
after-dinner sessions ridiculed by Persius (1.52), and the party-game
inflicted on her guests by Martial's Stella:

> *Lege nimis dura conuiuam scribere uersus*
> *cogis, Stella. 'Licet scribere nempe malos'* (9.89)

That rule whereby you compel your guests to versify, Stella,
is excessively cruel. 'You can always do it badly.'

Some writers, like Statius and his father,[1] could compose longer pieces in
that way – a habit which, according to Horace, accounted for much that
was slipshod in Lucilius (1.4.10). With others there might be several
stages in the process. When Virgil was writing the *Georgics*, he worked
out a large number of lines in the morning, dictated them, and then
spent the rest of the day 'licking them into shape' (Suetonius, *Life* 22).
Horace too, talks of composing in his head (1.9.2) and also of erasing,
correcting, and recasting.[2] As for 'the consumer', we think of him
nowadays as a solitary reader; but in Rome the situation was more
complex, for he was often part of an audience. From early times, teachers
had given lectures in which they recited and commented on well-known
poets like Naevius and Ennius – sometimes to quite large gatherings
(Suetonius, *Gramm*. 2). Later, the critic Valerius Cato, who spanned the
periods of Catullus and Virgil, was called 'the Latin Siren, who alone
reads and makes poets' (Suetonius, *Gramm*. 11). And Virgil's early works
were recited by Q. Caecilius Epirota, 'the nurse of young bards'
(Suetonius, *Gramm*. 16). When did poets begin to recite their own work?
It was, according to Suetonius (*Gramm*. 1), right at the start of Rome's
literary history: Livius and Ennius read their own compositions.
Subsequently private recitations became common. Yet the more
ambitious writers always intended their work to have a wider audience.

---

[1] Statius, *Silv*. 5.3.195ff. See Hardie, 76-85 and his General Index under 'Improvisation'.
[2] See, e.g. 1.10.72, AP 292-4, 438-50.

Two points are worth adding: when the purchaser bought a book, he would often have it read to him by a slave; and when he did read it for himself he would usually articulate the words.[3]

In the late republic a new departure took place. Probably in the 30s, when he had retired from public life and was writing his history, Asinius Pollio gave readings to a sizeable invited audience. Dalzell (1.26-7) has suggested that these formal occasions took place in the library which Pollio had founded in the *Atrium Libertatis* with the spoils of the Dalmatian campaigns. Others in quest of publicity had long adopted a less dignified procedure. They simply took their writing into the street and read it to passers-by. The Forum was a favourite pitch; but some preferred the baths because of their attractive resonance – *suaue locus resonat conclusus* (Horace 1.4.76). Others again, like the crazy poet at the end of the *Ars Poetica*, would fasten on some luckless wretch and 'read him to death'.

(i) Lucilius

In the case of Lucilius the evidence about his readership seems at first sight contradictory. In 1.10 Horace says:

> Don't seek mass adulation.

Be content with a small circle of readers (73-4).

He has just been talking about Lucilius, and he seems to have him still (at least partly) in mind. Such criticisms were made against Lucilius in his own day:

> You enjoy spreading abroad in your talks those tales about me (1085).

And Lucilius lent substance to the complaint by claiming that, unlike his critic's poems, his were popular:

> whereas mine alone of the many produced were now in demand (1091).

One should perhaps also consider 791-2:

> *rem populi salute et fictis uersibus Lucilius*
> *quibus potest impertit, totumque hoc studiose et sedulo*

Here Lucilius greets the state with verses of the utmost craft
and he does so in a spirit that is earnest and sincere.[4]

---

[3] See Knox's discussion.

[4] *Rem populi* is Lachmann's conjecture. For this use of *impertio* cf. Terence, *Eun*. 270-1. The translation assumes a play on *fictis* (carefully fashioned / false) and *sedulo* (sincerely).

But before concluding that Lucilius measured his success by his circulation, we have to take account of some information preserved by Cicero (*De Orat*. 2.25):

> C. Lucilius ... used to say that he wished to be read neither by the very ignorant nor by the very learned, since the former knew nothing and the latter perhaps more than himself. In this connection he also wrote 'I don't want Persius to read me' (*Persium non curo legere*) – Persius, as we know, was about the most learned of our countrymen – 'I do want Laelius Decimus to do so' (*Laelium Decimum uolo*). The latter was a worthy man and by no means uneducated, but he was nothing compared to Persius.

Finally, in Cicero, *De Fin*. 1.7, Lucilius is quoted as saying that he feared the opinion of Scipio and Rutilius and was writing for the people of Tarentum, Consentia and Sicily. This was clearly ironical, for the places in question spoke little Latin, but it does suggest that he was not a thoroughgoing elitist.

We can only make sense of all this if we recall the diversity of Lucilius' work. The letter which he composed when ill (or convalescing) was designed, at least in the first place, for its recipient (186-93). Short elegies, like the epitaph on his slave Metrophanes (524-5) were meant primarily for the poet's household. And the more academic pieces, such as the essay on orthography in Book 9, would have interested only the intelligentsia. On the other hand, the farcical and erotic scenes, the scandalous attacks on politicians, stories of gladiatorial encounters, and tales of personal adventures were doubtless enjoyed by the reading public at large – though that, of course, represented only a small percentage of the population.

(ii) Horace

In 1.4, where he is justifying his satire, Horace says he avoids giving public recitations for fear of causing offence – satire being, by its very nature, critical of human behaviour (23ff.). Later (71-2) he claims to despise publicity, declaring that his books will never hang in the stalls

to be mauled
by the sweaty hands of Hermogenes Tigellius and the rest of the mob.

One doubts if he quite meant it. In any case, within a few years he issued his first collection, thus entering on the second phase of publishing. This meant sending one's manuscript to a *bibliopola*, who would have it copied by a team of slaves and put it on sale. There were no contracts or royalties, and no copyright. So the only motive in publishing was to reach a larger audience.[5] Yet Horace remained selective: it was absurd to aim

[5] See the discussions by Kenney (2) and Quinn.

at pleasing the general public – why, one might end up as a text-book in elementary schools (1.10.74-5); better to concentrate on the knights. This attitude was closely bound up with Horace's view of his art. When he imposed restrictions on vulgarisms and importations, and insisted on correctness (good grammar, approved constructions, no dialect-words, etc.) Horace was upholding the standards of *Latinitas*; he was also practising what would now be termed 'cultural exclusivism'. That raises familiar questions. If certain qualities can be achieved only at certain moments in our cultural history, and appreciated only by a small number of people, should one insist on their importance? Or, a more radical question, are those qualities intrinsically excellent, or are they simply *described* as excellent by a privileged group? The way we answer such questions will affect our attitude to Horace, and to other exponents of classicism in literature and art.

Horace returned to the question of readership in *E* 1.19, about fifteen years after 1.10 and three or four years after the appearance of *Odes* 1-3. He is pleased with his reception by upper-class readers (33-4), but he complains of two categories which may well have overlapped: his slavish imitators and those who, while admiring him at home, denigrate him in public. Why are the latter hostile? Horace gives the reason:

> I'm not the kind to hunt for the votes of the fickle rabble
> by standing dinners and giving presents of worn-out clothes.
> I listen to distinguished writers and pay them back, but I never
> canvas the critic tribes on their platforms to win support.
> Hence the grief (37-41).

Horace has made his opponents' motives seem as mean and unfair as possible. One suspects they disliked him, not without reason, for being aloof and arrogant:

> If I say 'I'm ashamed to recite my writings
> in crowded halls (they don't deserve it) and attribute importance
> to trifles', 'You're teasing', they say; 'they're reserved for Jupiter's ear.
> You're so conceited you firmly believe that you alone
> distil poetry's honey' (41-5).

The evasion is not wholly sincere. Granted, such recitals were often associated with the grander genres which Horace avoided. But to call his odes trifles (*nugae*) was hardly quite candid, in view of his earlier claim to be the Latin minstrel (32-3). Diffidence was doubtless one side of the coin. (What if the hall were three-quarters empty?) But pride was the other. (What sort of people would be there if it were full?) As for cultivating the emperor, that was not a charge which Horace wanted to refute. All he could say was 'Pax!'

The tone of *E* 1.20 is very different. In publishing the first book of epistles, Horace wants to provide a 'seal' poem which will identify the author. At the same time, he remembers all he has said about the vulgar quest for publicity. So, to take account of both points, he develops an ingenious *double entendre* in which the book is admonished like a young slave-boy who knows he is good-looking and wants to be put on show. There are no apprehensions about an unfavourable reception, but the distant future is less exciting (11-13):

> When, having been through numerous dirty hands, you lose
> your charms, you'll be left unnoticed, gathering boorish maggots,
> or be banished to Utica, or firmly tied and sent to Ilerda ...

a piquant contrast to the bold prophecies of *exegi monumentum*. Horace then adds:

> This, too, lies ahead: when mumbling age overtakes you,
> you'll be teaching children how to read at the end of a street.

That, again, can be set beside the earlier scorn of 1.10.74-5:

> Are you so crazy
> as to want your poems recited in shabby schools? Not me.

The later thought is, of course, wryly ironical. One should probably decode it as something like: 'It'll hardly come to that; but if it does, so be it.' Whatever Horace's feelings, he was destined to be absorbed into the system. By the second century A.D. he had become a school text (Juvenal 7.226-7). He has been one ever since.

Horace's long-established status as a classic makes it hard to imagine that he was once a modern poet. Yet in his own day he had to contend with a public that 'knew what it liked' and was suspicious of anything unusual. Late in his career, the situation seems to have improved. In 17 B.C. he was invited by Augustus to compose a choral ode (the *Carmen Saeculare*) for the celebrations which marked the beginning of a new age. Not long after, in honour of his step-sons' Alpine victories in 15 B.C., Augustus commissioned further odes, which eventually gave rise to a fourth book. By now, Horace was a celebrity; but one can be 'a smiling public man', as Yeats was, without being read by the literate community at large. However famous he may have become by, say, 13 B.C., it did not prevent him from making a scornful attack on the conservatism of Roman taste in *E* 2.1.18-92. The case for modernism has never been put more clearly and concisely. Near the end of that section, Horace says of the traditionalists:

They seem to object to whatever hasn't appealed to *them*,
or else they're ashamed to heed their juniors and won't admit
that things they learned as lads should now be treated as rubbish.

Moreover, these readers have no *genuine* affection for the old:

In fact the man who praises Numa's *Salian Hymn*
and likes to pose as an expert on a work which he understands
as little as I do, is not the champion of the mighty dead
but our opponent; he's jealous, and hates us and our works.

Later (182ff.) Horace points out that these supposedly staunch defenders
of old poetry also form part of the audience which enjoys the jingoism
and vulgarity of stage performances. It is perhaps debatable how far the
endless rehearsals of military victories (190-4) anticipate our repeats of
war films; but there is something terribly familiar about the 'show-biz
personality':

He walks on stage and at once is greeted with frenzied applause.
'Has he said something already?
                         'No'.
                                    'Then why are they clapping?'
'It's his woollen coat, dyed in Tarentum to rival a violet.'

We almost expect the great man to beam at the audience and say 'Glad
you like the jacket, folks; 'cos let's face it, you paid for it!'

(iii) Persius

To judge from the frequency with which he mentions it, Horace was not
indifferent to the public. Strictly this was incompatible with his cultural
elitism, but he tried to reduce the difficulty by making the elite as large
as possible. Hence his interest in the young, e.g. *Odes* 3.1.4, 4.3.13-5,
4.6.31-2, *AP* 387-8. The *uirgines* and *pueri* were not only more flexible
and receptive than their elders, they would also be responsible for
Horace's future reputation. Persius seems to have been less concerned
with such matters. In his opening satire several types of audience are
described: the fawning and uncritical crowd that attends a public
recitation (15-21), the captive audience of a boys' school (29-30), the
over-fed guests at a dinner-party (30-40), the spectators at a trial who are
indifferent to the arguments and interested only in the speaker's
rhetorical flourishes (83-7). All these occasions of verbal communication
are ridiculed. According to the *Lifo*, Persius himself wrote seldom and
slowly (*et raro et tarde*). He did not live to publish his satires, but he did
give readings. We are told that after hearing him, Lucan declared with
impulsive generosity that these were true poems whereas his own were

but amusements.[6] The sixth piece, it seems, was not quite finished. Cornutus trimmed the loose ends and handed over the collection to Caesius Bassus for publication. Copies were snapped up at once, and throughout antiquity Persius was read with admiration by the intelligentsia.

That would probably have pleased him well enough. In 1.1-2 he claims to expect *no* readers, or at the most one or two. That can be set aside as just a rhetorical amplification of Horace's 'Be content with a few readers' (1.10.74). But what of the fable of King Midas? That, too, came in as an extension of a passage in Horace, namely the statement that Lucilius used to confide his secrets to his books, which he trusted like friends (2.1.30-1); yet as a result of that act of trust, 'the whole of the old fellow's life lay open' – *pateat*. I doubt if Horace meant us to worry about the paradox. If confronted with it, rather than admitting that to read Lucilius was a violation of trust (surely an absurd and pedantic idea), he might have said that by reading Lucilius' books we joined the number of his friends. Now the conclusion of the Midas story, as given by Ovid in *Met.* 11.190-3, was that the reeds heard the barber's secret and passed it on. So is Persius hinting that *his* secret will receive the same sort of furtive publicity? Not at once, for he adds: 'Slight as it is, I wouldn't sell [my secret] for all your *Iliads*' (122-3). Nevertheless, he does indicate that *some* people will be in the know. Those are the readers addressed in 123-5:

> If you've caught the spirit of brave Cratínus,
> or are pale from devotion to angry Eupolis and the Grand Old Man,
> if you've an ear for a concentrated brew, have a look at this.

The group includes all who value the sort of writing represented by Old Comedy – i.e. that which treats real life in an entertaining style and a spirit of moral candour. At the same time, Persius is claiming a place in the succession of Roman satirists; for Horace had found a spiritual ancestry for Lucilius, and hence for himself, in Eupolis, Cratinus, and Aristophanes (1.4.1). Then come examples of the reader who is *not* wanted:

> not the lout who is eager to jeer at Greek-style sandals,
> and can bear to shout 'Hey one-eye!' at a man with that affliction,
> who thinks he's somebody just because as aedile at Arezzo
> he has smashed a few short measures with full municipal pomp,
> nor the witty fellow who sniggers when he notices cones and numbers
> traced in the sand of the abacus, and is vastly amused if a Nones-girl
> cheekily pulls a philosopher's beard.[7] For them I suggest
> the law reports in the morning and *Callirhoe* after lunch.

[6] The text, however, is uncertain; see the apparatus on p. 32 of the OCT.
[7] A Nones-girl is a slave celebrating the festival of the *Nonae Caprotinae* on 7 July.

The whole passage offers an interesting contrast to the end of Horace 1.10. There the poet names fifteen of his friends and hints at several more – all at the centre of literary and political life. Persius, however, is quite unspecific. He did not need to assert his membership of a prominent clique, since he already enjoyed sufficient social status and had no political ambitions. Even if he had invoked some of the men listed in Chapter Two, it would have done little good; for such men were becoming increasingly disaffected and would soon pay a terrible price for their opposition.

(iv) Juvenal

While Persius occasionally gave recitations, he never mentions this, and the context in which he *thought* of his satires operating was that of a small reading public. Juvenal is different. The context in which we first meet him, and in which he brings his work before his fellow-citizens, is that of a recitation. Moreover, in spite of the occasional addressee's name, the style of the satires is most naturally seen as a special and original kind of declamatory rhetoric, and that implies not just a small gathering of friends, but a sizeable audience.

To obtain a little more information about the practice of public reading, we turn first to someone who approved of the system and worked successfully within it. According to the younger Pliny, people gave recitations not out of vanity, but to obtain advice and to provide themselves with a motive for self-criticism:

> I don't aim at winning applause from an audience but from my readers. So I take every opportunity to polish my work. First, I revise it myself, then I read it to two or three friends. In due course I send it for comment to others, and then, if in doubt, consider their remarks again with one or two people. Last of all I read the material to a larger audience. For them, I assure you, I edit it all most thoroughly. Anxiety lends care to my concentration (7.17.7).

Admittedly Pliny is talking of speeches, but poetry had long been recited, ostensibly for the same purpose. It was not entirely a pretext. Sometimes private readings did elicit genuine criticism, as we see from Horace's lines on Quintilius (*AP* 438-44); but in the main (and especially with the more public gatherings) these were occasions for advertisement rather than criticism.

Inevitably, people attended with varying degrees of enthusiasm and from mixed motives. Pliny, not wholly intentionally, shows the ambiguities involved:

> This year has brought a bumper harvest of poets. In the whole of April there was hardly a day on which someone was not giving a recital. I'm glad that literature is so much alive and that talent is emerging and being

presented to the public, even though people are reluctant to provide an audience. [They wander in late and leave early. Even those with lots of free time who have been given plenty of notice and numerous reminders don't show up; or if they do, they complain of wasting their time.] I have rarely let anyone down. True, most of the readers have been friends; for as a rule anyone who is fond of literature is also fond of me. [Now I'm off to the country to write something myself.] But I shan't read it; for it might look as if I had attended other people's readings not to listen but to put them under an obligation. In helping to provide an audience, as in other acts of kindness, a favour is worth nothing if you expect to have it repaid (1.13).

This is the one day which I must keep free. Titinius Capito is giving a recital, and I am obliged (and no less eager) to hear him ... He is a man of immense good will. He lends his house for readings and is regularly found in the audience both there and elsewhere. Certainly when in town he has always supported me. In a case where the reason for repaying a kindness is so excellent it would be discreditable not to do so (8.12.1-2).

A less favourable picture is presented by Marcus Aper, a successful barrister in Tacitus' *Dialogus*:

[After devoting so much effort to his work the poet has to] go round cajoling and soliciting to find people who will deign to listen to it. Even that costs money. He has to obtain the use of a house, furnish a recital room, hire seats, and distribute hand-bills ... He acquires no friends or clients, inspires no feelings of gratitude, and is rewarded only with fitful applause, meaningless compliments, and a short-lived pleasure (9).

From that we move easily to a passage of Juvenal which was probably based on it:

> If the sweet prospect of glory
> fires you to read, he lends you a building with damp-mottled walls –
> a house pressed into service though locked and barred for years,
> where the door emits a noise like a herd of pigs in a panic.[8]
> He's willing to provide freedmen to sit at the end of the rows,
> and to place his retainers' lusty voices around the hall.
> None of your lordships, however, will pay the cost of the benches,
> or of the seats perched on scaffolding hired for the day,
> or of the front-row chairs which have to be taken back (7.39-47).

There we have the performer's inconvenience; at the beginning of 1 we are shown the victims' ordeal:

> Shall I always remain a listener only? Never hit back,
> although so often assailed by the hoarse-voiced Cordus' *Theseid*?
> Shall I never obtain revenge when X has read me his comedies

[8] With some hesitation I have translated Jessen's conjecture *porcas* instead of the MSS *portas*.

and Y his elegies? No revenge when my day has been wasted
by mighty Telephus, or by Orestes who, having covered
the final margin, extends to the back and still isn't finished?
No citizen's private house is more familiar to *him*
than the grove of Mars and Vulcan's cave near Aeolus' rocks
are to *me*; what the winds are up to, what ghosts are being tormented
on Aeacus' rack, from what far land someone else has purloined
a bit of gold skin, how huge are the ash trees Monychus hurls –
the unending cry goes up from Fronto's plane trees, his marble
statues and his columns, shaken and shattered by non-stop readings.

In one of his most happily complacent letters, Pliny tells how he
decided to read his *Panagyric* of Trajan in a revised version. He did not
issue formal invitations or send out programmes; he just told his friends
to come along 'if convenient' and 'if they had nothing at all on'. The
weather was absolutely filthy (*foedissimis ... tempestatibus*), yet they
came two days running, and when he still hadn't finished they persuaded
him to add a third (3.18.1-4). One likes to think of Juvenal coming away
from some such occasion and resolving through gritted teeth to take a
terrible revenge. The result was an indictment of Roman life, including
public readings. And yet, as Juvenal was wryly aware, the indictment
was itself a recitation. The satirist could not escape from the institution;
he could only turn it upside down.

CHAPTER FOUR

Class and Patronage

(i) Lucilius

We begin by recalling in very brief outline the economic problems of the second half of the second century B.C. To fight Rome's wars in Africa, Greece and Spain, many small independent farmers had left their land. In their absence it deteriorated, or was taken over by others; and in some cases when they returned they no longer wished to work it. Those who did try to carry on found, at least in the districts around Rome itself, that their produce was undercut by cheap grain imported from Sicily and Sardinia. In time some of them gave up and drifted into the capital.[1] They also had other reasons. After relinquishing their land they were no longer liable for military service, and many no doubt hoped to make a living from the building boom which began after 146 B.C. The richer landowners had problems of a different kind. Frequently they owned several estates in different districts, and even if they were interested in doing so they could not supervise them all personally. Much responsibility and power was delegated to stewards or bailiffs, who sometimes exploited and intimidated their tenants, hired hands and slaves. The resulting hostility led to inefficiency, and this made it difficult for the landlord to collect his rents. Meanwhile, at least in certain areas, the pattern of agriculture was changing.[2] Large estates were developing, run by slave labour and devoted either to vines and olives (as in Etruria) or to stock-rearing (as in the south). In Sicily, where the problems were especially acute, the slaves revolted in 135 B.C., and were not finally subdued until 132, when they were met by P. Rupilius with reinforcements from the Spanish campaign.

Another, closely related, problem was that of public land (*ager publicus*), which Rome had acquired during her expansion in Italy. Some of this land had been used for colonies, and some had been sold; but a lot of the less desirable ground had been leased out by the censors. In 167 B.C. the maximum permitted to any individual was 300 acres, but over the years this rule was ignored, the rent was not collected, and many treated what was strictly public land as private property – a situation of

---

[1] I have worded these sentences cautiously in view of the articles by Garnsey and Skydsgaard, who have shown with the aid of archaeological evidence that the departure of the free labourer was more gradual and less complete than the literary sources suggest.

[2] See n.1 above.

central importance in the campaign of the Gracchi.

Of those who invested in land many, as D'Arms has argued, were also interested in trade. Although the upper classes would never have sailed on the merchantmen of the day, they did conduct business indirectly, through their agents, and so became involved in the banking, money-lending, and insurance which that trade required. More important than trade was the opportunity offered by various forms of contracting. The armies abroad had to be supplied, taxes had to be collected, and a whole range of public works had to be undertaken. Since there was no adequate civil service, and since (officially at least) senators were not supposed to engage in such activity, these important and lucrative functions were largely carried out by the equites. Thus the right to collect taxes in a given area of the provinces would be purchased from the censors in Rome by a syndicate of *publicani*, who would then make sure they didn't lose on the deal.

As noted earlier, Lucilius almost certainly had estates in the south. Fifty years after his death one of his relatives, C. Lucilius Hirrus, was renowned for his flocks and herds in Bruttium (Varro, *RR* 2.1.2). In addition, Lucilius probably had land in Sicily (before 94, and 143-5) and also in Sardinia. (Fragment 287-8 says: 'Lucilius from Sicily/to the land of Sardinia.') He will therefore have been affected by the slaves' revolt, and through Scipio he will have known P. Rupilius, the general who put it down. The revolt had serious consequences both in Sicily and in Rome. The grain tithe could not be collected, and the large quantities of grain which were usually purchased on the open market ceased to be available. Prices rose, the building boom petered out, and people began to go hungry. It has been suggested that Lucilius 214 refers to this crisis: *deficit alma Ceres, nec plebes pane potitur* – 'Nourishing Ceres fails and the people go without bread'.[3] But as the fragment comes from Book 5 it cannot be contemporary with events of 135-132 B.C., and there is no sufficient reason to take it as retrospective. It is perhaps more likely that in 768, as Warmington suggests, Lucilius is referring to the importation of grain from Africa. If the text is sound, he or one of his characters asserts that he would sooner have bought some commodity 'at whatever price he liked rather than bran and porridge from Mago's hand' (768). Like farmers at all periods, Lucilius complains about the weather: some of his crop is blown away by the wind; some of it is frozen stiff (654). Taxes on his Sicilian property were also a worry (655). Yet, a farm could still give satisfaction if the steward did his job energetically (557-8). As for the question of *ager publicus*, Laelius made an attempt to tackle it in 145 or 140 B.C., but withdrew his proposal when he saw the depth of the opposition. Whether Lucilius approved of his friend's efforts we cannot

[3] Boren, 62. I am also indebted to the articles by Brunt and Broughton in the same collection.

tell, but twenty-five or thirty years later he himself incurred
unpopularity by letting his herds graze on an area of *ager publicus* in
contravention of the *Lex Thoria* (Cicero, *De Orat.* 2.284). Unlike many
equites, Lucilius was not attracted by tax-farming or other activities of
the kind. In fact, he explicitly rejected that way of life as foreign to his
nature (650-1). When we add these fragmentary passages to the political
material mentioned in Chapter Two, it is clear that the disappearance of
Lucilius' satires is as sad a loss for the historian as it is for the student of
literature.

On the calculations of Brunt (3.79) there were, very roughly, 450,000
adult male citizens at the time when Lucilius began to write. Of these,
the senators and equites together formed only a minute fraction. Socially
there was a large overlap between the two classes. Lucilius' brother was a
senator, and he himself could presumably have been one had he wished.
While he did not actively participate in politics, he shared the tastes of
his aristocratic friends – the military life, horsemanship, the running of
an estate, a gentlemanly interest in scholarship, good food, and wine.
Occasionally he shows an amused disdain for rustic crudity. On his
journey south, for instance, he passed through a region in which, he says,
'A dirty pot and a stalk of rue are treasured like honey' (128-9); and he
describes a meal in terms of what wasn't available: 'No oyster was there,
nor any shellfish or mussel' (126). On another occasion 'One old couch
was laid out, tied together with string' (1025), and for the wine there was
'one tiny rickety table with rotten legs' (1027). Non-metropolitan and
'non-received' speech-habits are glanced at in 232 ('Cecilius' as *pretor
rusticus*), and we hear that a certain Vettius was taken to task for using
Tuscan, Sabine and Praenestine words (though the context of the
remark, as reported by Quintilian 1.5.56, is lost). Within the city the
same superior attitude is seen in the statement that the *uulgus* is holding
a levy (483) and in the comic coinage *mercedimerae legiones* (10)
'wage-earning battalions'. So much is general. In the case of Aeserninus,
the Samnite gladiator, Lucilius is more specific: he was a *spurcus homo,
uita illa dignus locoque* (173) – 'a filthy fellow, who deserved that life and
position'. One recalls that gladiators, like pimps, auctioneers,
undertakers and actors, were classed as *infames*. As such they were
debarred from holding office and forbidden to testify in court. In 652 we
hear of a *libertinus tricorius Syrus ipse ac mastigias* – 'a freedman with a
triple hide, a proper Syrian and a rogue'. Higher up the scale came the
rich auctioneer Gallonius who tried to impress his guests with a lavish
menu (including a sturgeon) and earned a priggish reprimand from
Laelius:

'*o Publi, o gurges Galloni, es homo miser*' inquit.
'*cenasti in uita numquam bene, cum omnia in ista
consumis squilla atque acupensere cum decimano* (203-5)

'Publius, glutton Gallonius,' he said, 'you're a wretched fellow.
You've never eaten *well* in your life, in spite of your spending
a fortune upon that crayfish and on a king-size sturgeon.'

Then as now, if you weren't *born* into the top set it was terribly hard to
get things right. In Gallonius' case nice people could not be expected to
forget that auctioneers made a lot of money by shouting in public.

When Lucilius is satirical about wealth his remarks often reflect
traditional class attitudes, as in 550-1:

> hi quos diuitiae producunt et caput ungunt
> horridulum

Those whom money advances, smearing their tousled tops
with brilliantine.

Since he does not condemn wealth as an evil in itself, or advocate its
redistribution, he can only deplore its abuse, as exemplified by gluttony,
extravagance, and ostentation. As these faults were widely associated
with the *nouveaux riches* like Gallonius, the effect of the satire was to
resist social change by demonstrating what happened when money got
into 'the wrong hands'. The account of the dinner-party which another
auctioneer, Q. Granius, gave to L. Licinius Crassus in 107 B.C. (Book 20)
seems to have been weighted rather differently. Again food, drink, and
service were all on a lavish scale, and at one point Granius announced
that 'he did not look down on himself and disliked arrogant magnates'
(610), which sounds like 'a self-made man and proud of it'; but since
Granius had a wide reputation as a wit, he can hardly have been mocked,
like Horace's Nasidienus, simply for naive pretentiousness. More
probably he was portrayed as brash but not stupid.

Just as wealth was not a boon when flaunted by vulgarians, poverty
was not a disaster if people had what they really needed. Several
fragments point to arguments like those found in Horace 1.1. Thus
(paraphrasing) although you take from your estates a myriad bushels of
corn and a thousand jars of wine (581-2), I enjoy [what I have] as much as
you do (583); [as the ant shows foresight] so you should collect what you
can use when winter comes (586-7); [the foolish never enjoy their
possessions, because they never stop amassing money;] when they are
wrinkled and shrivelled old men, they still try to acquire the same things
(590); for a fool, nothing is ever enough (591). So *making* money was the
trouble, rather than money itself. On this convenient principle the
aristocrat could often quite honestly declare that he was indifferent to
money: he simply never thought of it. This did not mean that the nobles
were necessarily misers. According to Cicero, it was perfectly
respectable, and indeed praiseworthy, to make gifts of money both
privately and publicly. In the latter case it was better to finance projects

like walls, docks, and harbours, or to ransom captives, rather than to provide public banquets, doles, or games (*Off.* 2.52-6). In many cases, no doubt, such generosity was prompted by a sense of civic duty; but it can rarely have been wholly disinterested, since it brought a valuable return in prestige, which could be converted into more political power, which in its turn would offer fresh opportunities for enrichment, and so on up the spiral. But all that kind of expenditure was very different from the sort that was lavished on bizarre and exotic dinners.

While Lucilius was aware, as he had to be, of the differences between one class and another, he was equally familiar with the dynamic relationship which enabled them to co-operate, namely *amicitia*. This certainly included 'friendship' in our sense of the word, but it also extended to relationships of a more emotionally distant kind (often between men of unequal status) based on the exchange of appropriate favours. As chance has it, very few of Lucilius' fragments have to do with *amicitia* between those of markedly unequal position. Examples include references to clients bringing thirty large fish as a present (159-60), to Coelius the hanger-on (*scurra*) who attended Gallonius (211), and to parasites or 'grubgrinders' (*cibicidas*) in a rich man's house (760). But we can make some reasonably reliable conjectures about Lucilius' friendship with Scipio. When all allowance has been made for youthful days in the country, for shared campaigns and leisure hours, Lucilius was quite clear about what he might expect from Scipio (e.g. encouragement and publicity for his writing, and the prestige of the great man's company) and also what Scipio would look for in return (e.g. help at election time, attacks on his opponents, and the polishing and mounting of his brighter sayings). We rather disapprove of such calculations, and when we go in for them we do not advertise it. But Cicero states in his *De Officiis* that in every act of moral obligation such matters should be taken into account 'so that we may become good reckoners of duty (*boni ratiocinatores officiorum*) determining by addition and subtraction what the final total is, with a view to assessing how much is due to each individual' (1.59). Just before this he has drawn up a list of priorities, in which country and parents come first, then children and household, and finally kinsmen (58). All this recalls Lucilius' lines on *uirtus*, which begin:

> Excellence is, my dear Albinus, being ready to pay
> what is truly due in our business dealings and daily life;
> excellence is knowing what every issue involves for a person

and end

> it means, moreover, putting our fatherland's interests first,
> then those of our parents, and thirdly and lastly our own (1196-1208).

As Cicero based his *De Officiis* on Panaetius' *Peri tou kathêkontos* the Greek philosopher may well have been the common source. But such principles were not just theoretical; they were carefully applied in the give and take of everyday life. A further refinement in the computing of social obligation was added by Gaius Gracchus and, a little later, by Livius Drusus. According to Seneca (*Ben.* 6.34.2), 'they began the practice of dividing their retinue, receiving some privately, others in groups, and the rest *en masse*'. Whether or not Lucilius had experience of the practice, it was still flourishing in the time of Pliny and Juvenal.

A certain amount, then, of what we find in Lucilius must be interpreted in the social context of *amicitia*. But a great deal more refuses to be confined in that way. Lucilius frequently says things unexpected from one of his class. For example, the fatuous luxury prevailing in Rome could not be attributed solely to upstarts like Gallonius. Nobles like Lupus (12, 13) and Scaevola (60, 70) had to take a share of the blame. They, to be sure, were just individuals; but sometimes criticism is directed at the senatorial order as a whole. Leaving aside what is said by other speakers, like the attack on the nobility in 270-1, one notes that the *patres* are included in the charges of swindling and hypocrisy made in 1145-51 (see p. 6 above); and the following fragment is largely directed at men of high ambition:

> *aurum atque ambitio specimen uirtutis uirique est.*
> *tantum habeas, tantum ipse sies tantique habearis* (1194-5)

> Gold and the scramble for office are the signs of a man and his manhood.
> Whatever you've got decides what you are and what you amount to.

In other respects too, Lucilius was untypical. We have already mentioned his lack of reticence in sexual matters. The same disregard of gentility can be seen in his willingness to talk publicly about the terms of his brother's will (1049) and his own financial decisions (656). But the most striking feature of Lucilius, considering his station in life, was his genuine and all-embracing interest in ordinary people and ordinary things. Discussing prices (365, 538-9), buying and selling (1160, 1237), making up accounts (906, 907, 908) – such things were normally beneath the notice of a gentleman. We even hear of:

> *illi qui inscriptum e portu exportant clanculum*
> *ne portorium dent* (753-4)

> those who take unregistered cargoes from the harbour secretly
> to avoid the customs duty.

More orthodox ways of earning a living are those of the fig-seller (221), the brickmaker (352), the dentist (434-5), the road-worker (436-7), the goldsmith (1097), the lumber-merchant (1170-1), the blacksmith

(1265-6) and the fowler (1267-8). Some such references, of course, are satirical, as in the case of the 'rotten no-good muleteer' (1172). But others are quite straightforward, as with the cook who doesn't care about a peacock's tail so long as the bird is plump (761). This range of interest on the part of a Roman poet was quite exceptional. If something like it could have been recaptured in the second century A.D., the decline which we designate by the word 'silver' might have been arrested. As it was, after the low-life novel of Petronius, literature was smothered by various conventions – literary, rhetorical and social. Of the poets, Juvenal managed to exploit those conventions ironically, producing an original kind of satire. But no one had the courage or the genius to attempt a fresh start.

(ii) Horace

In the year of Lucilius' death (102 B.C.) Archias, a Greek poet from Antioch, already well-known in Greece and Asia Minor, arrived in Rome, where he was received into the house of the Luculli and made much of by Roman aristocrats, including Q. Catulus (Cicero, *Arch.* 6). In return Archias probably helped Catulus with his writing; later he did much more for L. Lucullus by writing a substantial poem on the Mithridatic War. Cicero hoped for a tribute to his consulship from the same quarter, but failed to get it. Archias was just one of many Greek literary men who provided Roman leaders with congenial company and various kinds of cultural service, including recitals, discussions and tutorials. Such men (like Piso's friend Philodemus, Pompey's Theophanes, and Pollio's Timagenes) were also in a position to advise their patrons about conditions and attitudes in Greece. But not all literary clients were Greek. Caesar's successes were lauded by Varro of Atax and Furius (Bibaculus?), and Pompey had the support of the wealthy and scholarly knight Marcus Terentius Varro. These examples illustrate the continuity of literary patronage between Lucilius' period and that of Horace.[1] The qualities expected of an *amicus* remained the same. In fact, the ideal *amicus* had already been described by Ennius (*Ann.* 210-27) as one in whose company the patron could relax and speak freely, a reliable and discreet man who was both a good talker and a good listener. Then, as later, the client could be Greek or Italian, a freedman or a knight. A similar range of services was expected, and the same favours (legal, financial and social) were supplied in return. Lucilius, as we have seen, was something of an exception. In his social position he would have repudiated the name of client, but he would have readily conceded that in terms of power and prestige he was not on the same footing as Scipio,

---

[1] For detail see the papers by Treggiari (2) and Wiseman, and, on Pompey in particular, by Anderson (1).

Laelius, and the others.

Before discussing some of the nuances of Horace's friendship with Maecenas, it is worth looking at what he has to say about the main classes in Roman society, starting from the bottom. Morally, not much was expected of slaves.[2] As a class they were regarded as slothful, greedy, lecherous, and deceitful – just as well, for had they been thought virtuous it might have been hard to justify their position. As it was, the conditions in which they were kept and the punishments to which they were subjected ensured that traditional assumptions about their inferiority were not disturbed. In individual cases, of course, there was much variation. Horace's slaves were relatively fortunate. About 36 B.C. he had three to serve supper in his quarters in Rome (1.6.116). On the Sabine farm he had eight (2.7.118); some, perhaps all, of them were *uernae*, i.e. slaves who had been born within the household. In 2.6 they figure in a happy domestic scene in which they are given the same food as the guests; and since they are called 'cheeky' (*procaces* in v.66) they can hardly have been cowed.

Much later, writing from Rome, Horace addresses a man who has formerly been on the staff of his town house and is now looking after the country estate (*E*.1.14). We cannot tell how faithfully he depicts the steward's personality, for the purpose of the letter is not to provide a character-sketch, but to offer some comments on contentment. Still, the general picture of the slave, who has grown up in the city and now grumbles about the dullness and drudgery of farm-work, is quite convincing. Columella, writing about A.D. 60, says 'that type of servant is lazy and sleepy, being used to free time, the parks, the race-track, theatres, gambling, taverns and brothels, and is always dreaming about that kind of nonsense' (*RR* 1.8.2). Horace does not accuse his man of laziness, and when he criticises him for hankering after city life his tone is teasing rather than stern. Nevertheless, we are left with the feeling that Horace has not been quite fair. For what the city means to the bailiff now (drink and sex) is just a coarser version of what it once meant to Horace (wine and love); whereas what the *country* means to the bailiff now (hard work) is totally different from what it means to Horace (relaxation and the enjoyment of beauty). To be sure, a philosophical attitude may help everyone to accept his place, but there can be no doubt about who has been dealt the stronger hand. These reservations are, of course, largely a modern development. The place of such judgments has been touched on in the Preface and will be taken up again at the end of the final chapter. At present we will simply note that, although once or twice Horace gives us a chilling glimpse of what slavery could mean (e.g. the communal burials in 1.8.8-13, the gladiator pleading for his life in *E*. 1.1.6, the strap hanging ready on the wall in *E*. 2.2.15), he himself never

[2] See Wiedemann, ch.4.

abuses a slave for 'servile' faults. In 2.5.18 a speaker recoils with horror at
having to walk outside 'a filthy Dama', but that speaker is the
disreputable Ulysses, and at the end of Tiresias' instruction it is clear
that if he wants to be a successful legacy-hunter Ulysses must learn to
treat Dama as a 'friend' (101). In the one satire which deals with slavery
at length (2.7) the homily is delivered by the slave Davus, and the
intention is to show that someone who is dominated by his desires is the
equivalent of a slave; morally there is little to choose between Davus and
his master.

Brunt (3.383) has estimated that the total population of Rome at the
end of the first century B.C. was about 750,000, of which at least
two-thirds were slaves or freedmen. The latter were confined to the urban
tribes, where their influence was less effective; they were excluded by
custom from holding office; and they were not eligible for service as
iudices or legionaries. Less important, a *libertinus* could not record the
name of his father; he was usually identifiable by his servile *cognomen*,
and on certain formal occasions he wore the freedman's conical hat.
Nevertheless, freedmen worked happily alongside free-born citizens in a
wide variety of occupations, and in fact dominated some areas of
employment.[3] They were not resented except where they seemed to have
risen beyond their proper place. Pliny the elder (A.D. 23-79) mentions
Sulla's Chrysogonus, Catulus' Amphion, Lucullus' Hector, Pompey's
Demetrius, Antony's Hipparchus, Sextus Pompey's Menas and
Menecrates, and others 'who have grown rich from the blood of Roman
citizens and the chaotic illegality of the proscriptions' (*NH 35.200*). In
Epod.4 Horace speaks of the public indignation directed at a man who
had once been whipped and fettered as a slave but is now a wealthy
tribunus militum – a rank which has gained him admittance to the front
two rows of the knights' section of the theatre. While Horace was not
open to the charge of *tu quoque*, being himself free-born, it is true that
such crude, class-based, invective occurs only here in his *Epodes* and is
found nowhere else in his works.

In the *sermones* we shall leave aside the affectionate references to
Horace's father. One might also argue that the sketch of Volteius Mena
in *E*. 1.7 is so fully realised as to be comic rather than satirical. So we
start with a few passing gibes: the freedman who was slightly astray in
the head and used to pray for immortality (2.3.281-6); the clever type
who has gained an ascendancy over a rich old dotard (2.5.71); the
patronising reference to 'a dive from which/the cleaner sort of freedman
would blush to be seen emerging' (2.7.11-12). More interesting are the
lines satirising Tigellius the Sardinian for his ludicrously inconsistent
habits (1.3.1-19). Tigellius moved in the highest circles, being a friend of
Caesar, Cleopatra, and Octavian.[4] One notes, however, that his status as

---

[3] On the legal position and careers of freedmen see Treggiari (1), chs. 2 and 3.
[4] See Porphyrio on 1.2.1, and cf. 1.3.4-5.

a freedman (plausibly inferred from Cicero)[5] is nowhere mentioned and is hardly relevant to the attack; also Tigellius was dead (1.2.3). No doubt the raffish crew who used to benefit from his extravagance – 'the federated flute-girls' union, pedlars of dubious medicines,/holy beggars, strippers, comics, and all that collection' (1.2.1-2) – included many freedmen and freedwomen. One character whose status is mentioned is Sarmentus. According to the scholiast on Juvenal 5.3, this man was once the slave of M. Favonius but came into the possession of Maecenas, who emancipated him and got him a post as *scriba* in the treasury. In the journey-poem (1.5), Horace states that Sarmentus' lady owner is still alive (1.5.55); he then has him make an attack on Cicirrus' facial disfigurement. The latter replies by reminding Sarmentus of his former position as a slave. All rather boisterous knockabout stuff; but not, it seems, particularly offensive (*accipio* in 58, *iucunde* in 70). The scholiast also tells us that the following verses were circulating about Sarmentus:

> *aliud scriptum habet Sarmentus, aliud populus uoluerat.*
> *digna dignis: sic Sarmentus habeat crassas compedes.*
> *rustici, ne nihil agatis! aliquis Sarmentum alliget!*

Bundle is tied to a treasurer's post
(the public wished him another).
Let's give every man his due
(truss the Bundle up tightly).
Yokels, stand not idly by
(somebody bind the Bundle).

What occasioned those verses was the appearance of Sarmentus in the front row of the knights' seats at the theatre. As well as looking back to the *parvenu* of *Epod.* 4, the lines point forward to the taunt in 1.6.38ff.:

Do you, the son of a Syrus, Dionysius, or Dama, presume
to hurl Romans from the rock or hand them over to Cadmus?

The man addressed is a freedman's son who has become a magistrate. He replies:

Why not? My colleague Newman sits in the row behind me.
He is now what my father was.

In other words, he has a right to that position, more of a right than Newman, who is only a freedman. But the scoffer has the last word:

Do you think that *that*
makes *you* a Paulus or Messalla? If two hundred waggons collided

---

[5] Cicero, *Fam.* 7.24.1; cf. Porphyrio on 1.3.1.

with three enormous funerals in the Forum, Newman could drown
the horns and trumpets with his voice; at least he has that in his favour.

Perhaps, as the Ps. Acro suggests, Newman is supposed to have been a
crier or auctioneer before becoming a magistrate. At any rate, Horace's
point is that not only freedmen, but the sons of freedmen, are exposed to
opprobrium. Such taunts are unjust, because (as Horace has argued) the
status of one's father should not matter provided one is *ingenuus*.[6]
Nevertheless, unfair resentment of this kind is an inescapable feature of
politics, and so Horace himself prefers to remain a private citizen. The
satirist's attitude to those sons of freedmen who have persisted in trying
to make a public career is therefore somewhat complex. He objects to the
resentment which they have to face, yet he does not sympathise with
them; in fact, he regards them as fools. The case of the low-born Tillius
provides an illustration. After being expelled from the senate, Tillius
made a comeback and succeeded in reaching the level of praetor (1.6.24f.
and 107f.). Dislike accompanied his resurgence. In principle such dislike
was unfair, but that did not prevent Horace from ridiculing Tillius as he
travelled along the road to Tivoli, followed by five slaves carrying a
wine-cask and a portable lavatory.

Coming now to plebs, knights and senators, we find a number of
passages in which two, or all three, categories are combined. In *E. 2.1* the
emperor's *populus*, which is so foolishly mistaken about modern poetry,
includes knights and senators; in fact, most of the criticism is levelled at
the literate classes. When Horace goes on to talk about the
theatre-audience he does castigate the plebs:

> Often even the resolute poet is daunted and routed
> when those superior in numbers but not in worth or status –
> stupid illiterate men who are ready to start a fight
> if the knights oppose their wishes – call for a bear or boxers
> in the middle of a play. That's the stuff that appeals to the masses.

But then he immediately widens his attack:

> Nowadays even the knights have stopped listening, and all their
> interest is taken up with inane and ephemeral pageants (187-8).

Again, when Horace imagines Democritus laughing at the people as they
watch a show, the *populus* in question (197) is the whole community.

When the satire is directed at the rich, the target is seldom presented
in terms of class. An instance like the following is quite exceptional:

---

[6] In *E.* 1.1.62 the law of Roscius Otho (67 B.C.), which divided the seating in the theatre
and so put a disproportionate emphasis on rank, is contrasted with the children's chant
'You will be king if you do the right thing'.

Early to the Forum, home late – never let up,
or Mute may reap a richer crop from the fields he acquired
with his wife, and (horrid thought, for his people are lower class)
he may prove more dazzling to *you* than vice versa (*E*. 1.6.20-3).

The normal practice can be seen operating in numerous passages from
1.1.28-100 to *E*. 2.2.146-89. Even in a poem like 2.8, where class is at the
heart of the satire, it is not mentioned. Nasidienus embarrasses his
guests not because he is a knight, a fact which we have to infer from his
wealth,[7] but because he has not mastered the code of manners which
knights are supposed to have. On one occasion Horace speaks of a
millionaire's inability to enjoy his leisure (*E*. 1.1.82-90). Not only is there
no distinction drawn between knight and senator, but as if to stress that
the key to the problem is mental or spiritual, Horace adds:

And the poor man? Equally silly. He changes garret and bed,
baths and barber; he hires a boat and is just as sick
as the rich tycoon sailing along in his private yacht.

Even at a very humble level, a man like Ofellus, who has the *right*
attitude to getting and spending, can be contrasted with a wretched
miser like Avidienus (2.2.53-62; cf. *E*. 1.7.55-9).

The main area in which class-judgments are made is that of culture,
which in Horace's case is virtually equivalent to literature. Here the
masses are treated with contempt: Horace does not want to put his books
on sale to be pawed by the sweaty hands of the *uulgus* (1.4.72; cf. *E*.
1.20.11); nor does he deign to hunt for the votes of the fickle *plebs* (*E*.
1.19.37; but cf. *E*. 2.2.103). He advises the writer of satyr-plays not to
give the satyrs dirty jokes:

> *offenduntur enim, quibus est equus et pater et res,*
> *nec, si quid fricti ciceris probat et nucis emptor,*
> *aequis accipiunt animis donantue corona* (*AP*. 248-50)

Knights – free-born and men of property – take offence
and don't greet with approval all that's enjoyed by the buyer
of roasted nuts and chick-peas, or honour it with a garland.

When he attacks the *composers* of verse, instead of readers and listeners,
Horace moves up (necessarily) to the more educated classes. In *E*. 2.1.108
these enthusiastic, but largely incompetent, amateurs are just called
populus. Another passage is more specific:

---

[7] Ps.Acro calls him an *eques Romanus*. In regard to the end of 2.8, I was wrong, as
Shackleton Bailey (88) points out, to say that the guests rushed out of the house. That was
an over-translation of *fugimus* (93). 'We got away from him' would be better.

> qui nescit uersus tamen audet fingere. quidni?
> liber et ingenuus, praesertim census equestrem
> summam nummorum uitioque remotus ab omni (*AP*. 382-4)

The fellow who is useless at writing poetry still attempts it.
Why not? He's free, and so was his father; his fortune is rated
at the sum required of a knight; and his heart's in the right place!

Needless to say, Horace speaks rather differently of the upper classes
when he is claiming their support. Once, in reply to his critics, he says in
a somewhat lordly way: *satis est equitem mihi plaudere* (1.10.76) 'I'm
happy if the better classes applaud me'; but he at once softens the
crudity of the declaration by attributing the words to a disappointed
actress. Finally, at the end of 1.10, Horace mentions the names of several
distinguished friends who, he hopes, will enjoy the collection which is
about to appear. Some are equites (e.g. Maecenas and the two Visci) and
some are senators (e.g. Pollio, Messalla and Messalla's brother).

Of Horace's complaints about people's receptivity, then, some are
general and a few are directed at the upper classes. If rather more point
downward against the plebs, that is because cultural obtuseness was
most massively evident in that quarter. When he mocks the coarseness of
popular taste Horace is speaking primarily as an artist – an artist who is
confident of the superiority of the culture which he represents and is
piqued when he encounters indifference or hostility. The result is
sometimes arrogant, but Horace did not think it part of his business to
analyse the deficiencies of the Roman educational system.

Now it is possible to take a low view of some forms of popular
entertainment without making any general assumptions about the worth
of those who enjoy them. The distinction, however, tends to be rather
precarious; and it was hard to keep it steadily in view in a society where
honestus meant so much more than 'respectable' and the *optimates* or
'best people' belonged to the senatorial order. Occasionally Horace does
make a remark which shows he is thinking in social rather than cultural
terms. In 2.1.74-6 he says:

> Whatever I am, and however
> inferior to Lucilius in wealth and talent, Envy will have to
> admit, like it or not, that I've moved in important circles.

Cum magnis uixisse – the boast is somewhat irritating even when
prefaced with that modest concession. The same thing occurs at the end
of *E*. 1.20 where Horace addresses his slave-book:

> me libertino natum patre et in tenui re
> maiores pinnas nido extendisse loqueris,
> ut quantum generi demas uirtutibus addas;

me primis urbis belli placuisse domique,
corporis exigui, praecanum, solibus aptum,
irasci celerem, tamen ut placabilis essem

You will say I was born in a home without substantial possessions,
a freedman's son; that my wingspan proved too large for the nest
(thus adding to my merits whatever you take from my birth);
that in war and peace I won the esteem of the country's leaders;
that of small build, grey too soon, and fond of the sunshine
I was quick to lose my temper but was not hard to appease.

Here the claim to have pleased the great men of the day is less annoying, since it appears as just one detail in a charming self-portrait. In any case, Horace clearly attached great importance to his social success. It all started when his father took him to Orbilius' school, where he received the kind of education given to the sons of knights and senators (1.6.76-8).[8] In the same poem he claims that if things had turned out differently he would not have minded becoming an auctioneer like his father. Perhaps not. But as it is, he enjoys the reflected glory of his eminent friends, and it enables him to refer back with a superior smile to those 'important sergeant-majors' whose sons had swaggered past him on the way to school (1.6.73-5). If to these passages we add the complacent, but very amusing, satire on the pest (1.9), we must admit that Horace was something of a snob.

Before we judge him too harshly, however, certain points could be borne in mind. The first is that in Rome, more than in some other places, a man tended to be judged by the company he kept.[9] So although Horace never affected the life-style of a senator (and indeed explicitly rejected it in 1.6.100-4), nevertheless, by retaining the friendship and goodwill of Maecenas and the rest he gave public proof of his *fides*, or reliability. Periodically throughout his works he complains of the resentment he has experienced as the successful son of a freedman. Even when he has become a celebrity, some of the old sensitivity still remains, as in *et iam dente minus mordeor inuido* (*Odes* 4.3.16). The ancients were familiar with *inuidia* and other forms of personal attack, and they allowed a certain amount of self-praise by way of rebuttal.[10] This will not quite cover that piece of blatant name-dropping at the end of 1.10, but even that is muted in comparison with the blasts of self-approbation that issued so continually from Cicero's trumpet. Another important

---

[8] Suetonius (*Gramm*.9) says Orbilius taught for many years in Beneventum before moving to Rome. Beneventum was on the road from Venusia to Rome; so perhaps Horace's father had heard of him locally.

[9] In *Ep.* 4.15.? Pliny says he is very fond of Asinius Rufus. Rufus is a close friend of Tacitus. If one approves of Pliny and Tacitus, one is bound to approve of Rufus, because 'for cementing friendship the strongest bond is similarity of character'.

[10] See, e.g. Cicero, *Dom*.95; Quintilian 11.1.18; Plutarch, *De se ipsum citra inuidiam laudando* (*Mor*. 540C-F, Loeb, vol.7).

consideration is that from time to time Horace shows himself aware of his propensity and willing to laugh at it, e.g. at the end of *E*. 1.15:

> I admire the safe and humble
> when funds are low; I'm quite a Stoic with plain fare.
> But when something finer and more delectable comes, I say
> that the wise and the good life is only attained by those
> like you, whose solid wealth is reflected in splendid villas!

Finally, in his serious moods, Horace knows perfectly well that *sub specie aeternitatis* it is all vanity:

> *cum bene notum*
> *porticus Agrippae, uia te conspexerit Appi,*
> *ire tamen restat Numa quo deuenit et Ancus* (*E*. 1.6.25-7)

> Although you've provided
> a familiar sight in Agrippa's Porch and the Appian Way,
> you must still go down the road travelled by Numa and Ancus.

The discussion of Horace's social attitudes brings us back to his friendship with Maecenas. From the many lines dedicated to it I select just a few significant touches. First a point from the interview:

> *ut ueni coram, singultim pauca locutus,*
> *infans namque pudor prohibebat plura profari* (1.6.56-7)

> When I met you I managed no more than to gulp out a few words,
> for diffidence tied my tongue and stopped me talking freely.

So Horace was not quite at ease. But with all his experience of life and death was he quite so overcome? The exaggeration is surely a compliment to Maecenas' status. At first the friendship was limited to small-talk:

> 'What time do you make it?' 'Is the Thracian Chick a match for the Arab?'
> 'These frosty mornings are fairly nippy; you've got to be careful,'
> and other remarks that are safely lodged in a leaky ear (2.6.44-6).

Horace smiles in retrospect at Maecenas' caution; he was not yet sure of the poet's discretion (an essential quality in an *amicus*). At the same stage Horace hopes that if he is inadvertently tactless, blundering in on his patron when not expected, he will be regarded as just *simplicior* – 'a bit uninhibited' – rather than blamed for being totally lacking in *savoir faire* (1.3.63-6). The opening lines of 1.6 about Maecenas' ancestors, especially v.4:

olim qui magnis legionibus imperitarent

who held command over mighty legions in days gone by,

sound over-deferential. Heinze reminds us of Lucretius 3.1028: *magnis qui gentibus imperitarent*, and suggests a source in Ennius. But as Shackleton Bailey says, 'irony lurks' (17); and its function is to preserve Horace's self-respect. In 1.9, an insider's poem, vv.48-52 are directed over the poet's head to Maecenas himself, and they assure him that the poet takes nothing for granted:

> We don't behave up there in the way you imagine. Why nowhere
> is cleaner and more remote from that kind of corruption.
> I'm not worried, I assure you, that so-and-so's better read
> and better off than I am. We each have our own position.

For Horace to emulate Maecenas would be ludicrous – remember the fable of the frog (2.3.314-20). When Maecenas sends a last-minute invitation to dinner, Horace immediately leaves his own guest-parasites in the lurch and is roundly abused for doing so (2.7.32-42). In order to attend on his patron Horace has to put up with a good deal of unwelcome pressure (2.6.29-58). Passing over corroborative material in *Odes* 1-3, we come to *E.* 1.1, an affectionate poem which nevertheless indicates in passing that Horace has to take a certain amount of teasing from his fastidious friend about his hair-cut, his clothes, and perhaps even his finger-nails (94-105). The common thread in all these passages is a good-humoured acknowledgment of Maecenas' position. Horace owes him an incalculable amount and is not ungrateful. We shall bear this in mind when discussing *E.* 1.7.

Meanwhile, we must consider two very different epistles. In *E.* 1.18, Horace provides the young Lollius with tips for the aspiring client: watch what you say, don't gossip, and so on. So much is general. Then in vv.86-7 he says that attending a powerful friend is delightful only to those who have never done so; those who have are full of apprehension. (A little harsh, that, in a book addressed to Maecenas.) You must continually adapt your behaviour to your patron's moods and personality. Then some transitional lines: while you do so you should be considering what will bring you contentment

> prestige, or a nice little nest-egg,
> or the hidden path and the course of life that passes unnoticed (101-2).

Finally Horace discloses his own preference: the life of retirement. In particular he says *mihi uiuam/quod superest aeui* – 'May I live for myself what's left of my life'. That is not loud or emphatic, yet in its context it must intimate that Horace would like to have done with the whole business of *clientela* and its duties.

E. 1.17 is another unenchanted account of how to get on with the great. On the whole it is light and amusing, though (unlike *E.* 1.18) it tells us nothing about the addressee. Near the end, however, there is some cynical instruction on how to extract gifts from your patron (43-51). The tone is rather like that of Tiresias in 2.5. A squalid caricature, we may think, and quite unexceptionable since it is so obviously unconnected with Maecenas and Horace. But then, unfortunately, the client is told not to grumble about the road and the rainy weather when he is taken on a trip to Brundisium, which is exactly what Horace had done in 1.5.95-7. That, one must admit, is disconcerting. If it's a joke, our smile cannot be anything but uneasy. We then recall that whereas in *E.* 1.18 Horace is in a sort of half-way house, where a client's occupation can alternate with spells of retirement (*quotiens* in 104), in *E.* 1.17.6-12 the two life-styles are imagined as quite separate.

And so we come to *E.* 1.7, which is actually *written* in retirement. The tone is anything but hostile: Maecenas is addressed as *dulcis amice* (12); his generosity is contrasted with that of the Calabrian host (14); he has often been called *rex* and *pater* (37) – terms of affection and respect. Again, the illustrative material is charmingly presented – the fox in the corn-bin, Telemachus' polite refusal, the tale of Philippus and Mena. And Horace himself is never harsh or assertive. On the contrary, he is the self-mocking *uates* (11), who is now getting a bit short of stamina and a bit thin on top (26). So much recalls our first list of passages, where Horace was the dutiful, if sometimes reluctant, *amicus*. But underneath all the friendliness and good humour lies a stone-like refusal: Horace has finally said no. The years of his *obsequium* are over. He will, to be sure, see Maecenas from time to time, but

> *non regia Roma*
> *sed uacuum Tibur placet aut imbelle Tarentum* (44-5)

> It isn't royal Rome
> that attracts me now, but quiet Tibur or peaceful Tarentum.

There was no rift. Like *Odes* 1-3, the book was dedicated to Maecenas. But there had been a change. As John Owen wrote, in a famous line which Horace would not have despised: *tempora mutantur, nos et mutamur in illis.*

(iii) Persius

As we noted in Chapter Two, Persius was a Roman knight, related by blood and marriage to men of senatorial rank. His father died when he was six, and his step-father (another knight) died a few years later. The family was rich. Persius himself left a fortune of about two million sesterces – twice the sum required of a senator. This means that he wrote from a secure position within the social system and experienced neither the mingled elation and anxiety of Horace, who had moved upwards, nor the resentment of Juvenal, who felt he was on the way down. This position enabled him to take a rather detached view about the accident of birth. In 6 the satirist declares that if he can find no suitable kinsman he will go out and make some beggar his heir. The (fictitious) young man who was hoping to inherit says in horror: 'An offspring of the soil?' Persius answers:

> Ask who my grandfather's grandfather was.
> It'll take a while, but I'll tell you. Go back a stage – and another;
> we've now reached a son of the soil. So in point of kinship
> this 'Jack' turns out to be some kind of great-great-uncle (57-60).

The same coolness can be seen in the remonstrance addressed to the student in 3 by his stern companion. Referring to the parade of equites before the censor, he says:

> *an deceat pulmonem rumpere uentis*
> *stemmate quod Tusco ramum millesime ducis*
> *censoremue tuum uel quod trabeate salutas? (27-9)*

> Should you puff up your lungs till they burst
> because you, descendant one thousand, trace your family tree
> to Tuscan stock, and parade for your censor in full regalia?

Finally, we have the nobles and their decadent taste. True, the attack in 1 is not confined to them: *all* the citizens are confused and asinine. But with the phrase *Romulidae saturi* (31) we focus on the upper classes; *proceres* (52) 'leaders' points to the senators; and *patricius sanguis* (61) 'patrician blood' is unambiguous.

In the Roman value-system much store was set on freedom. The adjective *liberalis* connoted that which was worthy of a free man, hence 'gentlemanly', 'fine', 'noble', 'generous'. Horace could not accept this attitude in all its simplicity, because his father had been noble *without* being born a gentleman (1.6). Perhaps Persius came to feel the same misgivings in the course of his friendship with the freedman Cornutus. At any rate, in his fifth satire he enquired whether all these gentlemanly qualities were conferred merely by the process of manumission. At that ceremony a slave was touched by the praetor's rod, and his master turned him round saying 'I wish this man to be free'. But true freedom, as the Stoics insisted, was moral freedom, which inhered in a man's soul,

> *non in festuca, lictor quam iactat ineptus (5.175)*

> not in the piece of stick waved by a silly official.

This way of thinking was enlightened in so far as it stressed that in moral terms there was no necessary barrier between slave and free-born. Yet it could also be taken to imply that, since moral slavery was the real slavery, legal slavery didn't matter. Similarly, in a Christian context, the man who most often says 'We are all equal in the sight of God' is not always the one who tries hardest to reduce class distinctions. In fact, he may actually use the phrase as a way of referring the problem to a higher authority. Now for all we know, Persius *may* have been at ease with all sorts and conditions of men. But even allowing for the presence of Cornutus, who was an exceptional man and whose status, anyway, is never mentioned, that is not quite the picture that emerges from his satires. Consider the longer passage on manumission in 5:

> We need *freedom* – not the sort which Jack acquires
> when he figures as John Smith on the voter's list and is issued
> with coupons for mouldy bread. You haven't a crumb of truth:
> you create citizens by a whirl. Tom is a worthless yokel,
> bleary with booze; you couldn't trust him with a bucket of mash.
> Then his master turns him round; from that quick spin he emerges
> Tom Jones. What's this? You won't authorise a loan
> which Jones has guaranteed? You quail at the sight of Jones on the bench?
> It's true – Jones has said so! Would you sign this document, Jones?
> This is the real freedom, this is conferred by our caps (73-82).

While Persius' argument here is that moral slaves are to be found in every rank, a secondary conclusion insinuates itself, namely that often one who is a slave in law does not deserve to be anything else. In the same way, when that man in 3 has died from his spectacular seizure, and when

> *illum*
> *hesterni capite induto subiere Quirites* (3.105-6)

> he is raised on the shoulders
> of men whose caps proclaim them Romans – as of yesterday,

we are meant to find the sudden metamorphosis surprising, and rather ridiculous. Persius, then, shows little interest in slaves or in the kind of life they lived. Is it just due to chance, one wonders, that the word *seruus* never appears in his satires? At one point in 6 he gives a glimpse of the slave-market, speaking of the rich slave-dealer who is adept at 'slapping Cappadocians on the hard platform' (see Beikircher's note). He might have called the slaves *miseros* 'wretched'. Instead, he chose a more sensual word, which underlined the dealer's greed rather than his callousness, and which formally contrasted with the hard platform: *Cappadocas rigida pinguis plausisse catasta* (76). *Fat* Cappadocians.

The ordinary citizens usually appear as a collective mass. The reputation which they bestow on a man is ephemeral and based on a false

set of values (4.50). Their everyday life is something which Persius is glad
to ignore (*securus uulgi* in 6.12). Politically, when the *plebecula* 'rabble',
or the *calida turba* 'feverish mob', seethes with anger, it is soon quelled
by the lordly gesture of a high-born demagogue (4.6-8). They are also
easily wooed, being prepared to scramble eagerly for showers of peas
(5.177-8) and accepting handouts of oil and bits of meat (6.50). When a
figure does detach itself from the crowd, it is a clod-hopping yokel
(*peronatus arator* in 5.102), a centurian – whether smelly (*hircosus* in
3.77) or varicose (*varicosus* in 5.189) – or 'a wizened old Baucis' who
'hawks basil [reputedly an aphrodisiac] to a slob of a slave' (4.21-2).

In all this we are not, of course, asking Persius to be warm-hearted.
(That is not part of a satirist's duty.) We are talking about the level on
which he is standing. Consider these passages of Horace, one early and
the other late:

> I wander wherever I please
> on my own; I ask what price they're charging for greens and flour;
> in the evenings I often stroll around the Circus and Forum,
> those haunts of trickery; I loiter by the fortune-tellers; and then
> I amble home to a plate of minestrone with leeks and peas (1.6.111-15)

and

> A feverish builder charges past with his mules and workmen;
> a huge contraption heaves a beam and then a boulder;
> wailing funerals smash their way through lumbering waggons.
> There goes a mad dog; here's a muddy pig (*E.* 2.2.72-5).

Those lines, the first group favourable, the second comically critical,
come from the centre of an urban environment (McGann 2.61-70). They
are not exactly typical of Horace, but they are by no means uncommon.
They have no counterpart in Persius. One wonders if he ever did his own
shopping. This lack of the common touch is reflected in what he has to
say of other people's occupations. Politicians are interested only in
power; merchants are greedy for profits; soldiers are boors; housewives
(and indeed women in general) don't figure. The good life appears to
consist in having a comfortable income from land, which makes it
possible to spend one's time studying and discussing philosophy.

In accounts of patronage one sometimes comes across expressions of
regret that an institution, which in republican times encouraged mutual
assistance based on proper feelings of respect, degenerated into a kind of
sordid game in which the patron sought to retain his clients' services at
the minimum expense, while they concentrated on extracting the
maximum advantage. About the middle of the first century A.D. (i.e. in
Persius' adult life) the system had indeed many unattractive features.
Columella talks of clients being insulted by the rich man's porters (*RR* 1,

*praef.*10). In Seneca (*De Const. Sap.* 10.2) an aggrieved client complains
that he was not admitted though others were; that on another occasion
the patron haughtily ignored or undisguisedly laughed at his
conversation, and gave him the humblest place at the dinner-table. In
another passage (*De Brev. Vit.* 14.4) we hear of a guest being kept
waiting and then snubbed as the patron rushes past him; or else the
patron slips out the back door; or if he does admit his client to the
salutatio he frequently and pointedly forgets his name. The author of the
Laus Pisonis, a piece of protracted grovelling, sees it as a peculiarity in
his patron that he does not inflict arrogant witticisms on his guests or
allow their misfortune to be made the subject of merriment (115-16).

These, then, are not infrequently thought of as decadent features of the
system. But the trouble with decadence is that it always begins so early.
To every writer living under the empire the golden age of patronage was
the period of Maecenas; and his treatment of Horace and Virgil was
universally admired for its magnanimity. Yet it is clear from several, as it
were incidental, passages of Horace that, except in the case of a few very
lucky people, patronage had just the same degrading aspects then. The
second epode says that the truly happy man

> *forumque uitat et superba ciuium*
> *potentiorum limina* (7-8)

avoids the Forum and the lordly entrances
of influential citizens.

In an idyllic poem about the country, the phrase is easily overlooked.
Again, the phenomenon seems so much less objectionable when seen
from above. At the end of his invitation to Torquatus, Horace writes:

> *rebus omissis*
> *atria seruantem postico falle clientem* (*E.* 1.5.30-1)

Then drop what you're doing
and trick the client in the hallway by slipping out the back.

Horace himself dashes past his own guest Mulvius and his hangers-on
when he is hurrying off to dine with Maecenas. We think little of the
incident, because Horace turns it into a joke against himself (2.7.36).
Another beguiling passage, also about Maecenas, occurs in 1.9, where, on
learning that Maecenas is rather inaccessible, the pest sets his jaw:

> *haud mihi deero:*
> *muneribus seruos corrumpam; non, hodie si*
> *exclusus fuero, desistam* (56-8)

I shan't be found wanting.
I'll bribe his servants; and if today they shut me out
I'll persevere.

Very amusing; but it shows someone who desperately wants to become an *amicus* accepting that he may have the door shut in his face and be obliged to square the great man's slaves. We also tend to overlook the evidence of bribery, deception, flattery and pimping provided by 2.5, because that satire is about legacy-hunting. Yet *captatio* was a specialised form, however debased, of the behaviour of a client. So the golden age of patronage turns out to be something of a mirage.

In Persius we soon encounter the mercenary side of literary *amicitia*, albeit in a facetious context. The second part of the prologue states that the prospect of cash makes all kinds of people poetic. While Persius is referring here to his own work, which was *not* inspired by poverty, his words also ridicule, in a non-ironical way, those poems which were so inspired: they are the songs of ravens and magpies. Another half-serious passage which seems to imply that Persius was dependent on patronage comes in 1.108-9, where he is warned to take care that the thresholds of the great do not give him a chilly reception: *ne maiorum ... limina frigescant*. The warning itself, as we argued in Chapter Two, was not without foundation. But Persius' cautious adviser seems to draw his phraseology from the world of *clientela*. Horace had used the words *potentiorum limina* (*Epod.* 2.7-8); later, Martial would write from Spain picturing Juvenal, hot and uncomfortable, moving among the *limina potentiorum* (12.18.4). Within the class context of Roman society the *limen* was one of those all-important boundaries of which we have recently heard so much.

In those two passages from the prologue and the first satire, *clientela* is in the background. In another passage from 1 it is in the foreground, but the terms are reversed; for it is the patron who composes verse and the client who listens. As so often, we start from some lines of Horace, which I paraphrase: if a poet is well-off and in a position to serve a rich dinner (*unctum qui ponere possit*), to act as a guarantor, and to give legal assistance to a poor man, he will have difficulty in telling a true (*uerum*) friend from a false one. When you give someone a present, never ask him to listen to your verses; he is bound to praise them. As a hired mourner wails more loudly than the bereaved, so the fake admirer (*derisor*) demonstrates more enthusiasm than the real one (*AP* 420-33). Much earlier, in *E.* 1.19.37-8 he had said:

non ego uentosae plebis suffragia uenor
impensis cenarum et tritae munere uestis

I'm not the kind to hunt for the votes of the fickle rabble
by standing dinners and giving presents of worn-out clothes.

Drawing on the first passage, Persius wrote *calidum scis ponere sumen*
(53) – 'You know the trick of providing hot sow's udders'. (The specific
sumen for Horace's general *unctum* is characteristic.) He then took a
second type of favour from *E.* 1.19:

> *scis comitem horridulum trita donare lacerna*
>
> You know how to give a threadbare cloak to a shivering client.

(The shivering client is a new contribution.) But the main
thought-sequence still comes from the *Ars Poetica*, for Persius is
concerned with the difficulty of obtaining a sincere response:

> *'uerum' inquis 'amo, uerum mihi dicite de me.'*
> *qui pote? uis dicam?*
>
> You say 'I'm a lover of truth; tell me the truth about me.'
> How can he? Let me oblige.

Then, taking a hint, perhaps, from Horace's *derisor*, Persius proceeds to
ridicule the man as a pot-bellied doodler, and to describe the derisive
gestures made behind his back.

Given Persius' class, and his views of what poetry should be about, it is
easy to see why he did not portray himself as a serious participant in the
quest for patronage. In principle, no doubt he could have done so; for we
must not imagine that a poet's scope is necessarily confined to his
experience. But in fact he chose to show us just a few glimpses of the
relationship from outside. They are vivid and lively passages, and in
their own terms entirely successful. They do not, however, convey what it
felt like to be a client (literary or otherwise) with all the painful hopes
and apprehensions, the snubs and disappointments, and the continual
compromises with one's honesty and self-respect. For that kind of insight
we turn to Juvenal.

(iv) Juvenal

We begin with slavery, noting a few different kinds of remark and how
they are related to their context. Quite often Juvenal mentions the plight
of slaves, but usually in order to highlight something else. Naevolus, for
example, brings in the wretched ploughboy (*miser* in 9.45) not only for
the sake of a dirty joke, but also to claim that he himself is worse off. The
language at a rich man's dinner-party is filthier than that of a slave-girl
in her brothel (11.171-5). In 3.253 the 'poor blighter' (*infelix*) with the
dishes on his head is a detail from a comic scene; his discomfort is

secondary. In 6.331 the comedy is wilder: the slaves are imagined as suffering sexual assault from a horde of lust-crazed women. And yet they represent only the third point on a five-point rhetorical scale, which culminates in a donkey. One might argue, however, that in some instances of this kind, Juvenal shows that he at least *recognises* the slave's condition. In 1.93, for example, although the argument is primarily concerned with the obsessive gambler we are also left with the feeling that his shivering slave *ought* to have been given a tunic.

More remarkable are a couple of passages where the slave's suffering is in the foreground. In 6 a tyrannical wife says:

'Put that slave on a cross!'
          'What crime has he done to deserve it?
What witnesses are there? Who's his accuser? Give him a hearing.
When a human's life is at stake, no delay is excessive.'
'You fool! Is a slave human? What if he *hasn't* done wrong?
That is my wish, my order; my will is reason enough' (219-23).[1]

The male counterpart of this monster is the sadist in 14:

Does Rutilus foster a gentle temper and a mild reaction
to small transgressions, does he think the body and soul of a slave
are made of the same material as ours and the same constituents,
or does he impart a cruel streak when he thrills at the uproar
of a merciless flogging and prefers the crack of a lash to a Siren?
To his trembling house he becomes Antiphates and Polyphemus,
only happy when the torturer's called and someone is burnt
with the red-hot branding iron for stealing a couple of towels (15-22).

Those passages illustrate why it is inadequate to sum up Juvenal as a frivolous writer. Here we see him confronting evil – something that Horatian satire was not equipped to do. True, Horace envisaged such cruelty (a slave crucified for sampling his master's dinner), but he dismissed it as the action of a maniac (1.3.82-3). Good men tend to believe that atrocious behaviour *must* be insane. A generous mistake, but still, sadly, a mistake.

Juvenal, then, can view slaves without animus, and occasionally with compassion, when he is attacking someone else. If the period is sufficiently remote, he can even speak of them with approval. Back in the third century, a little slave-child (*uernula*) formed part of a happy rustic scene (14.169); earlier still, the last good king Rome had was the son of a slave-woman (8.259). But now slaves have become a nuisance: they are expensive to feed (3.167), they break or lose things (11.191), and they spread gossip (9.102-21). Worse still, they can be dangerous:

---

[1] Her brutal and capricious treatment of slaves, male and female, is further described in vv. 479-94.

> 'While he [Sejanus] lies by the river,
> let's all run and kick the man who was Caesar's enemy.'
> 'Make sure that our servants see us, so no one can say we didn't,
> and drag his terrified master to court with his neck in a noose (10.85-8).

Here the slave's right to bring a charge of treason against his owner contributes vividly to the general panic. Sometimes a rich man's slaves are mentioned simply as status-symbols (3.141, 7.141). But when they represent an affront to the satirist's self-respect, then he shows his characteristic indignation and dislike. What an insult that the son of freeborn parents should have to walk outside a wealthy man's slave (3.131), or tip him at a morning *salutatio* (3.189), or endure his supercilious insolence at a dinner-party (5.60-5)!

But Juvenal's most virulent hatred is reserved for those who have succeeded in escaping from the servile class and have joined other interlopers like Jews and Egyptians in challenging or usurping his own position. The most public demonstration of this social catastrophe takes place at the theatre:

> 'This won't do,' says the speaker,
> 'Out, if you please! When your means don't meet the law's requirements
> you have to vacate your knightly cushion. These seats are reserved for
> whoremongers' boys who first saw the light in some brothel or other;
> here the son of a sleek auctioneer can applaud, on his right
> a feather-remover's smart young lad, on his left a trainer's.'[2]

> Thus decreed the brainless Otho who assigned us our places (3.153-9).

Horace had portrayed a similar scene from the other side (1.6.38-44). Being the son of an auctioneer, he knew what this kind of denigration felt like. He did not actually invite it by attempting a political career, but he could not avoid it. Seeing him and Maecenas sitting together, people would murmur *Fortunae filius!* (2.6.49). Lady luck; that was it. Juvenal put it more savagely:

> cum sint
> *quales ex humili magna ad fastigia rerum*
> *extollit quotiens uoluit Fortuna iocari* (3.38-40)

> For these are
> the people fortune raises from lowly estate to the lofty
> pinnacles of worldly power, when she feels like playing a joke.

Well, no doubt the parvenu *was* ridiculous, but the real victim of the joke was the type whose viewpoint is so consistently represented by Juvenal –

---

[2] The term *pinnirapus* 'feather-snatcher' refers to a gladiator who after (or during?) the fight removed the plumes from his opponent's helmet.

the man who has known better days, whose income has dwindled, and who, lacking the right training and attitude for making money, must struggle to keep up appearances. As he does so, he thinks not only of spectacular figures like Tiberius Julius Alexander, the Jew who under Nero became Prefect of Egypt (1.130), or Domitian's favourite, the Egyptian Crispinus, who is mockingly styled *princeps equitum* (4.32), but of countless others who had become prosperous and achieved a significant position in society.

How have they done it? Could it have been through enterprise and honest effort? Pride will not countenance such an idea. Even luck on its own is too charitable an explanation. The only possible answer is crime:

> *criminibus debent hortos, praetoria, mensas,*
> *argentum uetus et stantem extra pocula caprum* (1.75-6)

> It is crime to which they owe their parks, mansions, and tables,
> their antique silver with a goat perched on the goblet's rim.

One had only to look around. The barber Cinnamus had become a knight through his mistress's generosity (1.24-5 with Martial 7.64.2); others had informed on their patrons (1.33), defrauded wards (1.46-7), lied in court (7.13), acted as go-betweens or gigolos (3.45f., 1.37ff.), accepted bribes (3.46-8), and forged wills (1.67-8). The city was in fact now entirely run by crooks (3.29ff.).[3]

As an aggrieved rentier, Juvenal might be expected to make frequent and contemptuous references to the plebs as a class. Yet such references are rare. When Democritus is said to have laughed at the *uulgus* (10.51), the word seems to be used rather vaguely of the public in general. So too, in 11.195-7, the plebs is equated with the whole population, which is supposed to be at the races. More precise is the statement

> *plebeiae Deciorum animae, plebeia fuerunt*
> *nomina* (8.254-5)

> The souls of the Decii, yes, their very names were plebeian,

a compliment which underlines the aphorism *stemmata quid faciunt?* (8.1), 'What do pedigrees count for?'. However, the most famous passage about the common people is undoubtedly contemptuous. Contrasting them with their forefathers, Juvenal says:

---

[3] Note the insinuation in 3.31-2 that civil engineers and undertakers are crooked. LaFleur (1) would identify Artorius (20) with a freedman architect who worked in Pompeii in the early part of the first century A.D. and then presumably moved to Rome, and Catulus (30) with L. Volusenus Catulus, a man who was connected with public works under Tiberius and was prosecuted on some unknown charge. If these suggestions are right, Artorius and Catulus in Juvenal 3 are types of dishonest public employees.

> *nam qui dabat olim*
> *imperium, fasces, legiones, omnia, nunc se*
> *continet atque duas tantum res anxius optat,*
> *panem et circenses* (10.78-81)

> The body which used to distribute
> commands, legions, rods, and the rest, has nowadays narrowed
> its scope, devoting its anxious attention to two things only –
> food and sport.

But here, as often, the satirist refuses to wax sentimental over the past. Instead of saying that this began ages ago, when the Romans were deprived of their voting-rights, he says

> *iam pridem, ex quo suffragia nulli*
> *uendimus, effudit curas*

> Ages ago the people cast off its worries,
> when we stopped selling our votes.

So the free republic had its share of corruption too.

Coming now to the aristocracy, we can easily find instances of vice and folly. A powerful passage in 8 begins with the thick figure of Lateranus, a consul, who frequents low dives (158-62) and behaves worse than a slave (179); it goes on to speak of other nobles who stoop to appearing on the stage, sometimes in the role of buffoons (185-92); and it culminates with Gracchus, who by fighting in the arena disgraced not only himself but his opponent (203-10). Such indignation must, one might assume, express a profound antipathy to the senatorial class. Yet, at least in the case of the men, that does not seem to be so. Certainly, Juvenal dislikes and despises them; but part of the reason at least is the fact that they are bringing their class into disrepute. It is significant that he makes Nero shoulder some of the blame: with a vulgar exhibitionist as emperor, perhaps it is not surprising that some of the aristocracy should demean themselves too (198-9). In Domitian's council (*Sat.* 4) there are half a dozen men like the deadly Pompeius and Catullus (110-13) who cannot be excused; but Juvenal deals gently with Pegasus and Crispus and the young Acilius: they were victims of the regime. The keynote of what Juvenal has to say about the order is struck early on, in 1.33, with the mention of the informer:

> *magni delator amici*
> *et cito rapturus de nobilitate comesa*
> *quod superest*

> one who betrayed his powerful friend
> and soon will be tearing away all that is left of the carcass
> of Rome's aristocracy.

The decline of the once-great order does not occasion glee; gloom, rather; and a feeling of aversion at having to live in an age of vultures. It is embarrassing and disconcerting to find nobles lining up for the *sportula* (1.100); depressing to contemplate a Corvinus reduced to the status of a herdsman (1.107-8); and of course it is deplorable that the new aristocracy should fail in its responsibilities to men of letters (7). Yet Juvenal never advocates that the class should be swept away. True, he mocks its monuments (all those mutilated portrait-busts at the beginning of 8, and the equestrian statue with a missing eyeball in 7.128), and he castigates numerous individuals who belong to it. But even when he is most indignant, part of his anger comes from the fact that the noble in question has betrayed the satirist's conception of the order. It was an old-fashioned conception, formed, perhaps, in the family circle at Aquinum; one which fitted the leaders of an earlier and simpler community of the kind described so well in 11.77-99 and 14.161-88. It is no accident that the idyllic picture of Juvenal's supper at Tibur (11.64-76) should be seen as a continuation of that venerable tradition. Not that he would have wished to go back. Too much history had intervened. He accepts the only kind of constitution he has known; his opposition is reserved for *bad* emperors. So although at times he (retrospectively) supports assassination, he should not be thought of as a sentimental pro-republican. While he is not concerned to give us a positive picture of society, his satires imply that he would have been less disaffected under a benevolent emperor, supported by a loyal yet independently-minded senate, and less greedy and ambitious knights; plebs, freedmen, and slaves would all have worked contentedly in their allotted stations. The harmony of the state depended on degree:

Take but degree away, untune that string,
And, hark! what discord follows.

Juvenal could not have written that speech, but he would surely have understood it.[4]

The vision of a stable and stratified society in which all movement took place according to the rules remains rather vague, and it is kept very much in the background. Present and real is a community in which the rules count for nothing. The implications of this are seen most vividly in the patron-client relationship. Before looking at particular passages, a few general remarks may be in order, beginning with the *salutatio*. To attend this function the client would have to rise before dawn and make his way up to the great man's house in all weathers.[5] In the rectangular area in front of the hall door, for long known as the *uestibulum*, he would

---

[4] Ulysses' speech on degree comes in *Troilus and Cressida*, Act 1, Scene 3, 75-137.
[5] Cf. Pliny *Ep.* 3.12.2; Martial 10.82; Horace 2.6.23-6.

find others already waiting. Not all were in the same category. Seneca distinguishes those admitted first and those admitted second (*Ben.* 6.33.4); earlier, the author of the *Commentariolum Petitionis* speaks of *salutatores*, who pay their respects and then move on, *deductores*, who escort the patron to the Forum, and *adsectatores* who stay with him all day (34-8).[6] Another classification, noted above, was attributed by Seneca to Gaius Gracchus and Livius Drusus: they used to admit some callers individually, some in groups, and the rest *en masse* (*Ben.* 6.34.2). Whichever method was used, attention was paid to rank. If the patron was a man of influence, enjoying the confidence of the emperor, he would be waited on even by members of the aristocracy. These might be eager to obtain his support for an important political post;[7] or they might want his help in a legal case (for powerful men, who possessed *gratia*, could always have a word with the judge);[8] or they might want to advance the career of a friend or kinsman,[9] or to arrange an advantageous marriage.

These aristocrats would naturally be summoned first; the rest would follow according to rank. Admission was not automatic. One had to get past the *nomenclator* with his book of names;[10] and recognition had sometimes to be assisted with a bribe.

The ordinary client's requests could take many forms, ranging from assistance in a law-suit or property deal, to a seat at the games. But to reach a position where he could make such requests he had to accumulate credit over a period of time by escorting his patron on his various calls, laughing at his jokes, and performing various minor but tedious services. Nor surprisingly, the client often felt he was wasting his time; Quintilian talks of the *uanus salutandi labor* (12.11.18), 'the futile drudgery of paying one's respects'. Sometimes the patron would slip away to attend on someone else (Martial 2.18). At other times he would fail to give the desired support, because he was unwilling to antagonise the other party (Martial 2.32). Nevertheless, patrons continued to perform a whole range of necessary functions which, as Saller (1.14) says, are fulfilled in our time by banks, solicitors, insurance companies and hotels. And of course the most important patron by far, only briefly mentioned in Juvenal 7, was the emperor himself.

In most respects poets were like other clients; but they offered a special kind of service, in that they could enhance the prestige of their powerful

[6] The pamphlet is translated in Cicero's *Letters to his Friends*, vol.4 (Loeb) 750-91.

[7] See e.g., Columella 1, *praef.*10; Martial 12.26.15; Epictetus 4.10.20-1.

[8] The corrupting effect of 'influence' in the Roman legal system is well expounded by Kelly, 51-5.

[9] Cf. Pliny *Ep.* 2.9.5, 2.13, 3.2. Horace too eventually reached a position where he was asked to write important references. (See the poetic version of such a letter in *E.*1.9.) That is yet another indication of the difference between an establishment figure (albeit an odd one) and an outsider like Juvenal.

[10] See Seneca *Ep.*19.11, *Ben.* 6.33.4; Epictetus, *Enchir.* 33.13.

amici and even confer lasting fame. I say *amici* in the plural because, as White (1 and 3) has emphasised, a poet might obtain support from a number of different sources in a given year. What forms of support? First, a patron could obtain publicity for the poet by introducing him to his friends and by organising recitations (often in his own house). From time to time, he would present him with gifts, ranging from a cloak to an item of silver or occasionally even a piece of property. He might secure him a post which carried a salary but involved only light duties. And if necessary, he could provide accommodation. It may be asked whether the rewards also included money. In the emperor's case they sometimes did, and although the aristocracy would be careful to avoid the appearance of trying to rival the princeps, they probably provided remuneration too, on a smaller scale. So on this issue Saller (2), I believe, is right. But White (2) is right to stress that the evidence is sparse and elusive. In 4.76, Martial tells us that he asked for 12,000 sesterces (as a loan or a gift?) and got 6,000; in 6.30 he has received a loan of 6,000 after a delay of nearly nine months and has no intention of repaying it. In Martial's eyes, as Saller mildly puts it (2.253), gifts and loans 'were not firmly distinguished'. In 12.36, among other presents, gold coins are mentioned. Martial, as usual, says they are not enough – they will only last a couple of months. Yet they must be regarded as payment in some sense. Expectation, one might argue, is another kind of evidence. In 6.5 and again in 6.20 Martial asks for a loan of 100,000 sesterces; in 10.14 he asked for 5,000. Throughout 7, Juvenal complains about the lack of financial support, a line which would be incomprehensible if there was *no* recent tradition of payment.[11] It is true, of course, that most poets we know of were equites and therefore by no means destitute. But while assets amounting to 400,000 sesterces would support a knight in his home town, it is not clear that the same sum would also have enabled him to maintain an establishment in Rome. Also, in Juvenal's case, we do not know if he actually possessed that minimum amount. So there were several reasons for attending on the rich. The alternatives were few, and not necessarily inviting. 'Apart from judicial oratory and the equestrian service, very few professions had evolved in which an educated man of modest means might secure his independence and at the same time avoid the stigma of working for hire' (White 2.85).

These rewards, whatever form they took, were distinct from the *sportula* that was distributed to clients at the morning *salutatio*.[12] The meaning of *sportula* varied and was probably not uniform in any period.

[11] In 9, to secure his future, Naevolus desires a modest income of 20,000 sesterces. He cannot hope to obtain such a sum from any source other than a patron. Later, Lucian talks of a regular stipend; but he is not referring specifically to poets (*De Merc. Cond.* 19-20).

[12] In Martial 10.70.13-4 and Pliny *Ep.*2.14.4 the *sportula* is handed out in the late afternoon. Braund and Cloud (198) maintain that Juvenal has put the *sportula* in the morning as a deliberate paradox.

In different contexts it could mean a food-basket, a picnic, a sum of money, a reward, or a person who had been bribed. In Juvenal 1.118 and 10.46 it is clearly a sum of money, which we are told amounted to 25 asses (1.120f.). This was in theory a substitute for the dinner which the client formerly expected as a reward for his attentions. Dinner invitations continued to be issued, but at the meal itself it was not uncommon for the host to distinguish between higher and lower guests by serving different grades of food and wine. Pliny (*Ep.* 2.6) mentions a man of still finer discrimination who operated a tripartite system: one wine for himself and the VIPs, another for the *minores amici,* and a third for the freedmen. Pliny congratulates himself on avoiding such invidious distinctions. He just serves poor wine to everyone.

In Juvenal, the various aspects of *amicitia* are accommodated within his general framework of complaint. One of Umbricius' laments is that, since he is honest, no one wants his services. He is not qualified to act as an astrologer or a go-between, and he has no prospects in the civil service:

> *nulli comes exeo tamquam*
> *mancus et extinctae, corpus non utile, dextrae* (3.47-8)

> I never go out on a governor's staff; you'd imagine
> I was crippled, with a withered hand – a totally useless body.

If he were so disabled, of course, he would be unable to accept bribes. Again, as he cannot stoop to insincere flattery, he is outmanoeuvred by unscrupulous Greeks (86ff.) and eventually dismissed on the strength of a lie:

> *limine summoueor, perierunt tempora longi*
> *seruitii; nusquam minor est iactura clientis* (124-5)

> I'm driven from the door; my long years of servile attention
> have gone for nothing; in Rome nobody misses a client.

In 9 we meet another client who is deeply sorry for himself. His pay is insufficient, and his services are grossly undervalued. Speaking, in imagination, to his patron, who is supposed to be a wealthy landowner, he feels he might at least have been given a few acres:

> *meliusne hic rusticus infans*
> *cum matre et casulis et conlusore catello*
> *cymbala pulsantis legatus fiet amici?* (60-2)

> Take this child in the country
> with his mother and little cottage and playmate pup – is it better
> to leave them all in your will to a friend who bashes the cymbals?[13]

---

[13] A eunuch priest of Cybele.

The new device in 9 is first to forestall our sympathy by describing how Naevolus looks and what sort of creature he is (1-26), and then to have him refer repeatedly, and without any apparent revulsion, to the various ways in which he has demeaned himself. In 7 the tension is less extreme. But it is still ironic that we should be asked to feel indignant at the neglect of professions which the satirist cannot quite bring himself to admire.

The *salutatio* and the *cena*, ceremonies designed to express respect and goodwill, are treated by Juvenal as occasions of humiliation. When he wants to portray the great Hannibal at the nadir of his fortunes, he imagines him sitting as a client at the palace of an oriental despot (10.160-2). In Rome Virgil's proud race – the *gens togata* of *Aeneid* 1.282 – has become a *turba togata* intent on grabbing the *sportula* (*rapienda* in 1.96). The steward has to check carefully to prevent impersonation (97-8). Then comes a passage containing that peculiarly Juvenalian concentration of prejudice and wit. A freedman, who has arrived first, refuses to give way to a tribune. He defends his position, but is made to condemn himself: he was *natus ad Euphraten* (i.e. 'at the back of beyond'), he has *molles fenestrae* 'fancy apertures' in his ears (and is hence outlandish and effeminate), but he possesses half a dozen shops which provide an income of 400,000 sesterces.[14] So, says Juvenal, the sacrosanct magistrate (a venerable but now severely attenuated idea) must give way to someone who only a short while ago came to Rome with chalk on his feet (the degrading mark of an imported slave).

It is stressed that the queue includes members of the aristocracy. Their presence is not surprising if they are just attending the *salutatio*. But Juvenal goes further, insisting that they are also collecting the *sportula*. This allegation, which is never made by Martial, is (I think) largely, but not wholly, satirical fantasy. What keeps it in touch with reality is the fact that a few noble families, which had fallen on hard times, received financial assistance from the emperor (e.g. Tacitus, *Ann.* 13.34). Even then the picture of Messalla Corvinus as a shepherd in the fields (*custodit* in 1.107-8) is surely to be compared to a passage like 4.32-3 where Crispinus is said to have sold fish in the street. Finally, we have the ridiculous scene where the client tricks the steward into handing over an additional allowance for his wife. The dialogue is brilliantly economical. The client points to what is in fact an empty litter:

---

[14] Or does the sum represent the man's capital? If the man has only the minimum equestrian census it is hard to see why tribunes give way to him on account of his wealth (109-10). If the 400,000 is his income, then his assets would amount to about 6½ million – a substantial sum, though still paltry in comparison with Pallas' 300 million. To explain why the man is in the queue at all, one may imagine that he came to see the patron, not really to collect the *sportula*.

'*Galla mea est' inquit, 'citius dimitte. moraris?*
profer, Galla, caput.'

                              '*noli uexare, quiescet.'*

'That's my Galla,' he says. 'Don't keep her too long. Are you worried?
Galla, put out your head.'

                    'Leave her, she must be sleeping.'

We come now to the *cena*. Addressing someone called Maximus in
2.53, Martial begins: *uis liber fieri?* – 'Do you want to be free?' He
continues:

> *liber eris, cenare foris si, Maxime, nolis*

You *will* be free, provided you're willing to dine at home.

Juvenal takes over this idea to construct a moral and social framework
for 5. By dining out, Trebius has forfeited his dignity (1-11); Virro, the
host, refuses to treat his guests as fellow-citizens (112); if you can endure
such behaviour you don't deserve to be free (161-73). Such a framework
ensures that the dinner is seen within a general context of social
relations, a context which links 5 to other passages on *amicitia*. It would
be going too far to compare this social framework with the mythological
framework of 6 (which starts with the regime of Saturn) or the
geographical framework of 10 (which begins by ranging from Cadiz to the
Ganges). But it would be fair to think of the historical introduction
provided in 4.37-8:

> *cum iam semianimum laceraret Flauius orbem*
> *ultimus et caluo seruiret Roma Neroni*

In the days when the last of the Flavian line was tearing to pieces
a half-dead world and Rome was slave to a bald-headed Nero.

That leads up to the trivial episode of the giant turbot (*nugis* in v.150).
Horace's *nugae* have no such setting. They are things that are talked
about in a barber's shop (1.7) or incidents that have taken place in the
street (1.9). His dinner-party is just an account of an evening's
entertainment gone wrong. We may, if we wish, provide a social
background and add moral reflections, but Horace does not invite us to
do so.

As for the dinner itself, Martial occasionally complains about not
receiving the same food and drink as his host (e.g. 3.60, 6.11). Juvenal
has expanded this idea so as to encompass an entire *cena*, including
drink and glasses, service, bread, fish, entrées, and dessert.[15] At every
stage Virro's meal is contrasted with what is served to the client; and the

---

[15] For detailed studies of the fifth satire see Adamietz, ch.3 and Morford (2).

grotesque polarities entailed give full scope to Juvenal's wit. The resources of the high, romantic style are employed to describe Virro's delicacies. One resource is geography – we hear of Getic frosts (50), Corsican mullet (92), Sicilian lamprey (100), and Libyan truffles (119). Another is myth – the daughters of Helios (i.e. amber) in v.38, the wine-waiter Ganymede (59), apples from the Hesperides (152). Another is epic – the jewels in Aeneas' scabbard (43-5), Meleager's boar (115), Phaeacian apples (151). Another, used satirically, is history – a vintage with traditions of *libertas* (36-7), Claudius' mushroom (147).[16] Such luxuries are contrasted with woefully common items, such as cracked cups (46-8), hard mouldy bread (67-9), and smelly oil (86-91). The last object mentioned is a rotten apple:

> *tu scabie frueris mali, quod in aggere rodit*
> *qui tegitur parma et galea metuensque flagelli*
> *discit ab hirsuta iaculum torquere capella* (153-5)

> You get a rotten apple, the sort that's gnawed on the rampart
> by a creature armed with a shield and helmet, who under the whip
> learns to propel a spear from the back of a shaggy goat.

Only in the last line does it become clear that the *qui* is an animal, a delay which strengthens the symbolic association of monkey and client.

While there is a direct line of descent from Gallonius, through Nasidienus, to Petronius' Trimalchio, Juvenal's Virro stands apart. The point can be made most briefly by contrasting him with Nasidienus. Both aim to enhance their prestige, but whereas Nasidienus attempts to do so by inviting important guests whom he tries to please and impress, Virro does so by humiliating men like Trebius in front of his friends (*Virronibus* in v.149). At Nasidienus' party lesser guests, like Vibidius and Balatro, are given the same food and drink, and they talk quite freely, in fact sarcastically, to the host; at Virro's they are too cowed to speak. If they do, they are flung out of the house (125-6). Though comically described by an allusion to Virgil's Cacus (*Aen.*8. 264-5), that is an act of deliberate arrogance. In Horace the violence, as represented by the collapse of the awning, is a piece of unintentional farce. Again, we hear something of what Nasidienus has to say. At the very centre of the poem, he launches into a boastful disquisition on the various courses served, revealing an obsession similar to that of Catius in 2.4. It is not exactly conversation – more a performance; but at least it is put on for the benefit of the company. In Juvenal, there is no communication at all. Virro says nothing, and the thoughts of his clients necessarily remain unexpressed. Finally, whereas Fundanius' narrative in Horace 2.8 brings before us a specific, if largely fictitious, occasion, where the guests are

---

[16] The mushroom was suggested by Martial 1.20.4.

named and given individual places at the table, Juvenal is describing the
sort of dinner-party that Virro gives. In other words, this dreadful
travesty of a social evening is continually re-enacted. What a thought.

The fifth satire, which ends ironically with the word *amico*, is a
powerful indictment of *amicitia* as Juvenal sees it. It can therefore be
related to several other satires, especially in Book 1. This theme has been
fully explored by LaFleur (2), and his paper is usefully complemented by
Seager, who documents numerous cases of hypocrisy and disloyalty from
Tacitus and Juvenal. Here is another passage which deserves
consideration, also cited by Seager:

> Ambition induced many men to become false, to hold one thing locked in
> their hearts and another ready on the tongue, to assess friendships and
> enmities not objectively but on the basis of self-interest, and to be
> well-disposed in their facial expression rather than in their feelings. At first
> these abuses developed slowly and were occasionally punished. Later, when
> the infection had spread like a plague, the country altered, and a
> government that was once exceptionally just and good became intolerably
> cruel.

Those words offer an excellent commentary, do they not, on Juvenal's
satire. Yet they were written by Sallust, probably before 40 B.C. (*Cat.*
10.5-6). And they sound very plausible; for the last century of the
republic, with its recurrent internecine strife, can hardly have promoted
fides, or reciprocal trust. Leaving aside the question of a possible revival
under Augustus, are we then to believe that there was no significant
difference between Sallust's time and Juvenal's? That may be going too
far. For all I know, *amicitia may* have sunk to new levels in the period
from A.D. 60 to 130. Everyone says so. But I have never seen any attempt
to prove it, and I fancy it would not be easy. One would have to find
appropriate evidence in both periods; but before that, one would have to
decide what kind of evidence *was* appropriate; and before *that*, one
would have to formulate the problem in precise and meaningful terms.
One factor, presumably, would be the increasingly frigid and impersonal
relations between patron and client. Disregarding the variations which
must have existed between patrons, one might want to relate this factor
to client numbers. But how many clients, one wonders, would have been
manageable? We are told that Scipio had 500 *amici* on his staff at
Numantia (Appian, *Iber.* 84). And they would not have included
freedmen. Since Scipio was not unique, that pushes the problem back to
a hundred years before Sallust. I am not suggesting that every complaint
about social and moral decline is merely a rhetorical topos. Clearly there
must have been changes. But, as in the case of luxury, the most radical
changes probably took place in the lifetime of Lucilius. Earlier, no doubt,
things were simpler. But before we form too rosy a picture of the system
as it functioned in the third and fourth centuries, we should perhaps

recall that in the fifth century one of the Twelve Tables laid it down that 'if a patron perpetrates fraud upon a client, he shall be accursed (*sacer esto*)' (*ROL* 3, Table 8.21). The need for such a law seems to suggest that even then the institution was far from perfect.

CHAPTER FIVE

Greek and the Greeks

(i) Lucilius

Disregarding earlier Greek influences, which came through Etruria, and more directly from colonies like Cumae, Paestum, and Croton, we shall take as our starting point the Roman victory over Tarentum in 272 B.C. This brought to the public a new awareness of Greek culture; Florus (1.18.27) speaks of the 'statues, pictures, and Tarentine luxuries' which were displayed in the ensuing triumph.[1] Awareness grew to familiarity during the long years of the first Punic war (264-241 B.C.), when thousands of Roman troops in Sicily came to know the temples and theatres of cities like Syracuse and Agrigentum. A year after the war ended, Livius Andronicus, a Tarentine freedman who had been teaching Greek in Rome, produced his first adaptation of a Greek play; he also introduced Homer to the public by his translation of the *Odyssey*. The same kind of career was followed with greater distinction by Quintus Ennius. Born at Rudiae in Calabria in 239 B.C., he served in the Roman army in Sardinia and impressed M. Porcius Cato, who brought him back to the capital to teach Greek. Although on the strength of the *Annals* Ennius was regarded as the father of Roman poetry,[2] a great deal of his time was spent in making Greek works available in Latin. These included not only tragedies and comedies but also compositions like 'Gracious Living' (a late fourth-century gastronomic poem by the Sicilian Archestratus) and 'The Sacred Writing' (a work of about 300 B.C. by Euhemerus maintaining that gods were deified men).

During the Hannibalic war, when Ennius was in his twenties, Syracuse was looted by Marcellus and his army; and before he died, in 169, Rome had been drawn into a series of conflicts in the east. Her armies won decisive engagements against Philip of Macedon (197) and Antiochus of Syria (190); they defeated Perseus at Pydna (168), and eventually occupied Corinth (146). Following these victories all kinds of plunder, including countless works of art, were shipped to Rome. Hundreds of Greeks (many of them prisoners of war) were employed as teachers in Roman houses; hundreds more set up as doctors, masons, and artists; and at the highest level men like Polybius and Panaetius lectured to

---

[1] Rome's acquisition of works of art is documented by Pollitt, 22-58.

[2] For *pater Ennius* see Horace, *E*.1.19.7. Even the *Annals* would not have been possible had not the soul of Homer entered the poet (*ROL*, 1, *Ann.* 5-13).

upper-class audiences. Travelling in the other direction, senators passed through Greece on various kinds of official business, and some of them, like Q. Metellus Numidicus and L. Licinius Crassus, listened to philosophers' lectures. Occasionally younger members of the aristocracy would stay longer. An early example was Titus Albucius, an Epicurean who played down his Sabine origins and in 121 or 120 lived in Athens as 'almost a Greek'.[3] He appears in the altercation with Scaevola in Lucilius Book 2.

During the same period other kinds of influence, no less important, were making themselves felt. A profitable trade in furniture, jewelry, silk, and wine was bringing elegance to Roman life. According to Livy, 'female flute-players and harpists and other types of festive entertainment became a feature of banquets; and from now on greater care and expense were bestowed on the banquets themselves. The cook, who in earlier times was regarded and treated as the cheapest kind of slave, began to be valued more highly, and what had once been a menial occupation came to be viewed as an art' (39.6.7-9). As the symposium and the gymnasium took root in the city, it became clear that in these areas too 'conquered Greece had taken her rough conqueror captive'.[4]

These were the conditions in which Scipio Aemilianus grew up. As a boy he received an exceptional education. Not only was he friendly with Greek artists and intellectuals (Plutarch, *Aem. Paul.* 6.5), he also had the use of King Perseus' library, which his father had brought back from Greece (Plutarch, *Aem.Paul.* 28.6). After 168 he was on close terms with Polybius, from whom he would have learned about history and politics.[5] Another of his foreign friends was the African Terence, whom he encouraged from 166 on to write plays adapted from Greek New Comedy.[6] Later, probably after his consulship in 147, he came to know the philosopher Panaetius of Rhodes, whom he took with him on an embassy to the east in 140-139.[7] Of Scipio's Roman friends the closest was the slightly older Gaius Laelius, who shared his cultural interests, being a friend of Terence and an admirer of the Stoics Diogenes and Panaetius.[8] Though less impressive as a general and politician, Laelius was at least as knowledgeable as Scipio about Greek ideas, and because of his scholarly mind and sound judgment he acquired the nickname of

[3] Cicero, *De Fin.*1.8-9, *Brut.* 131. On Romans studying abroad see Daly; for Rome's relations with Greek philosophers at this time see Jocelyn (4).
[4] Horace, *E.*2.1.156. Livy dates the beginning of decline from the return of Manlius Vulso's army from Asia in 187 B.C. For Polybius the significant date was 168 (Pydna). Piso the annalist chose 154. But after Sallust the turning point was usually put at 146. See Earl, ch.4. Later 'the development of luxury' became a rhetorical topos; but between 180 and 100 B.C. very marked changes did take place.
[5] Polybius 31.23; Diodorus 31.26.5. See Astin (1), index under Polybius.
[6] Suetonius, *Life of Terence* 1; cf. Quintilian 10.1.99.
[7] Cicero, *Acad.*2.2.5; Plutarch, *Mor.*200f. 777a; Athenaeus 12.549d.
[8] Suetonius, *Life of Terence* 1; Cicero, *Att.*7.3.10, *De Fin.*2.24, *De Orat.*2.155.

sapiens. Another member of the group was L. Furius Philus (consul 136) who, like Scipio and Laelius, had seen service in Spain. Furius, too, was a friend of Terence, a student of Greek philosophy, and an accomplished speaker.[9] According to Cicero (*De Orat*.2.154), these three men 'at all times and in public kept company with the most learned men of Greece'. Rather younger than these was P. Rutilius Rufus, who was military tribune under Scipio in Spain and eventually became consul in 105. In *De Rep*.1.17 Cicero pictures him at Numantia, talking with Scipio about the sun, a subject which he would have heard discussed by Panaetius (*De Rep*.1.15). Rutilius' interest in Greek literature, as distinct from philosophy, is also attested by Cicero (*Brut*.114); we know he wrote a historical work in Greek;[10] and after his unjust condemnation in 92 B.C. he retired to Smyrna (Cicero, *Balb*. 28).

Philhellenism, then, though certainly not the prerogative of Scipio's circle, was an important element in it and one which must be borne in mind in any study of Lucilius' work, for all its Roman originality. As well as being on close terms with the aristocrats mentioned above, Lucilius presumably knew Polybius and Panaetius, and probably Carneades. He certainly knew Clitomachus, who became head of the Academy in 127/6. We are not told where they met. (Athens is somewhat more likely than Rome.)[11] Nor do we know how long they were acquainted. But Clitomachus must have found the satirist capable of handling Greek ideas, for he sent him one of his books, which contained a discussion of probability (Cicero, *Acad*.2.102-3).

If Lucilius went to Athens, that may explain the mention of the Greek 'cadets' – *pareutactoe* – in 349 and 816, and the reference to Apelles' masterpiece – ἐπίτευγμα – in 954-5. There is also a glimpse of Rhodes 'sloping into the Carpathian sea' (498), but, as so often, we cannot be sure that this is a first-hand report. We have already noted the likelihood that Lucilius had estates in *Magna Graecia*. In visiting such places he would have spoken to his workmen in Greek. We hear of one such man, called Symmachus, in the journey-poem in Book 3. Other people with Greek names are the slaves Zopyrion (something of a bruiser to judge from 362-3 and 626), Metrophanes (affectionately commemorated in 624-5), and the agent Aristocrates (516-7). Some boys and girls will be mentioned in Chapter Six.[12]

[9] Cicero, *Rep*.3.5, *Brut*.108.

[10] Appian, *Iber*.88; Athenaeus 4.168e.

[11] In one of his writings Clitomachus repeated a verbal exchange that took place 'when Carneades and Diogenes the Stoic were appearing before the senate on the Capitol' (Cicero, *Acad*.2.137). That was in 155 B.C. But Clitomachus himself was not a member of that embassy. He probably heard of the incident from Carneades, of whom he saw quite a lot (Cicero, *Acad*.2.98).

[12] There is a general likelihood that Greek names signified Greek origin, but one cannot be sure in individual cases. Some non-Greek slaves were given Greek names because the slave-trade was run by Greeks. For debate see Gordon and Thylander, 178-85.

In discussing Lucilius' Greek vocabulary we may distinguish two categories.[13] The first is reserved for words which carry some special emphasis or nuance. The effect may be abusive, sarcastic, or humorous; or the word may merely be enclosed, as it were, between inverted commas. The second, which has been relegated to an appendix, includes words whose function appears to be neutral or else cannot be inferred from the context. Together the two lists testify to the immense variety of Lucilius' interests. Greek made its impact on every occupation from the humblest to the most refined. Nor did the range of occupations always correspond to modern notions of class. A Greek slave might be a teacher or a secretary; a freedman might be a doctor or a civil-servant. It need hardly be added that Greek influence went far beyond the purely linguistic usages which we shall be discussing. Lucilius presents a large amount of material in Latin form derived from Greek literature, philosophy, and social life. Sometimes the origin of an expression is acknowledged, as in *metuo ut fieri possit; ergo antiquo ab Arciloco excido* (786), 'I'm afraid it cannot happen, *pace* old Archilochus'. This alludes to the passage of Archilochus beginning χρημάτων ἄελπτον οὐδέν ἐστιν – i.e. anything *can* happen.[14] But far more often the subject-matter has been absorbed and turned into something Graeco-Roman. One thinks, for example, of the fable of the fox and the lion (1111-20), or the boisterous scene involving the storming of a house (793ff.), or the famous lines about *uirtus* (1196ff.).

Category A

We start from *androgyni* 'male-women' and *moechocinaedi* 'adulterer-sodomites' (1048), *blennus* 'blockhead' (1034), *malta* 'pansy' (744), and *mastigias* 'villain' (652). Whatever their context, such words were intrinsically rude. Somewhat milder were the nicknames *Pararhenchon* 'Snoring-partner' (after 251) and *Agelastus* 'Mirthless' (p.422). Often a noun which is not abusive in itself becomes so when used of people e.g. *cercopithecus*, 'long-tailed monkey' (1214); *cobium* and *thynnus*, 'goby' and 'tunny' of poor and rich fornicators (937); *rinoceros* (110), of a man with a protruding lower tooth; and *scorpios* (1079), of a malicious commentator. Slightly less unkind is ἀρθριτικὸς *ac podagrosus* (354), 'rheumatic and gouty' of a human wreck; *icterus morbus* (37), 'jaundice' describing a man's face; and *monogrammus* (56; cf.746), 'a sketch' of someone without colour, who is barely alive. Less often the prejudice is directed at a person's occupation: e.g., *sacer iste tocoglyphos*, 'that damned usurer' (540); so too we hear of the wily *propola*, 'fruit-vendor' (221f.), who sells early figs at an enormous price; and of *parasiti* (762) who are only interested in a person's money. Other phrases connected

---

[13] For a fuller treatment see Mariotti, 50-81.
[14] West, no.122, vol.1.

with comedy or working-class life include the army saying *scinde calam ut caleas* (981) 'Cut some wood to heat your blood', and an expression used by a man who is suspicious of people who hope 'to diddle him out of whatever haul he makes': *quouis posse me emungi bolo* (903).

In such cases it is sometimes hard to tell when Lucilius is being inventive and when he is drawing on a common fund of colloquial language. Take the following expressions: 'You filthy swine', 'You brilliantined stick-insect', 'You lousy bastard', 'You rancorous coiffured sow'. A native speaker knows that the first and third are conventional and the other two not; he may even remember that the second and fourth were created by John Cleese and Connie Booth in the TV programme 'Fawlty Towers'. But a foreigner might find it hard to see any difference. That is often our own position *vis-à-vis* Lucilius. And the problem is not limited to expressions of abuse. At one point Lucilius recommends engaging a *pistricem ualidam ... empleuron* (1055f.) 'a strong, broad-flanked bakeress'. The Greek word *empleuros* is not recorded in any other Latin writer. Is this just chance, or are we dealing with a novel locution? There are also some salacious and rather puzzling fragments about sex:

> *cum poclo bibo eodem, amplector, labra labellis*
> *fictricis compono, hoc est cum* ψωλοκοποῦμαι (331-2)

when I drink from the same cup and embrace the clever pretender, pressing her lips to mine, that is, when I'm racked with tension,

> *et cruribus crura diallaxon* (334)

and on the point of twining legs with legs

> *Hymnis sine eugio ac destina* (896)

(The line is corrupt, but Nonius, the fourth-century grammarian who preserves it, says that *eugium* is the middle part of the female genitalia.) In the second of these fragments *diallaxôn*, which should perhaps be written in Greek letters, sounds literary.[15] The Greek word ψωλοκοποῦμαι occurs again in a papyrus, where it is used in the active voice to express a vulgar imprecation: 'I cause (or want) the reader's organ to burst.'[16] Though not recorded in Greek, *eugium* is apparently connected with εὔγειος = fertile. It occurs only here and in two passages of the sketch-writer Laberius. As Adams infers (83), the word probably belongs to prostitutes' slang.[17]

---

[15] There is no other instance of διαλλάσσω in this sense, but πούς ἐπαλλαχθεὶς ποδί (Euripides, *Heracleid*.836) is not so very different.

[16] See Crönert 470-1, who compares a gloss of Hesychius: ὠτοκοπεῖ 'vexes the ears'.

[17] To these cases has to be added 1182: *haec inbubinat at contra te inbulbitat ille*, 'She bloodies you, but the youngster on the other hand muddies you'. This is Lucilius at his most disgusting. He has coined two compounds based on *bubinare* and βόλβιτον (properly

Several other Greek expressions can be grouped together, not because they are related to any one subject, but because they reflect the working of a learned and sophisticated mind. Fragments 675 and 674 seem to answer someone who had complained of Lucilius' critical rigour:

> *siquod uerbum inusitatum aut zetematium offenderam.*
> *quidni? et tu idem inlitteratum me atque idiotam diceres.*

The poet appears to be saying: 'I criticised you if I came across an unusual word or problematical construction. Why not? You'd have called me a mere uneducated amateur if I had made the same mistakes.' This is Lucilius in his role as the Roman Fowler. He was also interested in local history, as he showed in his travel-poem when referring to the inhabitants of Puteoli (originally a Greek colony) as *Dicarchitae* and calling the port 'a lesser Delos' (118). As we might expect, he alluded easily and amusingly to Greek philosophy. In 805-11, for instance, he speaks of Lupus the judge as sentencing a man to exile or death, describing the operation in terms of the four elements (ἀρχαί or *stoechia*); thus exile involves the loss of fire and water, death the loss of earth and air – body being earth (γῆ) and soul air (πνεῦμα).[18] In another place we hear of a man who, in view of the times, has apparently abandoned more lofty ideals and is taking Utility to live with him: *Chresin ad me recipio* (778).[19]

The figures of Greek religion and myth were an inexhaustible source. They could be used as satirical material in their own right, as when Hyacinthus is referred to as 'the Lord-of-the-tripod's [i.e. Apollo's] darling' (311-12). Or the appropriate mythological name could be applied to contemporary figures. Thus a man far gone in decrepitude is a Tiresias (229), and at a dreadful dinner-party

> *Tisiphone Tityi e pulmonibus atque adipe unguen*
> *excoctum attulit, Eumenidum sanctissima Erinys* (162-3)

Tisiphone, holiest Fury of all the Eumenides, brought us
oil obtained by rendering Tityos' fat and lungs.

---

cowdung). One wonders how many readers would have thought the word-play worth while. Lastly there is 1180, transmitted as *pudicis, Hortensi, est ad eam rem nata palaestra*. The first word is unmetrical and therefore wrong. If the restoration *podicis* (anus) is right, this, too, is obscene. *palaestra* 'wrestling-place' or 'wrestling' had become naturalised by Lucilius' time. Here it perhaps means 'adroitness', as it does later in Cicero. So the sense would be 'the adroitness of the anus, Hortensius, is suited to that purpose'

[18] For the punctuation of this fragment see Shackleton Bailey (1) 118. Another example of Greek used for stylishness is 869: *tum illud ἐπιφωνεῖ quod etiamnum nobile est*, 'Then he uttered that dictum which is still famous today'.

[19] *Chresin* is Lachmann's conjecture.

Lucilius' familiarity with Homer is sometimes conveyed in a single word, as when he calls the rather moderate hills at Sezze αἰγίλιπες *montes* (104-5) 'goatforsaken mountains' (cf.*Il.* 9.15). Or the allusion may fill a line, as in 491f., where Lucilius says it is better to be valued by the discerning few than to reign over all who are dead and gone; ἢ πᾶσιν νεκύεσσι καταφθιμένοισιν ἀνάσσειν – Achilles' words in Hades (*Od.*11.491).

This kind of intellectual play, which signalled the poet's membership of an educated elite, often took the form of parody, in which Homer was used as an instrument of satire. Thus Apollo is made to say that in beauty he does not wish to rival Leda, Thestius' daughter, and (Dia) the wife of Ixion: *Thestiados Ledae atque Ixionies alochoeo* (29). Or again, Homer may be both the instrument and in part the victim of satire. In 520-3 Lucilius says that people recognise Homer's monsters for what they are – creatures of the imagination, e.g. the two-hundred-foot Cyclops with his walking-stick the height of a ship's mast; yet they stupidly believe that gods actually reside in sculptors' figures (524-9, quoted on p. 6 above). Another instance is 567-73, where the reader is warned not to idealise the female beauties of the past:

> *Num censes calliplocamon callisphyron ullam*
> *non licitum esse uterum atque etiam inguina tangere mammis,*
> *conpernem aut uaram fuisse Amphitryonis acoetin*
> *Alcmenam atque alias, Helenam ipsam denique – nolo*
> *dicere; tute uide atque disyllabon elige quoduis –*
> κούρην *eupatereiam, aliquam rem insignem habuisse,*
> *uerrucam naeuum punctum dentem eminulum unum?*

Any woman with 'beautiful tresses' and 'beautiful ankles'
could have had breasts touching her womb and even her crotch;
Alcmena 'Amphitryon's spouse' could have been knock-kneed or bandy,
others too, perhaps Helen herself, that (better not say it,
decide for yourself and choose whatever disyllable's proper)
that 'daughter of noble sire' could have had some obvious blemish –
wart, pock-mark, or mole, or slightly prominent tooth.

The point is sharpened by using Greek for the ladies' perfections and Latin for their defects.

We turn now to a group of fragments about food and drink. The function of the Greek here is to suggest something exotic and delectable: *gigeria insunt / siue adeo hepatia* (337-8) 'There are giblets in it / or indeed *foies gras*'; ὠμοτριβὲς *oleum Casinas* (987), 'oil of Casinum pressed from immature olives'; *defusum e pleno* χρυσίζον ... *uinum* (1226) '*vin d'or*, poured from a full cask'; Χῖός τε δυνάστης (596) 'The Lord of Chios' [i.e. wine]. Given the nature of the genre, such references are likely to have been in some way critical. But is the speaker some solemn gastronome like Horace's Catius (2.4), or a guest describing a menu like Fundanius (2.8)? Or is Lucilius writing *in propria persona*? Again, is the satirist condemning such luxuries on principle, from the standpoint of an austere conservative? Occasionally his speakers seem to have taken that line, but Lucilius himself seems rather to have objected to the *abuse* of such commodities – the immoderate quantity, the expense, the vulgar display, the obsessive concern. It is hard to imagine him preaching against pleasure in itself.

Before concluding this section we must note one last group of fragments – those which indicate that in Lucilius' view the use of Greek could be inappropriate or excessive. In 186ff. Lucilius remonstrates with a friend for not coming to visit him when he was sick. After a few lines he says

> *ut periisse uelis, quem uisere nolueris cum*
> *debueris. Hoc 'nolueris' et 'debueris' te*
> *si minus delectat, quod atechnon et Eisocration*
> *lerodesque simul totum ac sit meiraciodes,*
> *non operam perdo, si tu hic.*

> [for I don't believe you're so ill-disposed]
> as to wish a person dead whom you would not come to visit
> when you should. If that 'would' and 'should' are not quite to your liking,
> because the effect is artistically flat and Isocratean,
> yes and entirely silly and puerile into the bargain,
> I shan't waste time if you're that sort.[20]

Lucilius' point seems to be that such formal criteria, derived from Greek stylistic theory, should not be used to assess a spontaneous letter from a friend.[21] Again, in 14 and 15f. we hear of people who pretentiously (*semnôs*) called water-pots *arutaenae* ('pots à eau') instead of *aquales*, the legs of a couch *clinopodes* ('pieds de lit') instead of *pedes lecti*, and lamps *lychni* ('chandeliers') instead of *lucernae*. One contemporary who overdid the use of Greek was Titus Albucius, the Epicurean mentioned earlier. He even preferred to be addressed as a Greek, at least when in Athens. And so when Scaevola met him in 121 B.C. he said: 'When you approach me, I as praetor greet you in Athens in Greek, as you have preferred. "*Chaere* (Bonjour) *Tite!*" I say.' Thereupon all Scaevola's retinue chimed in with '*Chaere, Tite!*', much to Albucius' annoyance (87-93).[22]

[20] For puerility see Longinus 3.4. The fault is attributed to Isocrates more than once by Dionysius. See his essay on Isocrates, sections 12 and 13, and that on Demosthenes, section 4 (cf.20, 21, 25).

[21] Cf. Demetrius, 225 and 231.

[22] I have translated Manutius' *cohors* for the *chorus* of the transmission. The instances of *chorus* in *OLD* 5a are either female or derogatory. Also Scaevola would hardly have used a Greek derivative in such a context. In 84-5 Scaevola mocks Albucius for his smooth style: his words are fitted together like the little cubes of a mosaic. The use of *lexis* for 'words' and *emblemate* for 'mosaic' suggests that here, too, there is a gibe at Albucius' passion for Greek. Cf. the ironical *rhetoricoterus* 86.

So there were limits to the acceptability of Greek. When technical criteria were misapplied, when ordinary objects were given fancy names, and when every other sentence was decorated with a hellenic flourish, then it was time to call a halt. Other aspects of Greek culture also posed problems. Singing and dancing were pleasant as entertainment, but no gentleman would have dreamed of performing – that was for slaves, freedmen, and the demi-monde; yet some people seemed intent on ignoring this distinction (33). Greek exercises were all very well (though not a patch on Roman military training), but gymnasiums did tend to attract homosexuals. Too often a symposium was an excuse for gluttony and drunkenness. And while the skills of rhetoric were admirable when used judiciously by a *uir bonus dicendi peritus*, what if the orator were an unscrupulous rogue?

Cato the Censor, who respected the Greeks of the past and was quite well versed in Greek literature, was convinced that modern Greek influence was wholly pernicious. The Greek race was 'utterly depraved and undisciplined' (*nequissimum et indocile*) and they should be expelled from Italy, the whole lot of them.[23] That degree of hostility was extreme. Most educated people no doubt had mixed feelings, valuing the skills of the Greeks and the culture which they represented, admiring and liking certain individuals, and yet distrusting them *en masse* as corrupt and unreliable.[24] Although he probably shared some of these misgivings, Lucilius seems to have taken a relatively favourable view: if the Romans became debauched by Greek habits and institutions instead of using them to enhance the quality of life, that was largely their own fault, and they deserved what they got. At any rate in the passages that survive there is no condemnation of the Greeks as a people. Where an individual is concerned, he is satirised as a rogue, not as a Greek.[25] On the positive side Lucilius had absorbed much of what was best in Greek literature; he knew and respected several exponents of Greek learning; and he used Greek spontaneously and effectively in many different ways. It is also worth recalling that the inventor of the only Roman genre ended his days in Naples, which in Nero's time and later was still regarded as a *Graeca urbs*.[26]

(ii) Horace

In the last century of the republic certain ways of thinking about literature developed. First, many Romans felt that, as they had conquered the world, their literature ought to be at least equal to

[23] Pliny the Elder, *NH* 29.14 and 7.113. For Cato's opinion of the Greeks see Astin (2) ch.8.
[24] This very large topic is studied by Balsdon and Petrochilos.
[25] E.g. the two pirates Rhondes and Icadion (197).
[26] Tacitus, *Ann*.15.33; see Hardie, index under Naples.

anything created in the past. The standards had been set by Greece, and so pride demanded that Roman writers should be brought into comparison with their Greek counterparts. In oratory Cato might be compared to Lysias (Cicero, *Brut.*63), Calvus was known to emulate the 'Attic' orators (Cicero, *Brut.*284), and Cicero himself could vie with Demosthenes (Cicero, *Brut.*253ff.). In the field of comedy Afranius had to face Menander (Horace, *E.*2.1.57), in epic Ennius was 'a second Homer' (Horace, *E.*2.1.50). However the Romans fared in these confrontations, the method gave them the assurance that Latin literature had achieved a separate and significant status. Hence such criticism was, at bottom, patriotic.

There was, however, one important group to which this patriotic method could not be applied, namely Catullus, Calvus, and the other writers of epyllia. These neoterics, or 'moderns', not only based their work on Greek models, they also stuck to Greek legends and characters, retained Greek settings, and did not hesitate to use names, words, and metrical effects with Greek associations. Examples are readily available in Catullus 64, e.g. vv.3, 30, 49, and 252. The result, though highly accomplished Latin poetry, was only in a rather loose sense Roman. No doubt the writers would have maintained that if being Roman meant churning out clumsy, pompous, and chauvinistic stuff in the style of Hostius and Volusius, then it was better to be something else.[1]

When Horace came to write satire, he knew that although Varro had linked Lucilius with Old Comedy, the genre was really a Roman creation (1.10.48, 2.1.63), and this seemed to carry linguistic consequences. Now it has often been remarked that in Lucilius' lines on *uirtus* (1196-1208) the diction is wholly Latin. This may mean that Lucilius tended to exclude Greek from his more formal and serious compositions. A similar habit is observable in Cicero. Hellenisms abound in his letters, but appear more rarely in his speeches. (An example is the attack on Clodius in *De Har. Resp.*44.) Even within his correspondence Greek words are much more common in the letters addressed to Atticus than in the more formal pieces addressed to figures like Lentulus, Sulpicius, and Appius Pulcher. In Horace's time Greek continued to be used in conversation and personal correspondence. Even someone like Augustus, who was not entirely fluent, would use Greek expressions for liveliness and wit (Malcovati, 2.6-28). No doubt Horace did the same, but where satire was concerned he took a different line, maintaining that, while akin to conversation, it was nevertheless a literary genre, and a Roman genre at that; it should therefore be written in Latin. He also seems to have felt that, as satire aimed to promote moral awareness, it was a kind of persuasion and was therefore related to oratory. Both points are made in 1.10. When Pedius and Messalla sweat to win their cases in court, they

---

[1] For Hostius see Morel, 33-4; for Volusius see Catullus 36 with Fordyce's note.

speak Latin and nothing else (28-9). That is the argument based on oratory.[2] If you had to speak in court would you forget about your fatherland and father Latinus and behave like a man from Canusium who was only half Italian (25-30)? That is the patriotic argument.

Satire 1.10, however, had another dimension, in that Horace's critics were not just admirers of Lucilius but were also in some way heirs of the neoteric tradition. The eight lines prefixed to the poem (which though probably spurious may be held to contain genuine information) tell us that one of these was Valerius Cato, who not only edited Lucilius but also wrote poems entitled *Lydia* and *Dictynna*.[3] The pretty Hermogenes and his ape-like friend are said to be capable only of crooning Calvus and Catullus (19). Another opponent with a Greek name (possibly the above-mentioned ape) was Demetrius (79). When these critics advocated mixing Latin with Greek, they did so, not on Lucilian grounds ('the mixture reflects spontaneous conversation'), but on neoteric grounds ('the mixture is more pleasant, like a blend of Falernian and Chian wine'). Since Lucilius did not use Greek for aesthetic or sentimental effects, the critics seem to have confused two different procedures.[4] Or was Horace presenting their position in a way which would make it easier to subvert? At any rate, one notes that in his reply Horace cleverly uses some neoteric devices against his opponents. First, like Callimachus, he compares rough verse to a muddy river (50-1; cf. *Hymn to Apollo* 108-9). Then, again like Callimachus (*Aetia* 1.1.21ff.), he describes how a divinity had intervened with poetic advice (31ff.). But whereas Callimachus had been advised by Apollo to keep his Muse slender, Horace was dissuaded by Quirinus (i.e. the deified Romulus, representing the citizenry of Rome) from writing in Greek – there was enough Greek literature already. Thus Callimachus' vision is made to serve the ends of a classical Roman purist. There is perhaps another point too. When the critic praises Lucilius for mixing Greek and Latin, Horace exclaims *o seri studiorum* (21)! That is a straight translation of the Greek ὀψιμαθεῖς (late-learners) and so illustrates the very procedure which he is advocating. Since the word was applied to people who had just acquired a skill long possessed by others and were eager to display it whenever possible, the implication was 'How very out of date!' An unkind cut, for there is nothing more out of date than yesterday's moderns.

After reading 1.10 one might imagine that the *sermones* were wholly free of Greek derivatives. This would be a mistake. A quick glance at

[2] Cf. Dionysius, *Isocrates* 12: rhetorical fripperies are useless to a statesman speaking about peace and war, and to a citizen defending himself on a capital charge.

[3] On Valerius Cato see Robinson, 98-116. His name has recently turned up in the Gallus fragment.

[4] There must have been some overlap. Cinna's fragments contain two Lucilian hellenisms: *anquina* (halyard) and *carchesia* (masthead); see Morel, 87-8.

Lane Cooper's concordance reveals at least 125 cases, not counting proper names. About 100 of these, however, are already used by Cicero, Lucretius, and Varro. Some go back much further. So the great majority of Horace's hellenisms had become naturalised and were no longer felt to be foreign. The same could apply to most of the remainder, but before reaching an opinion on that, we must consider *AP* 47-72, where Horace is discussing ways in which a poet can revitalise his language. First, he can revive old words no longer current (70; cf. *E.*2.2.115-8); secondly, he can use existing words in new combinations (47-8); thirdly he can bring in new words (48-59; cf. *E.*2.2.119). How could new words be brought in? Three possibilities were available: (a) to create a new word from a Latin root, (b) to use an existing word in a new sense, as the equivalent of a Greek term, (c) to import a Greek word into Latin. There has been some dispute about which of these methods Horace had in mind when writing 48-55:

> If novel terms are demanded
> to introduce obscure material, then you will have the
> chance to invent words which the apron-wearing Cethegi
> never heard; such a right will be given, if it's not abused.
> New and freshly created words are also acceptable
> when channelled from Greek, provided the trickle is small. For why
> should Romans refuse to Virgil and Varius what they've conceded
> to Caecilius and Plautus?

In vv.48-51 method (a) must be included, for it would be contrary to Horace's own practice to ban all new words except those based on, or derived from, Greek. Bo (1.391-5) lists about 150 such coinages, of which over 50 occur only once. One example is *cinctutis* 'apron-wearing' (50), which was surely manufactured to illustrate Horace's point. Similar arguments make it likely that method (b) is included in 52-3. Several examples of this procedure are mentioned by Bo (1.352-3), who confined himself to adjectives and verbs. Line 48 above offers an instance of a noun used in this way; for *indicia* is made to serve as the equivalent of the Greek σημεῖα 'verbal symbols'. Is method (c) included too? Heinze says no, but that is probably too strict. Let us think for a moment of other writers. It is clear from the early sections of *De Natura Deorum* and *Academica* that Cicero's usual way of extending the vocabulary of Latin was by employing equivalents – *prouidentia* for πρόνοια, and so on, i.e. method (b). But the rule was not quite rigid. 'When no Latin word is readily forthcoming, I think it permissible to use Greek,' says Cicero in *De Finibus* 3.15;[5] Atticus offers the same licence to Varro in *Academica*

---

[5] As a non-philosophical example Cicero gives *ephippia* (saddlecloth). The practice can be illustrated from Cato, *RR* 117 where there are half-a-dozen cases.

1.25.[6] Lucretius occasionally used Greek, not just when Latin failed him, as in *androgynus, cymbalum*, and *homoeomeria*, but also for aesthetic reasons, as in *ac musaea mele, per chordas organici quae ... figurant* (2.412f.; cf. 2,505), and for satire, as in the passage on sentimental endearments (4.1160-9). In the lines of the *Ars Poetica* under discussion Horace claims for Virgil the same right that had been given to Plautus. There are, in fact, a number of places in the *Aeneid* where Greek words are recorded for the first time, e.g., 3.533 (*eurous*), 7.84 (*mephitis*), 12.419 (*panacea*), or else appear for the first time in a particular sense, e.g. 8.402 (*electrum* as an alloy), 7.379 (*gyrus* as a circle), 7.753 (*hydra* as a snake). Finally, in Plautus the practice is so frequent that it requires no illustration. One concludes that in the *Ars Poetica* Horace meant to allow the occasional use of Greek words along with the other two kinds of innovation.

This, however, does not oblige us to believe that after 35 B.C. Horace relaxed the rule laid down for his *sermones* in 1.10. For in the *Ars Poetica* he is talking very generally, and in so far as he includes himself he may well be thinking primarily of the *Odes*. Therefore the 20-odd Greek derivatives found for the first time in the *sermones* were probably drawn from current usage. Even if one admits a couple of exceptions, like the unique *iambeus* (*AP* 253), Horace's objections to Lucilius are not undermined; for there are some 60 words in Lucilius (about 40 in Category A, nearly 20 in B) which occur only in him. Many of these, though probably not uncommon in fashionable conversation, were *felt* to be Greek – that was the point of using them; many others were straight quotations which were never intended to be admitted to Latin. Whatever functions they had in Lucilius, whether they were technical terms, connoisseurs' terminology, or satirist's ridicule, in Horace's view it was all the same: they had no place in the genre. Therefore they had to be altered or avoided. Sometimes this led to dilution, as when Homer's τὸν δ' ἐξήρπαξεν Ἀπόλλων (267) was rendered rather tamely by *sic me seruauit Apollo* (1.9.78); but often the Greek could be translated with little loss. Thus we find, not *Chresis*, but *Utilitas* (1.3.98), not *Eumenides*, but *Furiae* (1.8.45), not *meiraciodes*, but *puerilius* (2.3.250), not ψωλοκοποῦ-μαι, but *tentigine rumpor* (1.2.118). And whereas Lucilius had spoken of *eidola atque atomus* (820), when Horace wanted to express the Epicurean ideas of 'void' and 'full' he used the Latin equivalents *inane* and *soldum* (1.2.113). Again, to convey the notion of a mere amateur, Horace used *indoctus* (*E*.2.1.117) instead of *idiota*; for indigestion he called on the adjective *crudus* (1.5.49) instead of the noun ἀπεψία; for oil made from the first pressing he put the periphrasis *oleo quod prima*

---

[6] Varro says he will allow himself words like *philosophia* which are no longer thought of as foreign. In *Acad*.2.49 Lucullus explains the term *sorites* (the 'heap' argument) by the Latin *aceruus*, but later, in 92-3, he uses *sorites* by itself.

Venafri / pressit cella (2.8.45-6) instead of ὠμοτριβὲς *oleum*. On two occasions he even avoided Lucilius' *hexametro uersu*, which one might have thought permissible (1.5.87, 2.1.28).[7]

This purism, which pulled the *sermones* away from everyday speech and towards literature, must have required conscious discipline. For Greek influence now pervaded Roman life even more thoroughly than in the time of Lucilius. Documentation is readily available. Greek actors have been listed by Garton (267-83), Greek doctors by Scarborough (Appendix 1), Greek artists by Pollitt (237-8), and Greek members of the imperial household by J. Griffin (105). The last-named has also provided a useful collection of references ranging from art, bakery, and cooking to unguents, villas, and wines. All of which shows that Rome was on the way to becoming the capital lauded by Aelius Aristides and berated by Juvenal. The general effect on Horace is hard to assess. He enjoyed tragedies on Greek themes and despised chauvinistic pageants. (*E*.2.1.189-213). He recognised the work that lay behind a dancer's fluent agility (*E*.2.2.124-5), but he contrasted the discussion of individual performers unfavourably with the exploration of ethical questions (2.6.70-6). (One wonders whether the talk at the Sabine farm was always so high-minded.) Female singers are appreciated in the *Odes* (e.g., 3.9.10); male singers are mocked in the *Satires* (e.g. 1.3.1, 1.9.25, 1.10.91). As for painting and sculpture, Horace recognised that the Greeks were pre-eminent in those areas (*E*.2.1.32-3), and he occasionally praised famous artists (*Odes* 4.8.5ff., *E*.2.1.239-41). He also gave us the famous apophthegm *ut pictura poesis* (*AP*. 361) 'a poem is like a picture'.[8] On the negative side he speaks of an incompetent sculptor (*AP*. 32ff.), greedy collectors (2.3.20ff.), and an imaginary crazy painter (*AP*.1ff.); and there are some rather puritanical remarks about works of art in the *Epistles*.[9] Granted, such comments reflect the critical nature of the genre, and the items are being attacked as extravagant luxuries rather than as artistic creations. Still, on all the evidence one doubts if Horace was more informed about art than the average educated Roman of his day.

In addition to his own experiences in Greece as student and soldier, Horace had several acquaintances who knew the Greek east well, having served there in an official capacity, e.g., L. Cocceius Nerva (1.5.28), C. Fonteius Capito (1.5.32), C. Furnius (1.10.86), Q. Dellius (*Odes* 2.3), L. Munatius Plancus (*Odes* 1.7).[10] Also, as in Lucilius' day, educated

---

[7] Horace's practice is illuminated by comparing Lucretius 4.1160ff. with Horace 1.3.44-8, where the Greek is abandoned and certain adjectives (*paetus, pullus, uarus, scaurus*) are brought in, which indicate physical defects and are also current as proper names.

[8] For later developments see Hagstrum, index under *ut pictura poesis*.

[9] *E*.1.6.17, 2.2.180ff. Of the six instances of *pictus* in Horace five carry hints of frivolity and illusion, as though the word was thought of as in some sense the opposite of *uerus*.

[10] See Bowersock, ch.2.

Greeks lived in the houses of the aristocracy, writing books, tutoring the young, and in some cases giving diplomatic advice. In his late twenties Horace will have heard a lot about the Epicurean Philodemus, if he did not actually meet him, from Virgil, Varus, Varius, and Tucca.[11] He probably knew the famous Apollodorus of Pergamum, tutor and friend of Octavian; Valgius, one of Horace's friends, was a devoted pupil of Apollodorus,[12] and it seems likely that the rhetor Heliodorus who travelled with the company to Brundisium (1.5.2-3) was in fact Apollodorus. (The real name would not fit a hexameter.) Another distinguished Greek in Octavian's household was the Stoic Athenodorus of Tarsus. Horace does not mention him by name, but McGann (1.24-32) has argued strongly that his teachings on cheerfulness, prayers, and the quiet life had a significant influence on Horace's *Epistles*. Other Greeks who may well have been social acquaintances include the learned Areius of Alexandria, the rhetorician and historian Timagenes, the poet Crinagoras, and the librarian Pompeius Macer.[13] Nor must we forget Octavian's physician, Antonius Musa. With his dreaded cold-water treatment, which Horace grumbles about in *E*.1.15.2ff., this man could well have appeared in an ancient version of *The Doctor's Dilemma*.

Yet contemporary Greeks play little part in Horatian satire. A faintly derogatory reference is made to Greek exercises (*graecari* in 2.2.11) by the tough old Ofellus. In 1.6.38 an upstart is reminded that his father was a Dionysius, but again the attack does not come from Horace. Pantolabus 'Grab-all' is the typical parasite (1.8.11, 2.1.22). More specific is the gibe at Pitholeon of Rhodes for blending Latin with Greek (1.10.22). Personal antipathy is reserved for Pantilius 'Carp-all', the malicious louse of 1.10.78, and the singers Hermogenes and Demetrius. Yet their 'Greekness' is not underlined (1.10.79-80, 90). In fact no one is ridiculed for being a Greek, and there is nothing approaching the range of comment, some of it highly prejudiced, that we find in Cicero (see Guite).

The *sermones* show other signs, in addition to those already mentioned, of being rooted in a Graeco-Roman environment. For example, Marsyas had a statue in the Forum (1.6.120), Priapus in the park on the Esquiline (1.8); Aesculapius and Apollo had temples (1.3.27,

---

[11] See Frank, 48-54. In the papyrus fragment discussed by Körte, 177 'Plotie' (i.e. Plotius Tucca) seems more likely than 'Horatie'.

[12] Quintilian 3.1.18 and 3.5.17. See Nisbet-Hubbard, intr. to *Odes* 2.9.

[13] Areius knew Maecenas – see Aelian, *Varia Historia* 12.25 and Marcus Antoninus 8.31. Horace refers to Timagenes in *E*.1.19.15. Crinagoras' circle overlapped with Horace's. His epigram no.36 in *The Garland of Philip*, ed. Gow and Page, is addressed to Sallustius Crispus, recipient of *Odes* 2.2, and no.39 addresses Bathyllus the friend of Maecenas. For Dionysius see n.2 above and compare *The Second Letter to Ammaeus* 2 ἀσαφὲς γίνεται τὸ βραχὺ with *breuis esse laboro, obscurus fio* (*AP* 25-6). For Pompeius Macer see Suetonius, *Iul*.56.7. Augustus gave him the job of organising his libraries. Presumably Horace was, intermittently at least, a reader.

E.1.3.17); dancers mimed Cyclops and satyr (*E*.2.2.125); anecdotes were current about the miser of Athens (1.1.64), the lunatic of Argos (*E*.2.2.128), and the old woman of Thebes (2.5.84); Anticyra was the place for hellebore (2.3.83), and Boeotia bred dullards (*E*.2.1.244); proverbs were quoted directly – 'Not everyone can get to Corinth' (*E*.1.17.36) – or adapted – 'Poke the fire with a sword' (2.3.276), 'Get your sauce by sweat' (2.2.20-1); and Aesop's fables were a common source of worldly wisdom (2.6.79ff.).

As for the Greeks of the past, a vivid, if not wholly laudatory, description is given in *E*.2.1.93-101:

> As soon as Greece abandoned war and turned to amusements,
> lapsing into frivolity as fortune smiled upon her,
> she developed a feverish craze for either athletes or horses,
> or fell in love with craftsmen in ivory, bronze, or marble;
> she acquired a hang-up gazing at surfaces covered with paint,
> and became enraptured with pipers, or else with tragic actors.
> Just like a baby playing under her nurse's eye,
> she'd clamour for something, and then grow bored and leave it alone.
> Such were the blessings brought by the prosperous winds of peace.

That passage turns out to be a deliberate caricature – a foil to the Roman caricature which follows. But the picture is not ill-humoured or unfriendly. After all, the period in question, following the Persian wars, produced most of the *exemplaria Graeca* so warmly recommended in the *Ars Poetica* (268). Those examples showed the new age how to write. The characters they portrayed were also *exemplaria Graeca* in a rather different sense. Here genre was all-important. In epic the characters' virtues were given full weight; but in satire they became specimens of folly, crime, and even madness, as with Agamemnon in 2.3.199f. It is significant that, whereas Ulysses is praised for his resourcefulness in a moral epistle (*E*.1.2.17ff.), he is pilloried in a satire for his unscrupulous cunning (2.5), a fact which shows that Horace was fully alive to the ambiguities inherent in that hero's character.

Philosophers, on the whole, are treated with less respect than poets. When they are named, the context is usually in some way jocular or absurd. Hence Epicurus presides over a herd of pigs (*E*.1.4.16); Polemo suddenly caught philosophy on his way home from a party (2.3.254); Democritus' animals ate his crops while the sage was rapt in contemplation (*E*.1.12.12); Pythagoras is related to a plate of beans (2.6.63); Empedocles, formerly a fish (*E*.1.12.21), terminated his life by jumping into a volcano (*AP*. 465f). To an eclectic like Horace, each school had some characteristic which lent itself to ridicule. The dirtiness and rudeness of the cynics; the Epicureans' obsession with gastronomy; the Stoic doctrine that all sins were equally culpable and their contention that the wise man was a king – all these features were open to criticism.

To be sure, in certain cases the criticism was wide of the mark. Not all cynics in the tradition had been boors (one thinks, for instance of Crates); gastronomy was a perversion of Epicurus' teaching; the Stoics were not talking complete nonsense when they called the sage a king of men. Yet the various schools did have their eccentricities, and their self-righteousness and conceit were vulnerable to the satirist's clear-eyed realism.

Nevertheless, while the aberrations of Greek philosophy were laughed at, its central ethical ideas, which were often shared by two or more schools, provided a firm foundation for the *sermones*. Democritus' view of cheerfulness, Epicurus' idea of limit, Aristotle's mean, Aristippus' adaptability, Panaetius' decorum – these were sources from which Horace drew again and again, stressing now one idea, now another, according to his mood and situation. Nor should we forget the influence of those teachers who crossed the boundaries between the schools – men like Antiochus of Ascalon, whom Cicero heard lecturing in Athens, and the unorthodox Stoic Athenodorus, whom Horace almost certainly knew. Horace's *manner* in treating ethical ideas is informal and amusing, especially in the *Satires*. Even in the *Epistles*, where the satire is only intermittent, he explicitly related his talks to Greek popular philosophy by calling them *Bionei sermones* (*E*.2.2.60). Such a manner, however, did not mean that he took the ideas anything other than seriously. On the contrary, they represented an accumulated stock of wisdom which could help a man of good sense to cope with life. As such they were altogether more important than the verbal mazes constructed by over-subtle people to explain such elusive concepts as 'being' and 'the one'.

(iii) Persius

The Prologue has a striking concentration of hellenisms:

> *Nec fonte labra prolui caballino*
> *nec in bicipiti somniasse Parnaso*
> *memini, ut repente sic poeta prodirem.*
> *Heliconidasque pallidamque Pirenen*
> *illis remitto quorum imagines lambunt*
> *hederae sequaces; ipse semipaganus*
> *ad sacra uatum carmen adfero nostrum.*

I never drenched my lips in cart-horse spring,
nor dreamed upon Parnassus' two-pronged height
(I think) to explain my bursting on the scene
as poet. Pale Pirene and Helicon's Maids
I leave to those whose portraits are entwined
with clinging ivy. I present my song,
a semi-clansman, at the bardic rites.

Persius is not a 'true poet'; he has not undergone any of the usual rituals of consecration. The 'true poets' are not specified, but no doubt they include Ennius, who told how he had fallen asleep on the mountain of the Muses and received instruction from Homer (Skutsch, 126-8), and Propertius, who dreamed of meeting Apollo on Helicon (3.3). Both of these in their different ways were alluding to Callimachus, who had been transported in a dream to Helicon, where he had been instructed by the Muses.[1] That in turn recalled the *Theogony*, in which Hesiod had recounted how the Muses appeared to him on Helicon (22ff.). Persius is therefore undermining the pretensions of high-falutin Roman poets by satirising the Greek tradition in which they gloried. Hippocrene 'Horse Spring' dwindles into *fons caballinus*; Parnassus, which was called δίλοφος by Sophocles (*Ant*.1126) is *biceps* – an unprecedented word. *Heliconides*, i.e. the Muses, is given a Greek accusative ending, as is *Pirene*, the spring near Corinth where Pegasus was broken in.

> *quis expediuit psittaco suum 'chaere'*
> *picamque docuit nostra uerba conari?*
> *magister artis ingenique largitor*
> *uenter, negatas artifex sequi uoces.*
> *quod si dolosi spes refulserit nummi,*
> *coruos poetas et poetridas picas*
> *cantare credas Pegaseium nectar.*

Who coached the parrot to pronounce 'Bonjour!'?
Who helped the magpie mimic human speech?
Teacher of art, giver of genius' gift –
the belly, adept at bending nature's laws.
If cash sends out a tempting ray of hope,
then raven poets and magpie poetesses
you'd swear were singing Pegasus' nectar-flow.

Greek also plays a part here. The parrot (*psittacus*) is taught to say, not *aue* or *uale*, but *chaere*.[2] In the second last line, *poeta* had long been acclimatised, but *poetris* is a new creation. Finally, nectar is, of course, νέκταρ; but its epithet *Pegaseium* is another satirical coinage. The source of the last line may be found in a verse of Honestus: Πηγασίδος κρήνης νεκταρέων λιβάδων 'the nectar-flow of Pegasus' fountain',[3] but the new composite expression is Persius' own. The phrase 'poetess magpies' is worth noting. It recalls the story, told by Ovid in *Met*.5.300ff. and 664ff., of how the nine daughters of Pierus challenged the Muses and, on being defeated, were turned into magpies. The tale is told on Mount Helicon to

---

[1] Callimachus' dream is attested by *Greek Anth*.7.42 and Propertius 2.34.32.

[2] See Ovid, *Am*.2.6.48 and Martial 14.73.2. For a parrot which says *chaere* see Crinagoras 24.6.

[3] Honestus no.5 in *The Garland of Philip*, p.271. In no.4 he addresses both Pirene and Hippocrene.

Athene, who has come there to see the new spring created by the hoof of Pegasus. So the reference is entirely apt. It also provides a link with 1, which employs another myth about competent and less competent poets, namely the contest of Pan and Apollo and the unfortunate decision of King Midas.

In 1 Greek is used to underline literary affectation and moral decay. Labeo's translation of the *Iliad* is 'drunk with hellebore' (51) and therefore in some sense crazy. Yet Persius sardonically accepts that the new Troy – Polydamas and the Trojan ladies[4] – will prefer Labeo to him. People admire the would-be grand and try to write that kind of thing themselves. The falseness becomes apparent as the poet-reciter flashes his ring (*sardonyx*), prepares his voice with a warbling sound (*plasma*), and rolls his eyes in an emotional swoon. Another kind of poetry, whether in hexameters or elegiacs, deals with the sorrows of Phyllis or Hypsipyle (cf. Ovid, *Her.* 2 and 6). This is presented at rich dinner-parties, but the reciter is the same type as before. He wears a hyacinth mantle (*hyacinthina laena*) and has a voice to match. The host produces little elegies of his own. Persius coins a name for them to express his opinion – *elegidia* (51). This does not prevent them from being received with delighted cries of *euge*! The general public also admires the smooth style, a quality which it expects not only in elegies but also in grander works. These latter are produced by writers whose only apprenticeship has been doodling in Greek (70). They have never applied themselves to humble but solid subjects connected with the Italian countryside. The fancy style has also invaded the courtroom. Even a man on trial for extortion cannot defend himself without 'smoothly-shaven antitheses' (*rasis antithetis* in vv.85-6). The second was a genuine Greek word, but (as far as I know) it is not previously recorded in a Latin author. The insinuation of effeminacy is sharpened by the suggestive adjective *rasis*.

After this we return to poetry, in particular to precious treatments of Alexandrian subjects:

> cludere sic uersum didicit 'Berecyntius Attis'
> et 'qui caeruleum dirimebat Nerea delphin',
> sic 'costam longo subduximus Appennino.'

A metrical role has now been assigned to 'Berecyntian Attis'
and to 'the dolphin slicing his way through dark blue Nereus',
and to 'we stole a rib from the long spine of the Apennines'.

The tale of Attis, Cybele's favourite who castrated himself after breaking a vow of chastity, was morbid and unRoman (see Catullus 63). The adjective *Berecyntius* (of Mt. Berecyntus in Phrygia, sacred to Cybele) contained the Greek *y*, which sounded sweet and exotic to Roman ears

---

[4] 'Polydamas and the Trojan ladies' combines *Il.*22.100 with 22.105.

(Quintilian 12.10.27); and with *Attis* it formed a metrical pattern which Persius regarded as affected. Ovid had used *Cybeleius Attis* (*Met*.10.104) and *Berecyntius heros* (*Met*.11.106). *Delphin* is a later form of the Greek δελφίς. The metonymy Nereus = *mare* sounded silly when the divinity was being sliced in two (note the Greek accusative). And quadrasyllablic endings, like *Appennino*, were among the preciosities of the neoterics (see Catullus 64); Quintilian, who cites this very example (9.4.65) calls the effect *praemolle* 'over-effeminate'. By way of contrast Persius quotes the opening words of the *Aeneid: arma uirum*. Such poetry is now despised as old-fashioned – naturally, for as those two words make clear, it is essentially virile.

If Virgil is too dry, what then can be recited with a suitably limp wrist? More specimens follow:

> *torua Mimalloneis inplerunt cornua bombis,*
> *et raptum uitulo caput ablatura superbo*
> *Bassaris et lyncem Maenas flexura corymbis*
> *euhion ingeminat, reparabilis adsonat Echo.*

They filled their frightening horns with Bacchanalian brays.
The Bassarid carrying the head torn from a frisky calf
and the Maenad ready to guide the lynx with reins of ivy
cry Euhoe! Euhoe! The shout's taken up by restorative Echo.

The scene is wild and outlandish, the sound self-consciously musical, and the vocabulary markedly Greek. Nothing needs to be said about *bombis*, *Bassaris*, *lyncem*, *Maenas*, *corymbis*, *euhion*, and *Echo*; but the adjective *Mimalloneus* is unattested elsewhere. It comes from the Greek noun Μιμαλλών, a Bacchante, which in turn is derived, according to the scholiast, from the imitation (*mimesis*) of Bacchus.[5]

Even if we hesitate to ascribe these lines and phrases to Nero, there can be no doubt about Nero's neo-Callimachean taste. One fragment (Morel, 131) has a geographical conceit about the Tigris plunging underground, another speaks of the sheen on the neck of a 'Cytherian dove' (*Cytheriacae columbae*). He wrote verses on Poppaea's hair, and composed songs on the sea-deities Amphitrite, Poseidon, Melicerta, and Leucothea.

At the end of the satire Persius describes the sort of reader he wants: one who has studied Cratinus, Eupolis, and Aristophanes (123-4). So not all Greek poetry was corrupt. New Comedy was also acceptable, as appears from the scene in 5.161-74 taken from Menander's *Eunuch*. Menander was close to life in style and subject; he could also be admired as a critic of human follies. Reverting to 1, we find that Persius rejects as readers those who sneer at Greek sandals and at geometrical figures

---

[5] Ovid, *Ars* 1.541 has the noun *Mimallonides*.

described on a dust-table, and applaud when a tart is rude to a cynic preacher. The right entertainment for such provincial philistines is the *edictum* in the morning (a law-report or perhaps a play-bill) and Callirhoe after lunch. Was Callirhoe a music-hall actresss or the title of a poem or play? Since the whole satire has been about literature, it seems best to regard her as the heroine of some romantic piece without moral-intellectual content.[6]

So far, then, Persius dislikes most types of Graeco-Roman poetry, but makes an exception of comedy. We note too that when he defends Greek culture against ignorant mockers he is thinking of Graeco-Roman philosophy. This brings us to his other main concern with Greece. Of all the four satirists Persius was the most academic. His studies with Cornutus have already been mentioned. Through Cornutus he came to know two Greeks, Claudius Agathinus a doctor from Sparta, and Petronius Aristocrates, both of whom were keen philosophers. No doubt they further encouraged his interest in the subject, an interest reflected in his large library. The *Life* speaks of seven hundred volumes of Chrysippus. Still, it is well to remember that, in the poems he has left us, Persius is a philosophical *satirist*. While the sermon against sloth in 3 is predominantly Stoic in character, the system itself is not referred to in an excessively reverent spirit. Recalling his own school-days, the companion tells how he smeared his eyes with oil to get out of learning 'the dying Cato's magnificent speech' (45); his young friend, however, should not be so prone to laziness, having studied 'the doctrines of the porch with its mural of trousered Persians' (53). The sermon is also set against a background of popular contempt. At v.77 there is an interruption from a centurion – one of that smelly breed – who says:

> 'I know all I need to know. The last thing I want
> is to be like Arcésilas or a woebegone Solon – people who wander
> about with head hanging down, their eyes fixed on the ground,
> champing their silent mutterings in rabid self-absorption,
> pushing their lips out to serve as a balance for weighing their words,
> repeating over and over the dreams of a sick old fool:[7]
> "Nothing comes from nothing, nothing reverts to nothing."
> Is this why you're pale? Would this detain a man from his dinner?'
> That gets a laugh from the crowd, and the lads with the big muscles
> send peals of merriment ringing through their contemptuous nostrils.

That same device recurs at the end of 5, where another centurion greets Persius' homily with a vulgar guffaw and bids a clipped hundred-as piece

---

[6] In view of the anti-Ovidian ambience one thinks first of the daughter of Achelous (see Bömer on *Met*.9.414). But there are other possibilities, as is made clear by Smith's *Dictionary of Classical Mythology*. Chariton's novel *Chaereas and Callirhoe* has the right sentimental ethos, but one can hardly imagine Persius' loutish type reading Greek.

[7] The sick old fool was probably Epicurus. For the doctrine see Lucretius, *DRN* 1.150, 237, 248.

for a lot of a hundred Greeks. The Stoic diatribe lacks popular appeal, a
fact of which the satirist is defiantly aware.[8]

Satire 5 expounds the Stoic paradox 'Only the wise man is free, all
fools are slaves' (Cicero, *Par. Stoic.* 5). There is every reason to think that
Persius accepted the doctrine. With the other Flaccus one is less sure.
When he handled the same theme in 2.7 he avoided direct commitment
by employing a persona. Why, then, did Horace introduce Stoic
paradoxes into two of his major satires? The answer, probably, is that he
saw their potential as structural devices. In both 2.3 and 2.7 the paradox
functions like the hub of a wheel in which the vices are the spokes. 'All
fools are mad' is the central idea of 2.3 (Cicero, *Par. Stoic.* 4). Thus the
greedy are mad, the power-seeker is mad, the spendthrift is mad, the
lover is mad, and the superstitious man is mad. In 2.7 the hub is 'all fools
are slaves'. So sex is slavery, an interest in paintings is slavery, gluttony
is slavery, and the attempt to escape from *Angst* is slavery. In all these
cases the vices themselves and their representatives are more important
than the unifying motifs of madness and slavery.

Several new features appear in 6. It opens like an epistle: the first
eleven lines take a friendly interest in the doings of the addressee and
invite a reply. They also give a brief but pleasant description of Luna
(the modern Luni, now inland off the bay of Spezia), where Persius is
spending the winter. More important, the message of the poem (make a
sensible use of what you have) is one associated with Epicureanism and
popular philosophy rather than with Stoicism. Before postulating a
change of direction in Persius' thinking we should recall that the letter is
written to Caesius Bassus, a lyric poet interested in metres, who like
Horace had a Sabine farm. So it looks as if Persius has accommodated his
theme and treatment to the tastes of his correspondent. But how far does
this accommodation go? We start, as usual, from Horace, who in
*E.*2.2.190-2 said

> I shall enjoy what I have and draw on my modest resources
> as needed, without caring about what my heir may think of me
> when he finds the estate has not increased (Cf. *E.*1.5.12-15).

Taking up this idea in v.22 'For me it's enjoy what you have', Persius goes
on to expand it, anticipating the resentment of the heir, who will take
him to task for reducing the inheritance and will give him a paltry
funeral. In his complaints (37ff.) the heir connects the testator's
self-indulgence with the teachings of Greek intellectuals (*doctores
Graios*):

---

[8] Cf. Plautus, *Rud.*986 and 1103; *Capt.*284. In Lucilius 507-8 a solid, no-nonsense type
declares he has more use for a cloak, a gelding, a slave, or a straw cover than for a *sapiens*.
Trimalchio, whose creator was a contemporary of Persius, boasts at the climax of his own
obituary that he never listened to a philosopher (Petronius, *Sat.* 71).

That's how it goes;
since these fancy ideas arrived from abroad with the pepper
and dates our farmhands have spoilt their porridge with greasy sauces.

Persius has just told us of his own very moderate pleasures, which stop
well short of luxury: 'I can't feed my dependants on turbot, nor can I tell
the subtle flavour of a hen thrush' (23-4). To protect his position from an
ascetic's disapproval, Persius makes the attack extreme to the point of
absurdity, implicating unspecified and subversive Greek 'perfessers'. He
also suggests that the heir's complaints are motivated not so much by a
lofty Catonian anti-hellenism as by selfish greed. Yet we must still grant
that even this cautious gesture towards hedonism comes rather
unexpectedly from the man who wrote

The flesh has spoilt olive oil by mixing it into a perfume,
and soaked Calabrian fleece in unnatural purple dye (2.64-5).

(iv) Juvenal

With Juvenal the picture alters dramatically: *non possum ferre,
Quirites,/Graecam Urbem* (3.60-1) 'I cannot bear, fellow-citizens of
Rome ... ' a momentary pause, and then at the beginning of the next line
the monstrous paradox of 'a Greek capital'. After that, a further stroke:
'Yet how small a fraction of the dregs is from Greece proper?' The Syrian
Orontes has long been discharging into the Tiber – i.e. the newcomers are
so much filth and refuse. And if they're not washed down by a river
they're blown in by the wind (3.83). They come from Sicyon, Amydon,
Andros, Samos, Tralles, and Alabanda. As the attack widens, the
place-names become stranger and more outlandish. Here, then, is
another way of classifying Greeks: those from 'Greece proper' (i.e. the
province of Achaea), and those from the near east, which could be
regarded as Greek in a general sense since the time of Alexander. The
same distinction is found in a warm-hearted letter of Pliny (8.24.2). But
whereas Pliny calls Achaea 'the pure and authentic Greece', Juvenal
intimates that all Greeks are rotten, and those from outside Achaea are
the worst. The distinction, however, turns out to be another piece of
Juvenalian opportunism; no further use is made of it. From now on all
Greeks are treated alike.

For the first time, then, in Roman satire, Greeks are abused for being
Greek and living in Rome, regardless of the fact that their presence was
not illegal, and that many of their ancestors had not come there of their
own free will. Before looking at how this prejudice operates, however, we
should note one fact which is easily overlooked. Of twenty-six Greek
historical figures, seventeen are given favourable, or at least neutral,
mention. These include two statesmen (Solon and Pittacus), six artists,

and eight philosophers. The rest are not all villains. They range from the cruel and terrible (Phalaris and Pyrrhus) to the cunning and mendacious (Philip and Herodotus), and from there to the futile (Alexander, Demosthenes, and Milo of Croton) and the mildly absurd (Pythagoras). Usually the reference is very brief, and there is no retrospective animus of the kind directed at Hannibal.

Places of origin, as remarked above, are used to arouse ridicule. Sometimes an extra sneer is added. Corinthians have scented hair, and like the rest of the breed use resin as a depilatory (8.113ff.). An obsequious inn-keeper is a Syrophoenician, perpetually drenched in perfume (8.159). Another man was born by the Euphrates – you can tell by his pierced ear-lobes (1.104). At other times the ridicule centres on occupations. One thinks of the deliberately incongruous jumble in 3.76-7:

> *grammaticus, rhetor, geometres, pictor, aliptes,*
> *augur, schoenobates, medicus, magus ...*
>
> Teacher of grammar and speaking, geometer, painter, masseur,
> prophet and tightrope-walker, doctor, sorcerer ....

More often occupations are combined with names. The date of the person concerned hardly matters. Contemporary are Isaeus the rhetorician (3.74) and perhaps Themison, the doctor who helps to maintain the high mortality rate (10.221). The actors Demetrius and Stratocles (3.99) probably belong to the recent past, for Quintilian (11.3.178) speaks of them in the past tense. The powerful freedmen Posides and Narcissus (14.91 and 329) lived under Claudius. Thrasyllus the astrologer (6.576) was a companion of Tiberius; the dancer Bathyllus (6.63) was a friend of Maecenas. Clearly the combination of name and occupation is expected to reinforce the impression required by the context, whether that is criminal, sleazy, or merely ridiculous.

Clothes, too, can be the object of prejudice: *trechedipna* 'slippers' (3.67), *niceteria* 'medals' (3.68), *conchylia* 'purple garments' (3.81), *endromidem* 'athlete's wrap' (3.103 and 6.246). In the context of athletics the unique adjective *ceromatico* (3.68) is memorably effective: the peasant aping Greek fashions has a smear of mud (*ceroma*) on his neck to show he has been at the *palaestra*, hence *ceromatico collo*. Even musical instruments indicate the decline of *Romanitas*, e.g., the *sambuca* with its slanting strings (3.63-4) and oriental tambourines – *tympana* (3.64). These, however, are but the outward trappings of depravity. It is the personality and conduct of the Greek that make him really odious. He is quick-witted, glib, voluble, versatile, compliant, obsequious, insincere, lecherous, and vindictive (3.73ff.). Worse still, he is successful. He worms his way into the good graces of the patron, engineering *your* dismissal; and after making himself indispensable he ends up as master of the house. Trade is another road of advancement. Here is one who came to

Italy as a slave; now he has five shops and the fortune of a knight
(1.104-6). Another was once a barber but is now a millionaire (1.24-5). If
Juvenal is thinking of Cinnamus, his change of fortune was due to his
mistress, who, according to Martial 7.64, made him a knight. Such
creatures are always ready to ruin good citizens by telling lies in court
(7.13-4).

Most serious of all is the effect on native Romans. The Greeks carry
their language and habits like the plague. In 6.186ff. we see what
happens to women. The provincial from Tuscany is transformed into a
Graecula, the girl from Sulmo into a daughter of Cecrops.

> omnia Graece:
> *hoc sermone pauent, hoc iram, gaudia, curas,*
> *hoc cuncta effundunt animi secreta. quid ultra?*
> *concumbunt Graece.*

> Everything's done in Greek.
> In this they express their fears, anger, joys, and concerns;
> in this they reveal their hearts' secrets; what more can I say?
> They even make love in Greek.

Then, having glimpsed a new summit, Juvenal prepares for it by
pretending that the level he has just reached is not so very remarkable:

> *dones tamen ista puellis,*
> *tune etiam, quam sextus et octogensimus annus*
> *pulsat, adhuc Graece? non est hic sermo pudicus*
> *in uetula. quotiens lasciuum interuenit illud*
> ξωὴ καὶ ψυχή, *modo sub lodice ferendis*
> *uteris in turba.*

> Well, one may grant that habit to girls;
> but you, battered as you are by a series of eighty-five years,
> do you still employ Greek? Such language is simply not decent
> on an old woman's lips. Whenever that naughty endearment pops out –
> ξωὴ καὶ ψυχή – you are using in public expressions
> which should be confined to the sheets.[1]

Women have now taken over the appurtenances of both sexes. They wear
long thick sweaters (*endromidas*) and smear themselves with wrestler's
mud (*ceroma* in 6.246); but that doesn't stop them flaunting thin clothes
with fancy borders (*cyclade*) and silk flimsies (*panniculus bombycinus* in
6.259-60).

The effects on men are worse. Pseudo-philosophers have their houses
full of plaster casts of Chrysippus and Aristotle (2.4ff.). The most blatant
fraud amongst them has an original bust of Cleanthes. Then the two
terms of comparison (genuine Greek / Roman impostor) are brought

---

[1] 'Life and soul.'

together in a *iunctura* of adjective and noun, providing as often an obscene climax: 'Do you castigate vice, when you are the most notorious ditch among the Socratic perverts (*Socraticos ... cinaedos*)?' In 9, in a similar context, Juvenal again resorts to Greek, this time in the form of direct parody. Homer had said 'the steel itself lures a man on' αὐτὸς γὰρ ἐφέλκεται ἄνδρα σίδηρος (*Od*.16.294 and 19.13). After talking of a pervert who sends wheedling letters to the object of his desires, Juvenal adds by way of explanation 'the queer himself lures a man on' αὐτὸς γὰρ ἐφέλκεται ἄνδρα κίναιδος (9.37). We have seen something like that in Lucilius, but Juvenal's parodies have a more acid bite.

Our final examples are drawn from the area of food and drink. In 11.137-41 we hear of a carving school run by the expert Trypherus (Mr Dainty). Starting from the more familiar delicacies like sows' udders, hare, and boar, we progress to some wildly exotic dishes: antelope (*pygargus*), huge flamingos (*phoenicopterus ingens*), and African gazelle (*Gaetulus oryx*). As we should perhaps have guessed, they are all made of wood; for these are just students' models. In 5 the wit consists in the polar contrast between Virro's dinner and that of his client. Virro is waited on by a pretty boy – *flos Asiae* (56). The client is served by a dangerous-looking black (52ff.). These two bits of information prepare us subconsciously for the red-neck humour of *Gaetulum Ganymedem* (59) 'African Ganymede'. The host has a large cup (*phialas*) encrusted with 'the daughters of the sun' (*Heliadum*), i.e. amber, and inlaid with beryl (*berullo*); the client's beaker is cheap and chipped. Virro enjoys fruit like that from the orchards of Phaeacia or the Hesperides; the client must make do with a rotten apple (149-53). These illustrations remind us that however much of a hellenophobe Juvenal may have been, he could not dispense with the Greek cultural tradition, for that provided him with standards. Chrysippus and Cleanthes must be seen as genuine philosophers if the Roman fakes are to appear in their true light. And those legendary apples must represent perfection if Virro's mixture of extravagance and meanness is to be fully perceived.

Turning now to the use of contemporary names, we start with 3.120, a line charged with xenophobic contempt: *Protogenes aliquis uel Diphilus aut Hermarchus*. The names are clearly types, as we see from that dismissive *aliquis*. Other probable types include Hedymeles the musician (6.383), Trypherus the carver (11.137), Psecas the hairdresser (6.491), Cyane the waitress (8.162), and the whores Chione and Lycisca (3.136, 6.123). In several other cases the name is taken from an individual and yet still functions as the representative of a type, e.g. Asylus the gladiator (6.267), the musicians Echion and Glaphyrus (6.76f.), the singer Chrysogonus (6.74), the actor Haemus (6.198), and the doctor Archigenes (6.336, 13.98, 14.252). A glance at the occupations shows that when an individual's name is used he is not a man of any social or political consequence. This corroborates what was said in Chapter Two about Juvenal's avoidance of dangerous targets. But if he did not incur danger, he must still have given offence. For people who do not matter are nevertheless people.

But what about those Greeks who did matter? One of the large and profoundly important processes that had been taking place in the first century A.D. was the decline of Roman predominance in the senate. The corollary was the increasing influence of the provinces, including the provinces of the Greek east. Of provincial senators 15 per cent were of eastern origin under Domitian, 36.6 per cent under Trajan, 46.5 per cent under Antoninus Pius, and 53.7 per cent under Marcus Aurelius.[2] This reflects the area's growing social and economic importance, and the need to find suitable administrators. Outside the senate there had long been another avenue to power, namely the favour of the princeps. The position enjoyed by Pallas and Narcissus under Claudius was still remembered. (One thinks of Pliny's indignant onslaught on the former in *Ep.8.6.*) A dozen or more Greeks were appointed by Nero to the important imperial procuratorships;[3] others followed distinguished careers in the *militia equestris*. Domitian showed his admiration for things Greek by instituting quadrennial games, including competitions in music and declamation, over which he presided in Greek dress. True, he punished philosophers for their connection with dissidence, but not all Greeks were philosophers. Some, like Julius Celsus and Julius Quadratus, advanced to positions of considerable power.[4] Trajan, rather surprisingly, doubled the number of eastern senators. And Hadrian 'was so devoted to Greek pursuits that in some quarters he was called a *Graeculus*'.[5] In view of his many-sided personality, his admiration of artists and intellectuals, his Greek verses, Greek titles, and Greek boy-friend, the charge was not unfounded.

Greek influence continued to make itself felt at every level. In law the most distinguished advocates were, indeed, Roman or Italian, but freedmen were often employed in more humble positions; also some of the most eminent jurisconsults came from the east (Duff, 120). Thanks to Roman snobbery or stupidity the other professions were largely left open to the Greeks, whether freedmen or *peregrini*. The same applied to the worlds of business and entertainment. And Greek lecturers and essayists were frequently employed as diplomats. Evidence for these large and complex trends comes from various sources – coins, inscriptions, historians' statements. But occasionally we find a Greek author filling out Juvenal's picture from his own experience. Plutarch, who was born in the early 40s into a distinguished family at Chaeronea, visited Rome where his friends overlapped with those of Tacitus and the younger

[2] The figures are supplied by Mason Hammond, 77.
[3] They are named by Momigliano, 727.
[4] See Syme, (2) 510.
[5] Aelius Spartianus, *Hist. Aug., Life of Hadrian* 1.5.

Pliny.[6] Trajan gave him the *ornamenta consularia* and Hadrian made him procurator of Greece. He did a great deal to promote concord between Rome and her Greek subjects, and much of his success came from following one of his own Precepts of Statecraft: 'Not only should a statesman show himself blameless towards our rulers; he should also have a friend among the men of high station' (814C).

Dio of Prusa, a wealthy Greek rhetorician and philosopher, was about fifteen years older than Juvenal. Though exiled by Domitian, he returned to favour and became a friend of Trajan,[7] whom he praised discreetly in a number of speeches, especially the first oration on *Kingship*. When he says he has 'known the houses and tables of the rich, and not private persons only but also satraps and kings' (*Or.*7.66), we believe him. The Phrygian Stoic Epictetus, Juvenal's contemporary, had once been a slave. Emancipated by Nero's freedman Epaphroditus, he made a name by his writings and eventually became a friend of Hadrian. In his *Encheiridion* or *Manual* he advises the reader to prepare for rebuffs: 'When you go to see an influential man, imagine that you will not find him at home, that you will be shut out and the door slammed in your face, or that he will take no notice of you' (33.13). Again, 'Have you failed to be invited to someone's house? Naturally, for you did not pay the host the price for which he sells his dinner. He sells it for praise; he sells it for being made much of. Pay him the price, then, if it's in your interest to do so. But if you want to get what he offers without paying the price, you're a fool as well as a glutton' (25.4).

Then we have the testimony of Lucian, who was born about A.D. 120 in Samosata on the Euphrates. His Nigrinus, like Juvenal, castigates the arrogant rich of Rome and describes the indignities which they heap on their clients. Like Juvenal too, he insists that the parasite and sycophant deserve all they get. The theme is taken further in *Dependent Scholars*. There, basing himself on the experiences of numerous victims, Lucian deplores the miseries of the client's life. But again we are struck by his impartiality. The Romans are indeed crass and insensitive, and some of them complain openly about Greek competition. But the Greeks themselves are not attractive, and the scholar who is speaking turns out to be rather a snob. He has to endure the porter with his horrible Syrian accent (10), he may be confused with low Bithynians (23) and be outshone by some vile Alexandrian (27). The Greeks are despised for trafficking in prophecies, philtres, love-charms, and incantations, and in many cases their low reputation is justified (40). By an ironical twist of fate, Lucian was later appointed to a secretaryship in the prefecture of Egypt. His essay was now an embarrassment, and he had to laugh it off as best he could in his *Apology*.

[6] See C.P. Jones (2), ch.6.
[7] See C.P. Jones (3), ch.13.

Other names could be mentioned, such as Favorinus, the hellenised Gallic eunuch, and Polemo the Laodicaean, who travelled with a large retinue of slaves, horses, and dogs (Philostratus, *Lives of the Sophists* 489-91, 530-44). Both were twenty years or so younger than Juvenal, and both made brilliant careers as orators and writers, receiving generous favours from Trajan and Hadrian. These are just some of the better-known Greeks who managed to use the imperial system to their own advantage. Many of them, of course, would not have read Juvenal. Those who did doubtless shrugged him off with contempt. It was all they could do, for he had made no specific attack on *them*. This failure to insult the powerful is sometimes held against him. 'Juvenal,' says Syme (2.511), 'derides the needy adventurer – smooth, versatile, corrupt – outwitting by low devices the ethical and dignified Roman. Superior material was waiting for a genuine satirist, namely the great sophists in their greed and vanity – the voluble Favorinus ... the intolerable Polemo ... the virtuous Dio ... Juvenal did not dare to use it.' True, he did not dare to use it. Nevertheless, I do not see how anyone reading the third satire between, say, A.D. 112 and 140 could have avoided including such men in Juvenal's attack. Then there is that phrase 'a genuine satirist'. One must not make too much of it, for Sir Ronald may just have thrown it in to annoy Gilbert Highet. But the assumption behind it should not pass unquestioned: under an autocracy the only genuine satirist is one who is prepared to risk his life.

Given, then, that Juvenal's indictment of Greek residents, however prejudiced and exaggerated, was based on fact, one wonders how many Romans felt quite as intensely about the matter as he did. The nearest parallel, perhaps, is the tirade of Cn. Piso against the Athenians, as reported in Tacitus, *Ann.*2.55.1. Tacitus' own attitude seems to have become more hostile with the passage of time (Syme, 2.512-3). Or perhaps his antipathy was just given more opportunity for expression by the philhellenic antics of Nero. In Martial there is less evidence than one might have expected. In 12.82 he describes the sycophantic Menogenes who

> plies you with admiration and praise, till after enduring
>   countless boredoms you finally say 'Come and dine'.

One might, I suppose, add the lines on Hermogenes the napkin-thief, where the name is almost used as a refrain (12.29). But those are isolated instances, and even they do not contain any derogatory remarks about the Greeks in general. For stereoscopic vision we must combine Juvenal's viewpoint with Pliny's. The *Epistles* show Pliny treating his freedman Zosimus with kindness and affection (5.19), praising the Syrian philosophers Euphrates and Artemidorus (1.10, 3.11), and admiring the eloquence of Isaeus (2.3), whom Juvenal mocked as 'torrential' (3.74). To be sure, even the bland Pliny sometimes betrays annoyance. In the case which the Bithynians brought against Rufus Varenus, Pliny appeared for the defence and, needless to say, spoke with telling effect. Fonteius Magnus conducted the prosecution with many words but few points of substance. 'Most Greeks are like him. They mistake volubility for fullness of expression, pouring out long boring sentences in a torrent without pausing for breath.'[8] Greek advocates, however, are a minor irritation. On the whole Pliny takes a generous view of the Greeks, partly, no doubt, because they pose no threat to his position.

It is otherwise with Juvenal. The resentment which he so pungently conveys must surely come, to some extent at least, from feelings of insecurity. Gaston Boissier put it thus: le motif qui le fait gronder est moins élevé qu'on ne pense, et il n'y a au fond de cette colère qu'une rivalité de parasites. Le vieux client romain, qui s'est habitué à vivre de la générosité des riches, ne peut pas supporter l'idée qu'un étranger va prendre sa place (318).[9] That states very sharply the view as seen from above, and it does contain part of the truth (cf. Marmorale, 35-6). Yet Serafini, siding with Genovese and Marchesi, whose remarks he quotes, finds it quite unacceptable. In his interesting eighth chapter (Giovenale e il mondo greco) he presents Juvenal as a high-minded conservative, passionately attached to Roman traditions, and implacably hostile to the Greeks, who have brought corruption. After quoting anti-Greek sentiments from a long line of Latin writers, he says: Ma è sopratutto con Catone che Giovenale è spiritualmente collegato (375).[10] Later he adds: La fiera protesta giovenaliana è illuminata da un ideale: quello di salvare, con sforzo disperato come dentro l'ultima trincea, l'orbe romano dall' esiziale tabe ellenica (378-9).[11] This view is supported by quotations from 11 and 14 in praise of the old republic. That too contains some truth. It recognises that the satires project a genuine moral protest. ('Fighting for an ideal in the last ditch', however, seems to go too far. As we argued in Chapter One, the ideal is rarely visible and Juvenal has no illusions about turning the tide.) In assessing Juvenal's antipathy to the Greeks it is possible to make room for some of the cynical self-interest

[8] *Ep.*5.20.4. Cf. Pliny's account of a similar case in 4.9. There the prosecuting counsel, Theophanes, who was a most unmannerly fellow (*impudentissime*), spoke far too long (14). We have just been told that Pliny's own speech went on for three and a half hours before being interrupted by nightfall. He then continued for another hour and a half by lamp-light.

[9] 'The cause of his complaint is less noble than one imagines. His anger is based simply on the rivalry which one parasite feels for another. The old Roman client, accustomed to living off the generosity of the rich, cannot bear the thought of being supplanted by a foreigner.'

[10] 'But Juvenal's main spiritual affinity is with Cato.'

[11] 'Juvenal's fierce protest is inspired by an ideal: to save the Roman world, by a desperate last-ditch effort, from the Greeks' deadly corruption.'

detected by Boissier and also for a certain amount of Serafini's moral protest; for people's attitudes in such matters are capable of more than one explanation. It is of more importance, perhaps, to recognise that in Juvenal's view the Greeks were only partly responsible for the state of affairs in the capital; anti-Greek sentiment appears sporadically in 6, and in a famous passage of 3; elsewhere it is negligible. Moreover, like other contemporary evils, the 'Greek problem' was created by Roman armies. Hence it was only a single aspect, albeit a conspicuous one, of a much vaster process. What Juvenal was witnessing, as he well knew, was the nemesis of world conquest:

> *saeuior armis*
> *luxuria incubuit uictumque ulciscitur orbem* (6.292-3)

> More devastating than armies,
> luxury has fallen upon us, avenging the world we conquered.

CHAPTER SIX

Women and Sex

(i) Adultery

The second epode of Horace paints an idyllic picture of the small
independent farmer and his wife. While he goes about the seasonal tasks
of the countryside, she attends to the house and children; she also drives
the animals into their stalls and milks them, carries in firewood, sets out
the wine and cooks a meal. It goes without saying that she is *pudica*
'chaste'. Later, in *Odes* 3.6, we hear of a stern mother ordering her sons to
fetch firewood in the evening – sons who will eventually fight against
Pyrrhus, Hannibal, and Antiochus. That is a traditional picture, going
back to the early third century and beyond. As the pattern of
land-ownership changed and fewer people came to have more
(MacMullen, 38), in certain areas at least the independent farmer began
to be superseded by the tenant, or by the bailiff, who was usually a slave.
Yet the work still had to be done, and its strenuous nature can be inferred
from the instructions in Cato's *De Agricultura*. Most of the treatise is
concerned with the bailiff and his tasks, but chapter 143 is devoted to the
bailiff's wife. She must have food available for her husband and the other
hands; she must also look after the poultry, see to the preservation of
fruit, and grind flour. Spinning and weaving are not mentioned, but may
be assumed. And as if all that were not enough, she has to keep herself
and the farmstead neat and clean. Cato lived until 149 B.C. and so
overlapped with Lucilius.

The next important agricultural writer, Marcus Terentius Varro, was
fourteen when Lucilius died. Amazingly, he lived on until 27 B.C., and his
Res Rusticae appeared when Horace was writing his *Satires*. In his
old-fashioned way Varro complains about modern villas with all their
new-fangled Greek appointments (2, Introduction 2), and he alleges that
most of the *patres familiae* have abandoned sickel and plough and now
use their hands in theatre and race-course rather than in the grain-fields
and vineyards. Columella, an older contemporary of Persius, writing
about A.D. 60, says that the old kind of free farmer could still be
remembered by his father's generation – i.e. in the early Augustan
period. Now they have gone, and the wives who used to help them have
become fastidious, regarding farmwork as dull and dirty (*RR* 12.*Pref.*9).
As we noted in Chapter Four, these statements exaggerate the flight from
the land, but no one denies that the process was taking place. More

important, no one doubts the fidelity of the account which they give of life on a small holding.

If we try to imagine the kind of work traditionally done by the farmer's wife, it is clear that she was by no means a chattel. She took practical decisions all the time, and her effort was vital to the success and survival of the enterprise. Columella agrees that she was the equal of her husband in memory and diligence, and did her best to make the household prosper. It is perhaps naive to speculate on how happy she was. Much would have depended on the health of herself and her family. Probably most of the time she was too busy to think about the matter. As for the permanence of marriages, while we should allow for the occasional village scandal, adultery and divorce would not have been common. Marital problems, like the weather, would have been coped with by endurance and resignation, as they were for centuries up to our own time. However crude and limited such a life may have been, the toughness, thrift, piety and fidelity of those country folk were remembered with admiration, and were sometimes praised in passages of real eloquence. One thinks of the lines in the second Georgic beginning *o fortunatos nimium, sua si bona norint, / agricolas!* (458-9). Juvenal too could pay tribute, as in 11.64-76 and 14.161-72. Yet few would have wanted to go back. As Ovid put it:

> *prisca iuuent alios, ego me nunc denique natum*
> *gratulor: haec aetas moribus apta meis* (*Ars* 3.121-2)

Let others take pleasure in olden days; I am delighted
to be living now. The present suits my character.

It suits him, he says, not because of its gold and marble,

> *sed quia cultus adest nec nostros mansit in annos*
> *rusticitas priscis illa superstes auis* (*Ars* 3.127-8)

but because culture is here, and the boorish life which existed
in our grandfathers' time has not continued to ours.

This cultivated life which developed in the second century, was enjoyed by the senatorial class, which had consolidated its power during the Hannibalic wars, and by the equites, whether country squires or city businessmen. But the farmers who moved into the capital were poor and had to make a living as best they could. In many cases their wives took jobs. Literature has little to say about what these women did, but inscriptions show that they worked in the clothes trade (making, mending, dyeing) and in cosmetics and jewelry. They were also active as midwives, hair-dressers, and shop-assistants. Often they ran businesses with their husbands, though (as now) they received no public acknowledgment for doing so (Treggiari, 3). As for accommodation, most of them had to put up with the squalor and discomfort of tenements.[1] But if our own nineteenth-century history is anything to go by, such places may well have been superior to the hovels they left behind in the country. Finally, a moment's thought will make it clear that, far from being sheltered, those women were familiar with every aspect of life in the raw.

Upper-class wives, with their city houses and country villas, were in a very different position. Their material comfort can be taken for granted, but any discussion of their relations with men must start from the fact that Rome's political organisation had always centred on the clan or family. Marriages were arranged to increase its wealth and political influence, and to provide sons who would perpetuate its name. The partners themselves were seldom in a position to make an informed choice, especially as the girl was often married in her early teens. While mutual respect and affection were encouraged, and seem in fact to have developed more often than we might imagine, romantic love and sexual excitement must have been rather exceptional, at least until the last century of the republic. It was partly because of this defect in the marriage-system that, after the victories over Antiochus (190) and Perseus (168), and following the sack of Corinth (146), a Greek-style demi-monde established itself in Rome.[2] This meant that well-to-do young men could pursue affairs with attractive and sophisticated partners. Moreover, as such women, unlike slave-girls and common prostitutes, were in many cases well enough off to say 'no', the men could persuade themselves that when the answer was 'yes' they were being accepted for their own sake, not just for their money. Though not welcome, such liaisons were tolerated by the older generation in the hope that they would be temporary and not too ruinous, and that in due course the young men would settle down to marriage and a public career (see Cicero, *Cael.* 40-3).

The upper-class girl had no such opportunities either before or after marriage. Though less secluded than her classical Greek counterpart, she was raised in the belief that her main duties were to run her household smoothly and to remain faithful to her husband. This emphasis on *pudicitia*, which corresponded to a man's *uirtus*, may in part be explained by male possessiveness and the half-conscious fear of female irrationality;[3] but there was also a basic factor of a social and biological kind, namely that Rome was a patrilinear society and a wife's chastity was the only guarantee of her husband's paternity. This presented a serious obstacle to the social emancipation of women. Yet, if it was never

---

[1] In visualising tenements it is easiest to think in negative terms: no sanitation, no running water, no window-panes, no fireplaces ... See Carcopino, 31-44; Yavetz, 166-79.

[2] These women were called *meretrices*. The word had a wide range, including prostitutes of a poorer kind.

[3] The trouble with such a fear, then as now, was that it tended to be self-validating.

removed, it was gradually eroded as a result of those same conquests which led to the rise of the demi-monde. While their husbands were away, wives had to face more responsibilities at home, and this engendered a spirit of independence. Under the free marriage-custom that now prevailed women retained control of their own property, and it was not difficult to obtain a divorce. As Rome grew rich, houses became larger and more comfortable. Domestic chores could be left to slaves or ex-slaves. The birth-rate declined, and those infants who were allowed to survive could be handed over to nurses. The resulting leisure could be devoted to the refinements of cultivated life, and in the course of time many *matronae* came to surpass the demi-monde in their sophistication and accomplishments. One may also infer that an aristocratic marriage now allowed greater scope for romantic feelings of the kind so delightfully portrayed in Catullus 61.

Nevertheless, in the sexual sphere women on the whole never obtained the freedom enjoyed by men. Granted, if they tired of their husbands they could insist on a divorce; and if they were sufficiently daring and unconventional they could take lovers. But there was no male class corresponding to the demi-monde. And although a young woman might occasionally take some of the liberties so luridly described by Juvenal, none of her elders would smile indulgently and say 'When she has finished sleeping with such-and-such an actor she will doubtless settle down and make a good wife and mother'. Society, then, did not allow women the same licence as men. And 'society' included large numbers of conservative women who believed in *pudicitia* and who, like their spiritual descendants in Victorian times, scornfully accepted male promiscuity simply on the grounds that the poor creatures couldn't help it.

In surveying how the four satirists treat adultery we start with a short fragment of Lucilius: *non omnibus dormio* (251), 'I do not sleep for the world at large'. The words are attributed to one Cipius, who feigned sleep to facilitate his wife's adultery but apparently woke at once when someone tried to steal the wine. He was nicknamed 'Pararhenchon', 'The Snoring-Partner', presumably on the analogy of παρακοίτης or παράκοιτις, 'sleeping-partner' or 'spouse'. The story became traditional, as may be seen from Marx's note on Lucilius 1223 and Courtney's on Juvenal 1.57. Juvenal speaks of the husband as

> *doctus spectare lacunar,*
> *doctus et ad calicem uigilanti stertere naso*

> trained to gaze at the ceiling,
> trained to snore over his wine through a wide-awake nose.

Such behaviour was not a mark of gentlemanly tolerance. It was inspired by greed; for the conniving husband shared in the adulterer's gifts and so was nothing better than a pimp. Another Lucilian fragment speaks of a man who castrated himself with the intention of punishing his wife for some sexual misdemeanour (303-5). An observer remarks that the knife was used on the wrong person (306-7). In these two cases Lucilius was satirising both wife and husband. In Book 29 he attacked men who pursued other people's wives, urging his listener *eicere istum abs te quamprimum et perdere amorem* (920), 'to cast that passion away and destroy it as soon as may be'. But in most of the marriage-fragments it is the wife who is ridiculed. She decks herself out in all her finery for visitors, but not for her husband (534-5); she is unfaithful, and the rest of the household impure (639); she thinks up excuses for going out – to the goldsmith, to her mother, to a relative or friend (1096-7); when her husband is away, her housework is neglected (1104); wives, as Metellus conceded, were really a great nuisance (644-5).

In Horace, on the other hand, little is said about either wife or husband. It is indeed pointed out that 'Helen wasn't the first bitch to occasion a war / by her foul behaviour' (1.3.107-8); and according to Tiresias, Penelope, that exemplar of wifely virtue, resisted the suitors simply because

> when those lads came, they were rather mean with their presents;
> it wasn't sex that enticed them so much as the palace cooking (2.5.79-80).

Nevertheless, adultery is considered mainly from the point of view of the lover. The youthful Horace was warned against such activity by his father:

> *ne sequerer moechas, concessa cum uenere uti*
> *possem: 'deprensi non bella est fama Treboni'*
> *aiebat* (1.4.113-5)

> To stop me chasing wives when legitimate sex was available,
> 'A name like that of Trebonius isn't nice,' he would say.
> 'He was caught in the act.'

And most of 1.2 aims to dissuade men from becoming involved with married women. The topic is broached in a stately parody of Ennius:

> *audire est operae pretium, procedere recte*
> *qui moechis non uultis, ut omni parte laborent* (37-8)

> 'Tis worth your while to give ear, ye who wish ill success
> to adulterous men, how on every side they are beset by troubles.[4]

---

[4] Ennius had written: *audire est operae pretium, procedere recte / qui rem Romanam ... uultis* (*ROL*, vol. 1, *Ann.* 471-2), ''Tis worth your while to give ear, ye who wish all success / to the Roman state.'

There follows a catalogue of reprisals, which becomes increasingly bawdy and finishes with a swipe at the aristocratic Galba:

> One has jumped from a roof, another has been flogged to death;
> one while running away has blundered into a gang
> of violent thugs; another has traded cash for his life;
> another was soaked by lecherous louts; there was even an instance
> where a party mowed the lover's balls and randy prick
> with a sword. 'Perfectly right,' said everyone. Galba dissented (41-6).

A similar technique is employed in the closing scene, which depicts in the idiom of wild bedroom farce the hazards which can be avoided by eschewing married women:

> No fear, when I'm fucking, that her husband will hurry home from the country,
> the door crash open, the dog bark, and the house resound
> with an awful din; that the woman, her face as white as a sheet,
> will jump out of bed, her accomplice shriek, and we'll all be in terror –
> the maid for her legs, the wife for her dowry, and me for myself.
> I have to escape barefoot, with my clothes at sixes and sevens,
> or else my cash or my arse or my reputation has had it.
> It's tough to be caught; I could prove it even in Fabius' court-room
>   (127-34).

The same kind of scene, with its mixture of brutality and humiliation, is referred to again, though in a less dramatic style, in 2.7.56-61:

> As you're led in you are nervous,
> and your whole body trembles as fear struggles with lust.
> What matter whether you're handed over to be seared with the birch
> and killed with a sword, or whether you're bundled into a box
> by a maid abetting her mistress' sin, and forced to cower
> with your head stuffed between your knees?

Setting and tone recall the traditional adultery mime, in which the return of the husband and the concealment of the lover in a chest provided a recurrent motif.[5]

The language is suited to the boisterous crudity of the action. *Perminxerunt* (1.2.44), like *meiat* (2.7.52) confuses ejaculation with micturition. According to Adams (142) such usages 'seem to have been applied particularly to squalid or humiliating sexual acts'. The confusion was not due to ignorance; it was a deliberate obscenity. *Testis* (1.2.45) apparently never quite lost its connexion with the literal sense of

---

[5] See Juvenal 6.44, and the article by Reynolds. An aimiable variation of 'lover hides in chest' is to be found in Boccaccio, *Decameron*, Eighth Day, Eighth Tale.

'witness'; Adams (67) describes it as having 'a risqué and jocose quality'. *Cauda* (1.2.45; cf. 2.7.49), which normally means 'tail' occurs only here in the sense of *penis*, which had undergone a similar process. Adams (37) is inclined to see the use as an innovation by Horace. I wonder. It sounds like the sort of thing that might turn up in the next discovery of Pompeian graffiti. Horace did not use the vulgar *futuo* again (1.2.127), nor did he revert to *puga* (1.2.133; cf. *depugis* in v.93). A handful of other such words (*permolere, cunnus, muto*) are also confined to 1.2.

That early satire may be set beside *Epod.* 8, a nasty piece in which a well-to-do married woman (13f.) is subjected to abuse because she has complained about the poet's unresponsiveness. The comparison suggests an inconsistency between Horace's preaching and his practice. Yet people *are* inconsistent, and as far as the 'message' is concerned the ugly episode with the *moecha* could be said to reinforce the text of 1.2: *desine matronas sectarier* (78) 'stop chasing married women'. In taking this line are we supporting autobiographical literalism and ignoring the influence of the genre? Not quite. While it is wrong (I think) to imagine that the iambic tradition of Archilochus somehow compelled the poet to write a piece of vulgar abuse which was foreign to his nature and experience, one can still believe that, having chosen that genre as a suitable vehicle for his thought and feeling, he then heightened or dramatised the more lurid elements in keeping with his Greek 'models'. In 2.7, which is about eight years later than 1.2, Horace denies that he is an adulterer (72). The practice is treated as a public abuse in *Odes* 3.6.17-32. And the topic is avoided in the *Epistles*.

Returning to 1.2, we observe that the arguments are entirely prudential: think of the waste of time and effort – all those attendants, coiffeuses, and female hangers-on (98); if that doesn't deter you, think of the disgrace and the mocking laughter; think of the appalling dangers; only a fool will pursue *matronae* when he can so easily find satisfaction elsewhere. No similar arguments are addressed to the wife. More significant, the lover is never reminded that he has any obligation to the husband. The special status of marriage in law and custom and religion is simply ignored. Yet, given this narrow angle of approach, Horace is not unfair. He assumes that the adulterous intention comes from the man. The *moechus* takes all the initiative; and he bears the brunt of the satirist's ridicule. Morally, the later satire (2.7) is rather more sophisticated. Whereas in 1.2 we are told simply that the wife is worried about her dowry (131), in 2.7 she is guilty – *peccati erilis* (60), *matronae peccantis* (62). The lover is also guilty – *peccat* (47). In fact he is *more* guilty, because he is the corruptor (63) and inflicts the sin on her.[6] Both deserve to be punished by the husband, and such punishment is eminently just (62-3). So justice does come into it. The point is only

---

[6] 'Inflicts' is an attempt to reproduce the *double entendre* in *peccat superne*.

touched on. Horace does not go on to explore how legal rules reflect the basic needs of a community. Nor does he enquire *why* the adulterer is treated with such derision. By following that line he might have developed the argument that every act of adultery causes, as it were, a tear in the social fabric. Such reasoning might have held some attractions for the Roman mind; yet it could not easily have been related to the satire's theme, which was that of servitude. So instead Horace introduced a very different kind of argument, which *was* immediately relevant, one which had to do with the nature of the human individual. Having spoken about the dangers of adultery, he goes on to say that the good man will resist such temptations even when there are *no* dangers:

> Who then is free? The wise man who is master of himself,
> who remains undaunted in the face of poverty, chains, and death,
> stoutly defies his passions and despises positions of power,
> a man complete in himself, smooth and round, who prevents
> extraneous elements clinging to his polished surface, who is such that
> when Fortune attacks him she maims only herself (83-8).

On this view all desires (not just sexual passion) are unruly and must be kept in check by reason. That, of course, raises other, deeper, questions; but 'the morally free man' was a serious and important concept, with the authority of Plato and the Stoics behind it; and in so far as it implied that sexual restraint was more than a matter of avoiding unpleasant consequences, it raised the discussion of adultery to another level. That level, one must add, is not achieved elsewhere in the *Satires*, and it is not maintained for long in 2.7. (Davus soon passes on to lower things.) As for the more positive side of sexual 'pairing', that is not a satirical motif, but one recalls the concluding stanza of a complex and delightful ode:

> *felices ter et amplius*
> *quos irrupta tenet copula nec malis*
> *diuulsus querimoniis*
> *suprema citius soluet amor die* (1.13.17-20)

> Thrice happy, more than thrice, are they
>   who, by an unbroken bond made one,
> live in harmonious love, and stay
>   united till life's day is done.

The worldly-wise bachelor might almost have been talking about a happy marriage.

Persius shows no interest in the topic of adultery, but one brief passage in 6 does appear relevant. Addressing his (fictitious) heir, the satirist demands to know why he should stint himself just so that his heir's descendant may enjoy the *dolce vita*;

> Shall I on my holiday
> eat boiled nettles and a smoked pig's cheek with a hook-hole in the ear,
> so that one day your young wastrel may gorge on goose's liver,
> and when the fastidious vein throbs in his roving cock
> relieve himself into an upper-class pouch? (69-73)

The coarse coinage *inmeiat* in v.73 is a typical intensification of Horace's *meiat* (2.7.52). But the violent heterosexuality is most unusual. One other passage calls for mention, not because it concerns adultery, but because it implies a certain assumption about a Roman wife – an assumption which one tends to forget when reading satire. Nothing, says Persius, can be more terrifying

> than for a man to say to himself
> 'I'm falling, falling headlong!' and blanch in his heart, poor devil,
> as he thinks of a crime which the wife beside him must never hear of
>
> (3.41-3).

After a nightmare, the man lies sweating with fear, unable to confide even in his *proxima uxor*. She is closer to him than anyone else. The fact that he cannot confess to her shows the appalling nature of his guilt.

In the context of marriage Juvenal makes some telling attacks on men. Unlike Horace, however, he does not treat their behaviour as a kind of folly which can easily be avoided with a little common sense; nor does he try to deter them by employing an urbane ridicule. Instead he presents their conduct as a breach or reversal of some accepted norm – an action which appears as paradox, absurdity, or outrage depending on the satirical context. *Cum tener uxorem ducat spado* (1.22) 'when a flabby eunuch takes a wife' – that is the first of many factors that drive Juvenal to satire. Clearly it is a ludicrous defiance of nature, like the pig-sticking lady, and it establishes at the outset the theme that Roman life has somehow been turned upside down. Soon after comes the man who lives off the immoral earnings of his wife (55). Ovid had complained about a husband who made things too easy: *Quid mihi cum facili, quid cum lenone marito?* (*Am.* 2.19.57), 'Why should I talk to a pliant husband who is simply a pander?' Juvenal goes one step further by dropping the word for husband: *cum leno accipiat moechi bona* (1.55), 'when a pander takes gifts from a lover'. We have to make the disgraceful equation of 'pander = husband' for ourselves, and are rewarded with confirmation in the next line. Finally comes that sign of unnatural precocity, the *praetextatus adulter* (78), 'an adulterer still in short trousers'.

In 6, after an introduction in which the praise of golden-age chastity is characteristically undercut by his mockery of primitive life, Juvenal begins his declamation thus: *anticum et uetus est ...* (21), ''Tis an old and time-honoured custom ...' In Roman terms that must be the prelude to

something noble. Aware of this, Juvenal continues *alienum ... lectum /
concutere*, 'to rattle another man's bedstead'. The one crime of the silver
age – in other words the original sin, for the golden age was chaste – was
that of adultery. So *moechi* have been around a long time. But now, what
an astonishing thing, one of them intends to get married! And, what
lunacy, he's looking for a virtuous wife! The climax of this paradoxical
technique comes in 9, where so far from wrecking a marriage the
unspeakable Naevolus takes the credit for saving it. He even becomes the
spokesman of his profession, putting on record the services which too
often go unacknowledged:

> *instabile ac dirimi coeptum et iam paene solutum
> coniugium in multis domibus seruauit adulter* (79-80)

> A tottering, crumbling marriage, now on the verge of collapse,
> has, in the case of many a house, been saved by a lover.

As with Lucilius, however, the main weight of Juvenal's attack falls on
wives. Isolated shots are heard throughout, from the *matrona* who
poisons her husband (1.69) to the 'generous' Larga, who sets her daughter
an example of promiscuity (14.25). But the real bombardment takes
place in 6, a satire so long and so unrelenting that many have taken it as
a proof of almost pathological misogyny. In answer to this it is sometimes
pointed out that in the other fifteen poems Juvenal's targets are male.
And it may indeed be that, like Hamlet, the satirist is proclaiming 'Man
delights not me, no, nor woman neither'. Yet 6 differs from other pieces
in that, while men are exposed as greedy, vainglorious, dishonest, and so
on, women are attacked solely in their capacity as females. Perhaps this
was inevitable. Since women's activities were virtually limited to private
life, it followed that their delinquencies had to be domestic. But Juvenal
actually narrowed the restriction even further by choosing to concentrate
largely on wives, and on upper-class wives at that.

As the piece develops one notices how often a complaint about some
other kind of defect begins, or more frequently ends, with a sexual
reproach. Thus the lines on Caesennia start with her wealth and then
reveal that she bribes her husband to connive at her adulteries (136-41);
the passage on Bibula starts with her sexual domination over her
husband and ends with her greed (142-57); the description of the
fashionable philhellene ends with her attempts at seductiveness, even at
the age of eighty-five (184-99); the attack on the female sadist ends with
her antics on the matrimonial merry-go-round (219-30); the mother-in-
law, who might have been criticised for just interfering, turns out to be an
accomplice in her daughter's adultery (231-41). All this might perhaps
have been expected in the long section on the disappearance of *pudicitia*
(1-285); but the same orientation is observable in what follows. A wife's
drunkenness is not sufficient; it must be seen as leading to sexual

degradation (301). The worship of the Bona Dea is seen as an excuse for an orgy (329-34). The woman attends the games, not as a frivolous diversion, but so that she can squander her money on an athlete (356). An effeminate companion in the household is really an adulterer in disguise (025). A wife's interest in music is not to be trusted – it leads to infatuation with performers (379-92). Even a visit to the baths involves sexual gratification from the masseur (423). Along with this obsessive emphasis goes a concentration on physical minutiae: Tuccia's *uesica* 'vulva' (64), the smell of the stews which Messalina brought home (132), the grotesque urination scene (310), the involuntary noise produced by the masseur (423),[7] the nauseating behaviour in the dining-room (432). The intention seems to be to reduce women to a series of physiological reactions.

I realise that a selective summary of this kind omits the element of humour. Yet when the poem is taken as a whole I cannot persuade myself that the humour cancels out the hostility. It seems indeed that by harping on woman's uncontrolled animality Juvenal may well be indicating a fear of her full potentialities as a person. One such fear is that women may try to assert themselves physically in certain areas monopolised by men. We have already noted the pig-sticker in 1.22-3. Related to her is the woman who goes in for gladiatorial exercises in 6. That was the most extreme example Juvenal could find; and again he adds a sexual note: 'You might think,' he says in effect, 'that a female gladiator would prefer to be a man. Not a bit of it. That would mean forfeiting her woman's sexual pleasure, which is so much more intense than ours (254).'[8] Then, having portrayed this woman as a parody of a man, he explodes the whole charade by having her reach for a chamber-pot. Another fear is that the woman may display her intelligence. What a mortifying experience for her husband when she talks to generals in uniform (400). Then the sexual comment; 'without any expression of deference on her face (*recta facie*) and with her breasts dry (*siccis mamillis*).' In other words she should be nursing children. Later we hear of that negation of femininity, the literary critic. It would, one assumes, be in order for the lady to memorise and recite Virgil; but to contest Dido's guilt and to embark on a comparative discussion of Virgil and Homer – that really is an affront to decorum. As for eloquence, logic, and grammar, those are men's concerns. If she wants to go in for that sort of thing she should

---

[7] Cf., with Ruperti, Martial 7.18. On Martial's sexual attitudes see Sullivan.
[8] That was the opinion of Tiresias, who had been both man and woman (at different times). See Ovid, *Met.* 3.320-33 and Ruperti's parallels. I refer without comment to some statements by a modern psychologist, which include the phrase 'the female's more intense experience of pain and pleasure' (Charlotte Wolff, 50).

hoist up her tunic so that it reaches just to her knees,
offer a pig to Silvanus, and pay a quarter to bathe (446-7),

that is, transform herself into a man. None of this, of course, prevents Juvenal from complaining later on about women who surrender their intellect to oriental superstitions. That kind of dabbling is dangerous for several reasons. One is that it leads to the purchase of magic spells and philtres which enable the woman *mentem uexare mariti / et solea pulsare nates* (611-2) 'to unhinge the mind of her husband / and lather his bum with a slipper' (another hint of fear, with markedly Freudian overtones). The whole satire then concludes with a grotesque and ferocious coda designed to show that by abandoning *pudicitia* and succumbing to *luxuria* Roman wives have become enemies of life itself. They pay abortionists 'to murder human creatures in the womb' (596); they administer aconite to their children (639-42); and they dispose of their husbands by devices ranging from a mushroom to a slice of toad's lung (621, 659).

Unless the satire is taken as pure fantasy (which is, I think, an unwarranted and reductive reading), Juvenal's women must be seen as in various degrees impatient with the role which had been assigned to the upper-class wife in early times and which had been universally accepted until the last century of the republic. That role was part of a beautifully simple division of responsibilities between the sexes – a simplicity which we can apprehend the more clearly because we have abandoned it and have to cope with the consequences. Unfortunately, in addition to being simple, that division was also unjust. This comes out in one arrestingly modern phrase in the sixth satire:

>   'olim conuenerat' inquit
> 'ut faceres tu quod uelles, nec non ego possem
> indulgere mihi. clames licet et mare caelo
> confundas, homo sum' (281-4)

>   'Long ago,' she says, 'we made an agreement
> that you should do as you liked and I too should be able
> to please myself. You can rant and rave till the sky falls,
> *I am a person!*'

That last fact has been borne in on us since Ibsen's heroines first appeared on stage; and every aspect of our national life has slowly been taking account of it. That was not so in Rome. There, if a woman did shake off the shackles of domesticity, there was nothing for her to do. Law, government, finance were all equally unthinkable. (The influence exerted by dynamic women in politics remained a backstage affair.) Apart from a few clerkships in the civil service, which in any case were given to freedwomen, there was nothing available in administration. As

for the professions, even those which have been most accessible in our
own recent history – teaching and nursing – offered no opportunities. It
followed that if a woman could not find fulfilment within her traditional
sphere – home, family, polite accomplishments – she was condemned to
frivolity. Because of this, in spite of what Juvenal avers, the liberated
woman was never in the majority. Granted we all remember Catullus'
Lesbia; Juvenal too could not forget her (6.7-8). But even within the
metropolitan upper class her set can hardly have been typical. Since
there was no reliable contraception, that stubborn biological fact (that
chastity was needed to establish paternity) ruled out any prospect of real
equality. At the beginning of our period Cato declared that a husband
might kill a wife caught in adultery; she, however, could not lay a finger
on him (Gellius 10.23.5). At the end, i.e. in the mid second century, the
civilised Plutarch was still urging the wife to turn a blind eye to her
husband's escapades (*Mor.* 140B).[9] So the double standard prevailed. It
is significant that in the whole of Roman satire no man is ever criticised
for being false to his wife.

(ii) Fornication

One day, the story goes, Cato saw a young man leaving a brothel. 'Well
done,' he said. 'That's better than chasing other men's wives.' But after
seeing him emerge on several subsequent occasions, he said 'Look here,
when I commended you for visiting that place I was not suggesting you
should take up residence.'[10] Authentic or not, the story does imply that
young men were not censured too harshly for occasionally visiting
prostitutes. Such indulgence was not extended so readily to older men,
and it always presupposed a context of friendly feeling. In the case of an
enemy, charges of fornication were entirely in order. Thus, addressing
one of his critics, Lucilius refers to *quem sumptum facis in lustris circum
oppida lustrans* (1071), 'the money you spend on brothels, whoring
around the race-track'. The attitude of the speaker was all-important,
and that depended on the situation. We would like to know how Lucilius
treated the subject in his so-called *Fornix* 'The Brothel' (before 910).
Perhaps that was the satire in which, like Cato, he recommended
fornication instead of adultery. In 921-2 we have

> *at non sunt similes neque dant, quid si dare uellent?*
> *acciperesne? doce*

---

[9] The rationalisation is interesting: it is out of respect for his wife that the husband shares
his debauchery with another woman. Later, however, Plutarch does say that a husband
should not vex his wife by pursuing extra-marital affairs (144D).

[10] Ps.Acro on Horace 1.2.31.

You say they're different and don't deliver. Suppose they were willing;
tell me, would you accept?

This sounds as if it referred to married women. The point would be that
even if they were willing, they should still be avoided because of the
attendant risks. On the other hand,

> hic corpus solidum inuenies, hic stare papillas
> pectore marmoreo (923-4)

Here you will find a firm body, a chest like marble
with jutting breasts.

'Here,' I take it, is the brothel, a place in which you can find women

> quae et poscent minus et praebebunt rectius multo
> et sine flagitio (927-8)

who will ask for less and deliver their wares much more straightforwardly
without bringing scandal.[11]

Whereas the poorest prostitute, who was usually a slave, rarely
provided comic material, the more classy type of *meretrix* could be
satirised for her cunning and avarice. In 937, for instance, we hear of
those who *thynno capto cobium excludunt foras*, 'on trapping a tunny,
shut the door in the goby's face'. The male clients, for their part, were
open to ridicule for their infatuation and extravagance. In castigating
Scaevola, Albucius listed some of the items which he had stolen for his
mistress: *chirodyti aurati, ricae, toracia, mitrae* (60), 'sleeved,
gold-threaded tunics, veils, bodices, hairbands'. Another speaker
attacked his opponent (L. Cotta?), saying *nec mihi amatore hoc opus nec
tricone uadato* (443), 'I've no use for this lecherous fellow, this
bound-over twister'. Those charges were directed at real-life characters,
and the women in question were probably courtesans.

The *meretrix* also, of course, figured in comedy. Now even if, for
chronological reasons, Lucilius never met Terence, he still knew his
plays. This was to be expected, since they both belonged to Scipio's
circle. And in fact the satires include more than one scene containing
Terentian material. Here entertainment seems to have taken precedence
over censure. In Book 27 a lover confides in a friend, very much as
Phaedria confides in Parmeno at the beginning of the *Eunuch: pacem
cum peto, cum placo, cum adeo et cum appello meam* (737), 'when I sue
for peace, appease her, go to her, and call her mine'. The same character
wonders if he can ever achieve success: *ego enim an perficiam ut me*

---

[11] The MSS reading *quiete*, however, points to *qui* rather than *quae*, in which case
Lucilius is urging the claims of boy prostitutes. For *pueri meritorii* see Krenkel (4).

amare expediat? (741), 'Can I contrive that loving me should suit her interest?' Yet whereas Terence, after placing the lover in a perplexing situation and allowing various characters to criticise his behaviour, eventually made sure all would end well, the satirist probably dwelt more on the young man's silliness. It is hard to imagine a Lucilian lover marrying and living happily ever after. Another comic writer used by Lucilius was Caecilius Statius, who was a generation older than Terence. One of his plays, *Hymnis*, based on Menander's play of the same name,[12] had the line *mihi sex menses satis sunt uitae; septimum Orco spondeo* (*ROL* 1, p. 490) 'I desire six months of living, and the seventh I pledge to Dis'. This reappeared in Lucilius as *qui sex menses uitam ducunt, Orco spondent septimum* (659), 'Men who live six months of pleasure and the seventh pledge to Dis'. One detects a note of criticism here, and in fact Cicero calls the expression the motto of the dissolute (*Fin.* 2.7.22). Another fragment of Caecilius' play runs as follows:

> You've a lassie from Miletus, haven't you?
> I'll betroth her to this fellow and frustrate my son's designs (*ROL* 1, p. 490).

A father, presumably, is talking to a brothel-owner. His intention is to prevent his son from getting involved with a girl (doubtless Hymnis). Now in the course of a comic scene in Book 29 of Lucilius, a speaker says:

> *facio ⟨ilico⟩*
> *ad lenonem uenio, tribus in libertatem milibus*
> *destino* (893-5)

> I act at once.
> Going to the pimp I purchase [that young slave-girl's] liberty
> for three thousand.

That sounds very much like the action envisaged in Caecilius. Moreover, at least three fragments from the same book contain the name Hymnis (887-8, 889, 896); and another, unassigned, may also belong here: *Hymnis cantando quem adseruisse ait ad se* (1168) 'one whom Hymnis says she captured by her singing'. So the Lucilian scene appears to be largely literary. There is, however, another, very corrupt, fragment, this time in hexameters, which is generally thought to conceal the name Hymnis. In Marx's restoration it goes:

> *at Hymnidis acri*
> *ex facie florem delegeris* (1166-7)

> but if from Hymnis' radiant face
> you picked the bloom [her beauty would still remain?]

---

[12] See Körte (2), vol. 2, 144-6.

Was this Hymnis related in some way to the girl in the comic scene? Or
was she a girl-friend of the poet? No answer is possible.

But the question has brought us to Lucilius' love-life. In 1039-40 we
find:

> cuius uultu ac facie ludo ac sermonibus nostris
> uirginis hoc pretium atque hunc reddebamus honorem

This was the prize I gave the girl for her face and appearance,
this the reward I paid in the form of my light-hearted talks.

For once we can be confident that Lucilius himself is speaking. The
following pieces, also from Book 30, may belong to the same poem, in
which case Lucilius indulges in some repartee with a spirited young girl:

> ante ego te uacuam atque animosam
> Tessalam ut indomitam frenis subigamque domemque (1041-2)

You who have been till now unpartnered and skittish,
like a wild Thessalian filly, I'd love to master and break you.

Then, I suspect, came another line or two in which the image changed to
that of an ox. This brought forth the reply:

> tune iugo iungas me autem et succedere aratro
> inuitam et glebas subigas proscindere ferro?

Yoke me to the yoke, then, would you, and make me, despite my struggles,
submit to the plough and cleave the clods with its metal share?

That was Book 30. Book 16, according to Porphyrio (on Horace, *Odes*
1.22.10), was entitled 'Collyra', because it was about Lucilius' mistress of
that name. Unfortunately none of it survives. Varro (*LL* 6.69, reported
after 897) mentions another girl called Cretaea, who, when she came to
sleep with Lucilius, was induced of her own accord to remove her tunic
and the rest. That may be the context of

> mihi commodum
> statuerat dare, uestimenta et in toro reposueram (898-9)

She had just made up her mind
to oblige me, I had stripped and laid my clothes upon the bed.

Whether the poet's autobiographical writings included the more
drastically explicit lines quoted earlier (p. 166) must remain
uncertain. Two other, equally obscene, fragments will illustrate the
problem: *perminxi lectum, imposui pede pellibus labes* (1183), 'I
thoroughly soaked the bed, messing the clothes with my member',[13] and

---

[13] For a Greek parallel to *pes* = *penis* Marx cites the scholiast's note on Euripides, *Med.*
679. See also Haupt, 166.

at laeua lacrimas muttoni absterget amica (335), 'but with her friendly hand she will wipe the tears from one's organ'. The former is in the first person and was quoted by Porphyrio on a first person passage of Horace (1.6.22); the latter is not in the first person, nor is the Horatian passage on which Porphyrio is commenting (1.2.68). But these points do not provide an adequate base for an argument. Autobiography aside, the bawdy unabashed tone of some of these fragments foreshadows Catullus' invitation to Ipsithilla (32) and that demanding woman's complaints about Horace's lack of virility (*Epod.* 12). The milder fragments look forward to Propertius, Tibullus, and Ovid. True, *their* metre was the elegiac couplet, and the first two often struck a romantic note which was quite foreign to the satirist. Nevertheless, in view of the frank and personal way in which Lucilius wrote about *amor*, he does claim a place in the pre-history of Latin love elegy.

When Horace took over the tradition of Lucilian satire, he gave it a more consistently moral/didactic slant. Part of this process was his decision to write and publish love-poems as 'iambics' rather than 'satires'. Hence in *Epod.* 11 he looks back to his affair with Inachia (cf. *Epod.* 12.15), in *Epod.* 14 he is consumed with ardour for the unreliable Phryne, and in *Epod.* 15 he is furious at having been jilted by Neaera. Even if these girls are wholly fictitious (which I doubt), they all belong to the class of *meretrices* with which relations are recommended in 1.2; so there is no inconsistency of the kind noted in connexion with *Epod.* 8. Yet the poet's *attitude* is appreciably different; for in the satire he claims to preserve the detachment appropriate to a perfunctory commercial transaction. Are we then to reflect with Fulke Greville on the 'wearisome condition of humanity' and on 'passion and reason, self-division's cause'? Nothing quite so grave seems to be called for. The notion of genre is elastic enough to stand the tension. In the personal medium of the epode Horace confesses that he has been prostrated by passion and has been quite unable to write. But there is a penumbra of self-mockery. We are pretty sure he will get over his obsession with Phryne and will survive to concoct other excuses for his laziness (cf. *E.* 2.2). As the form of the epode heightens his infatuation, so the satire, and the sort of writing that lay behind it,[14] projects a cynical sensuality which is only relieved by the clever wit, which draws on New Comedy (20-2), epic (37-8), epigram (105-8, 120-2), and finally on mime (127-33). It may be assumed that this difference in emotional perspective was less marked in Lucilius.

It is time now to look at 1.2 in a little more detail. It begins by pondering on the folly of extremes. In the way people behave there seems to be no middle way *nil medium est* (28). The next illustration of this polarity is sexual: one man pursues married ladies, another confines his

[14] For references to Cercidas, Diogenes, Philemon, and others see Rudd (2), 277.

attention to the stews. How much more reasonable to have dealings with the intermediate class of freedwomen (47). Granted, they also present a risk, for if a man falls under their spell they can deprive him of his money and reputation. But this risk can be neutralised if one acts coolly and circumspectly and chooses *meretrices* who are not too expensive (121-2).[15] The commercial aspect is never forgotten. Dealing with freedwomen is a relatively safe transaction – *tutior merx* (47); a prudent level of expenditure is quite possible (52-3). The right sort of girl

> *mercem sine fucis gestat, aperto*
> *quod uenale habet ostendit* (83-4)

> carries her wares without disguise, revealing
> what she has for sale.

This leads naturally to the horse fair, where the buyer can appraise all the animals' points. Like the horses, the girls are virtually naked, which is surely as it should be:

> *an tibi mauis*
> *insidias fieri pretiumque auellier ante*
> *quam mercem ostendi?* (103-5)

> Or perhaps you'd rather be taken in and fleeced of your money
> before you inspect the goods?

After that, a few minutes of fantasy. (Let her be Ilia or Egeria or anyone you like.) And then good-bye. The coldness is uncharacteristic, but it is partly mitigated by the farcical conclusion.

In the long homily, 2.3, love appears as a form of lunacy.

> If a man old enough to shave enjoyed playing odds and evens,
> building houses for dolls, riding a big cock-horse,
> and harnessing mice to a tiny cart, he'd have to be simple (247-9).

Such childish behaviour is also typical of the lover:

> When you press an apple on a sulky child he won't accept it.
> 'Take it, pet!' He says 'No'. If it wasn't offered he'd want it.
> Likewise the lover, lately shut out, ponders the question
> whether or not to call at the place he had meant to revisit
> until he was asked. He dithers at the hated door. 'Should I enter
> now she invites me? Or make an effort to banish my suffering?
> She snubbed me; she calls me back; should I go? Not if she begged me!'
> Here's a slave with a lot more sense: 'Now sir, a problem
> which doesn't admit of method or system cannot be handled

[15] The inexpensive *meretrix* blurs the distinction between the smart freedwoman, who may be too dear, and the common whore.

by rules and logic. In love there are two afflictions: warfare
and peace, two things which alter very much as the weather ...'
When you pick the pips from a Cox's apple and go into transports
if you manage to hit the ceiling, are you in command of your senses?
When you let a stream of baby-talk trip from your silly old palate,
have you more sense than the child with its doll's house? (258-75)

So, within the framework of the doll's house, apple, and contrary child,
Horace has staged part of a famous scene from Terence's *Eunuch*, in
which Parmeno advises the love-sick Phaedria. The same scene lies
behind 2.7.89-92, where Davus, after abandoning the charge of adultery
returns with a different accusation:

> A woman demands
> a small fortune, bullies you, slams the door, saturates you
> with freezing water – and invites you back. Tear that degrading
> yoke from your neck.

In those comic scenes, as elsewhere in the *sermones* (e.g. 1.3.38-40), the
lover's state of mind is seen as ridiculous. It is very exceptional when
Horace notes that such feelings can lead to tragedy, as in the case of
Marius, who stabbed his mistress and then jumped to his death
(2.3.277-8). It is also unusual for Horace to adopt a more condemnatory
tone. This is what happens in vv.23-6 of *E.* 1.2, a poem with a discernible
Stoic colouring. In that passage, however, the theme is rather the
servitude of lust. Praising Ulysses, Horace says:

> You have often heard of the Sirens' song and Circe's cups;
> if *he* had been foolish and greedy enough to drink, like his comrades,
> he'd have fallen under the brutish degrading spell of a whore,
> living the life of a filthy dog or a wallowing pig.

The *sermones* as a whole, then, concentrate on the silliness of love, and
occasionally on its dangers and degradation. Such onesidedness was to be
expected from poems written in the tradition of Greek popular
philosophy. (Horace calls them *Bionei sermones* in *E.* 2.2.60.) In the
Odes, however, love's ambiguities, sweet and sour, are explored with
great charm. Since the poet is now forty, or thereabouts, he seldom
portrays himself as in love, though one must not forget his interest in
Glycera (1.19 and 3.19). More often he reflects on his past loves (e.g. 1.5,
3.26), or comments on the affairs of other people (e.g. 2.5, 3.7). Over the
years he has developed, if not a philosophy of love, at least a half-tender,
half-ironical, attitude of mind which can take account of its vagaries and
locate it in a general pattern of experience. It never had the consuming
intensity that it had for Catullus, and its place was never central. (The
central positions were occupied by poetry and friendship.) But it was not
wholly peripheral either. Cinara, who died young (*Odes* 4.13.22-3), seems

to have awakened stronger feelings than the rest. Her memory lingered, and no one quite took her place. But casual diversions were still feasible. In his forties Horace contemplates a holiday on the coast. He sees himself as setting out (still optimistic, in spite of expanding waistline and receding hairline) to try his luck with the girls of Lucania (*E.* 1.15.21). Later he reflects sadly how

> *singula de nobis anni praedantur euntes:*
> *eripuere iocos, uenerem, conuiuia, ludum* (*E.* 2.2.55-6)

As the years go by they rob us of one thing after another:
already they've taken fun, sex, parties, and sport.

But in his last collection of odes, which appeared a few years before his death, he could still send an invitation to Phyllis:

> *age iam meorum*
> *finis amorum –*
>
> *non enim posthac alia calebo*
> *femina – condisce modos, amanda*
> *uoce quos reddas: minuentur atrae*
> *carmine curae* (*Odes* 4.11.31-6)

End of my loves' story, Phyllis,
(for no other woman's cheer
after this my heart will brighten)
   come, my dear,

learn a melody and sing it
with that voice I love to hear.
Song, and song alone, can lighten
   clouds of fear.

Unlike Horace (2.7.88-94), Persius may have lacked the confidence to portray himself as a comic lover. In any case the casting would have been implausible. Cornutus had managed to protect him from all that kind of thing (5.32-6). He does, however, provide quite an interesting adaptation of the opening scene of the *Eunuch*. Talking of the lover's servitude, he launches abruptly into a speech in which a young man vows to pull himself together:

> *Daue, cito, hoc credas iubeo, finire dolores*
> *praeteritos meditor* (5.161-2)

Davus, look here – I really mean it – I'm putting a stop to
the hell I've been through.

Following Menander's play of the same name, Persius calls the slave

'Davus' and the lover 'Chaerestratus'.[16] The latter, unlike his Terentian or Horatian counterpart, has already formed his intention when he appears. His reasons are also new:

> *an siccis dedecus obstem*
> *cognatis? an rem patriam rumore sinistro*
> *limen ad obscenum frangam, dum Chrysidis udas*
> *ebrius ante fores extincta cum face canto?*

> Why should I bring disgrace to my decent relatives,
> earning a bad name, squandering the family fortune
> outside a house of ill repute, drunkenly singing
> in front of Goldie's dripping door when my torch has gone out?

That element of remorse is not in Terence, or in Horace's comic scenes.[17] The slave then says, in effect, 'Good for you, you're well out of it'. Whereupon Chaerestratus at once begins to waver:

> *sed censen plorabit, Daue, relicta?*

> But Davus, do you think she'll cry when I leave her?

There is no crying in Horace, but crocodile tears are mentioned by Parmeno in Terence (67-8). Davus has a crisp answer:

> *nugaris. solea, puer, obiurgabere rubra*

> Nonsense, my boy! She'll give you a whack with her red slipper.

That, too, may well come from a passage near the end of Terence's *Eunuch,* where Gnatho the parasite says he'd like to see Thais pulping Thraso's head with her sandal (1027-8). Davus continues:

> Now you're wild and fierce; if she called, at once you'd say:
> 'What'll I do? Not go near her, not even now
> when she asks me – begs me?'
> > Not even now, if you've made a clean
> and genuine break.

Here again Persius is sterner and more decisive than his predecessors. Terence and Horace both allow their slaves to indulge in some aimiable, roundabout, reflexions on the psychology of love. Davus, however, sticks to his text, which is true, Stoic, freedom as distinct from the formal emancipation conferred by the praetor:

---

[16] So says Persius' scholiast. Menander's play has not survived.
[17] But see 1.2.61-2.

> hic hic quod quaerimus, hic est,
> non in festuca, lictor quam iactat ineptus

> There, I tell you, is the freedom we're after,
> not in the piece of stick waved by a silly official.

While Persius gives the scene from New Comedy a sterner, more puritanical, slant, Juvenal avoids it altogether. Semi-indulgent banter was not his metier. He has, in fact, less to say than one might imagine about relations with prostitutes. The remarks he does make are intended, at least ostensibly, as illustrations of some other theme. In 3.58-125 the theme is the influx of Greeks and orientals. Along with the language, customs, and musical instruments washed to Rome by the Orontes come the harlots, whose employers make them stand at the race-track:

> ite, quibus grata est picta lupa barbara mitra (66)

> Go, if you fancy a foreign tart with a coloured turban.

After objecting to these girls, however, Umbricius later complains only of their price:

> at tu
> cum tibi uestiti facies scorti placet, haeres
> et dubitas alta Chionen deducere sella (134-6)

> However,
> when *you* like the look of Snow-White's face, you must stop and think twice
> before helping the dolled-up whore down from her chair.

This type of inconsistency has been mentioned in Chapter One. It cannot be resolved by postulating a distinction between Juvenal's views and those of Umbricius; for here Umbricius is inconsistent with himself. Other passages also suggest that Juvenal never really thought out his objections to prostitution. When he resents equestrian theatre-seats being taken by *lenonum pueri, quocumque ex fornice nati* (3.156) 'whoremongers' boys who first saw the light in some brothel or other', he is using the brothel simply as an insult – the ultimate example of 'a low background'. In 10.236-9 the rhetoric seems intended, rather, to generate aesthetic disgust. The old man forgets his kith and kin:

> He forbids his blood to inherit; his entire estate is made over
> to Phiale; such is the power of the breath of that expert mouth
> which stood for sale for so many years in the cell of a brothel (237-9).[18]

But what about *meretrices* with artistic accomplishments, who could

---

[18] The sense of these nasty lines seems to be 'Such is the influence of the *fellatrix*, with her stinking breath, who etc.'

offer a less squalid kind of satisfaction? There is an interesting passage in 11 (162-70) where Juvenal invites his friend to a simple meal. Certain kinds of diversion will *not* be available:

> Perhaps you expect a group of girls who, singing together,
> will start a lascivious Spanish dance and then, encouraged
> by the diners' applause, will sink to the floor with shimmying buttocks –
> a stimulant, that, to jaded appetites, used by the wealthy
> as a sharp aphrodisiac. (Yet, that particular pleasure
> is more intense in the other sex; their excitement increases
> and they end by wetting themselves in response to sight and sound).[19]

Juvenal refuses to have such girls, not because they are too expensive (though in fact they are), but because they are obscene. Why, then, does he object to their obscenity? Not for any philosophical reason, such as the Stoic view that appetite should be suppressed by the rational soul. So perhaps for a social reason; is their act vulgar, the kind of thing that only plebeians would enjoy? On the contrary, he says in effect 'Leave the appreciation of such an act, which is accompanied by words more lewd than anything one would hear in a brothel, to the rich man, *qui Lacedaemonium pytismate lubricat orbem* (175), 'who greases with spits of wine his circular Spartan inlay'. He then concludes:

> Gambling is shameful,
> adultery, too, is shameful for ordinary people; when *these* chaps
> follow the same pursuits they're thought of as smart and lively.

There is no point in pretending that Juvenal is inviting sophisticated laughter at all this. He explicitly condemns such performances as obscene and licentious – *uocibus obscenis omnique libidinis arte* (174). Yet there is a trap which awaits all those who inveigh against debauchery: they may describe it in such graphic detail as to incur the suspicion of desiring it. With his account of the girls' bumps and grinds, and his gratuitous comment on female physiology, Juvenal has not wholly escaped that suspicion. Another kind of ambiguity is apparent in his sneer at the rich – a sneer which both censures their dissolute habits and envies their privileged position in society. When those moral and social ambiguities are combined, we get a picture of the speaker which strongly resembles a middle-class puritan.

(iii) Homosexuality

'Did the Romans approve or disapprove of homosexuality?' Like most

---

[19] Verses 165-6 are somewhat inapposite, and even when enclosed in brackets they interfere very harshly with the syntax. They have therefore been omitted.

questions about 'the Romans', it cannot be given a straightforward answer. First, nearly all our evidence has to do with *male* homosexuality; we know very little about the practice of lesbianism.[20] Then, are we talking about sentimental attitudes or certain kinds of physical intimacy? If the latter, then we must ask further questions. Assuming the evidence is verbal, who is the speaker, and whom is he addressing – friends, readers, or a court of law? What is his tone? Is he joking, or expressing admiration, or is he delivering censure and abuse? Are the alleged acts supposed to have taken place between men, or between a man and a boy? If the first, is the person addressed reputed to have been the active or the passive partner? If the second, was the boy freeborn or a slave? Several situations and several responses have to be considered.

Within the area of satire, the most varied material comes, ironically, from the most fragmentary source. Speaking of Socrates, Lucilius says:

> *sic Socrates in amore et in adulescentulis*
> *meliore paulo facie; signat nil quem amet* (959-60)

That's Socrates' way with love and the somewhat handsomer
young men; no feature characterises his beloved.

In other words, he loves them all alike, whatever their differences. Here we have Socrates' affection for young men – an affection which, by all accounts, he transfigured into spiritual love. Rather the same sort of affection is referred to in 822-3, which has to do with Polemo, Crates, and the headship of the Academy:

> *Polemon et amauit, morte huic transmisit suam*
> *scolen quam dicunt*

And Polemo loved him; after his death he handed on
to him his 'school', as they call it.

Although no more details are provided, we may safely take it that these fragments imply approval.

Something very different happens in Book 1. According to Servius (before 28-9), in the council of the gods Apollo says he does not wish to be given one of his traditional epithets, namely *pulcher* 'fine'. The reason is that the word is now applied to *exoleti* (adult pathics) in the sense of 'pretty'. So – a mildly disrespectful joke. But also more than that, for Lucilius was almost certainly taking a swipe at Appius Claudius Pulcher, one of Scipio's most powerful opponents. The mention of *exoleti* – men who a few years before would have been *pueri delicati* – 'boy favourites' – brings us to the fact that homosexual relations, however deprecated and concealed in earlier periods, had now become familiar, and in some

---

[20] See Citroni, 281-2.

quarters fashionable. Familiarity is indicated by the fact that Plautus (late third, early second, century) throws in an occasional homosexual joke, e.g. in *Asin*, 703, *Most.* 845-7, *Pseud.* 1181. Presumably he knew what he was doing. More significant is the fact that Afranius, roughly contemporary with Lucilius, is criticised by Quintilian (10.1.100) for staining his plots with 'filthy pederastic love-affairs' (*puerorum foedis amoribus*). While it would be silly to ascribe this process entirely to the influence of Greek habits, that influence does seem to have been a major factor. Among the people who make this point is the Greek historian Polybius. He says that in the period after Pydna many young Romans abandoned themselves to boy-friends (*erômenous*) or prostitutes (*hetairas*). Scipio is said to have rejected such behaviour, thus winning a reputation for self-control (31.25.2). A few of the remarks which Scipio directed at passive homosexuals have been preserved. In 142 or 141, at the review of the knights, he attacked P. Sulpicius Galus, saying that one who put on make-up in front of a mirror, plucked his eyebrows, and wore a long-sleeved tunic must be presumed to behave like a *cinaedus* (Gellius 6.12.5). In another speech he expressed horror that well-born boys and girls should be attending dancing-classes and mingling there with *cinaedi* (Macrobius, *Sat.* 3.14.7). These speeches were in line with his decision to expel all prostitutes from the camp, when he arrived at Numantia in 134 B.C. (Appian, *Iber.* 85.)

Lucilius echoes Scipio's contempt for *cinaedi* and for those who went dancing with them: *stulte saltatum te inter uenisse cinaedos* (33). In Book 2, however, we find an attack on the active role. This comes in the lines which Warmington assigns to Albucius in his speech against Scaevola (61, 62, 63). The first two are obscene: *in bulgam penetrare pilosam*, 'to penetrate into a hairy bag', and *si natibus natricem impressit crassam et capitatam*, 'if with a thick and headed snake he has butted his buttocks'. The third says: *pedicum iam excoquit omne*, 'Now he exhausts his lust for boys'. The boys in question are unknown. In such circumstances, slave-boys, of course, had no choice; but compliance on the part of free-born boys brought them into disrepute. Thus Quintus Opimius as a boy is said to have been both *formosus* and *famosus* 'well-formed' and 'ill-famed' (450-2; cf. 453). Finally we have another line, which refers to *inberbi androgyni, barbati moechocinaedi* (1048), 'beardless men-cum-women, bearded adulterer-pathics'. That seems to take account of pretty well everything. Accusations like these indicate hostility, at least among respectable conservative readers, to homosexual vice. How many of the same readers would have approved of Lucilius' indecency is another question. From Cicero, *De Off.* 1,104 it is clear that Panaetius disliked coarse humour.[21] He also banned any reference to the private parts and their functions (127). While it is true that Panaetius'

[21] Cicero's terms are *illiberale, petulans, flagitiosum, obscenum.*

ideals were beyond the reach of most Romans, nevertheless some
standards of decency were acknowledged, and it seems certain that many
people in Lucilius' own time, as well as later, thought he went too far.[22]

One of the later critics was Apuleius. Defending his own erotic verses in
the mid second century A.D. as part of a much larger defence against the
charge of magical practices, Apuleius reads out two of his poems
addressed to Charinus and Critias. His first argument is that these are
not the boys' actual names; they are pseudonyms, like 'Lesbia' and
'Cynthia'. 'And indeed I should be inclined to find fault with Lucilius,
even though he was writing in an aggressive genre, for smearing the boys
Gentius and Macedo in his poetry under their own names' (*Apol.* 10). By
way of contrast Apuleius points to Virgil, who in *Ecl.* 2 decorously
referred to himself as 'Corydon' and to Pollio's boy as 'Alexis'. Two
relevant fragments of Lucilius have survived, the first of uncertain
meaning and the second impenetrable. The first, on the most likely
punctuation and reading, runs:

> *nunc, praetor, tuus est; meus, si discesseris horno,*
> *Gentius* (308-9)

> Gentius, praetor, is yours for now; but soon he'll be mine,
> if you depart this year.

In spite of Apuleius' implication, we cannot be sure that the speaker was
Lucilius himself. Nor do we know whether the context was one of
approval. If Lucilius did write approvingly of a boy-friend called Gentius,
he might, I suppose, have defended himself, as Apuleius did in *Apol.* 11,
with the argument that his sportive verses were not a *specimen morum*;
i.e. they did not reflect his own behaviour. But that seems unlikely.
Another possibility would have been to point out that the names Gentius
and Macedo were non-Roman. If they were slaves, relations with them
would have been treated much less seriously. One may contrast the fate
of Valerius Valentinus, who (about 111 B.C.) lost a case because he had
claimed in a frivolous poem to have debauched a free-born adolescent
(Valerius Maximus 8.1.8), with that of Calidius Bononiensis who was
allegedly acquitted of adultery because he maintained he had gone to the
other man's house *ob amorem pueri serui*, 'to pursue an affair with a
slave boy' (Valerius Maximus 8.1.12). Elsewhere in Lucilius there seems
to have been a debate about the relative advantages and disadvantages
of girls and boys. A markedly unappealing fragment from this discussion
(1182) was translated above (Ch. 5, n.17). We have tried to illustrate the
wide range of tone and attitude found in Lucilius. The state of the text
precludes anything more detailed, unless we want to do what Housman

---

[22] One recalls the defensive remarks of Trebonius in his letter to Cicero (*Fam.* 12.16.3).
Porphyrio, on Horace *E.* 1.19.34, says there was a lot of dirt in Lucilius (*multa ... spurca*).

suggested to Marx: write a novel.

In Horace, of course, the various references *can* be related to their context. When that is done we find that, as with the heterosexual material, there is a certain amount of inconsistency. But where does it lie and what does it amount to? *Maltinus tunicis demissis ambulat* (1.2.25), 'Maltinus minces around with his tunic trailing low'. The name is chosen for its associations with *malta*, which meant a 'pansy' (cf. Lucilius 744). A character called *fragilis Pediatia* 'the petite Miss Pediatius' is mentioned in 1.8.39. An invert with the disastrous name of 'Jumbo' (Barrus) tries to compete with the girls in attracting men (1.6.30); his condition is described as a disease (*morbus*).[23] The pest hopes to ingratiate himself by boasting of his sinuous dancing – *quis membra mouere mollius* (1.9.24-5)? All these are satirised as effeminate. No problem so far. As for relations with boys, free-born Roman boys were supposed to be protected,[24] but others were much more vulnerable. The elder Seneca has a revealing story here. He quotes the declaimer Haterius as saying that submitting to a male's lust is criminal in a free-born Roman, compulsory in a slave, and a matter of duty in a freedman (*Contr.* 4, *praef.* 10). According to Seneca the reference to a freedman's 'duty' (*officium*) caused much laughter. But no one is said to have laughed at the slave's compulsion. That was merely a truism. Hence Horace could recommend casual intercourse on impulse with a slave-boy or girl (1.2.117). He does not say that he ever took such advice. Still, he is responsible for giving it, and many people would regard that line as the low point of the *sermones*. Only slightly less unpleasant is the cynically witty counsel given in *E.* 1.18:

> Don't let any maid or lad arouse your desires
> within the marble hall of the friend who commands respect.
> The owner may *give* you the pretty boy or the darling girl
> (and add nothing of substance), or cause you pain by refusing (72-5).

Even the clever double-entendre of book and slave-boy in *E.* 1.20 leaves a faintly unpleasant after-taste.

Occasional recourse to boys is, therefore, condoned, provided discretion is observed and one's emotions are not seriously involved. It is obsession that incurs ridicule (*insanit* in 1.4.27). But again it appears from *Epod.* 11 that Horace did not always manage to remain as cool as he ought. Lyciscus has taken over from Neaera, and there is no prospect of

---

[23] If, as some think, the name Barrus occurred in Lucilius and referred to Betutius Barrus, Horace has changed the character's sexual orientation. For Betutius Barrus was prosecuted for seducing three Vestal virgins. See Heinze's note.

[24] Horace himself was protected by his father (1.67.81-4). Sometimes the threat came from the school-teacher. See Pliny, *Ep.* 3.3.3-4, Quintilian, 2.2.15, 1.3.17; and Juvenal 10.224.

release – except through a new attachment to another girl or boy.[25] The same sort of self-mockery, though less specific, occurs in 2.3.325, where Damasippus makes the poet out to be a bi-sexual maniac: *mille puellarum, puerorum mille furores*. Later, in the *Odes*, we hear of Alcaeus' boy Lycus (1.32.11-12) and of Pyrrhus' Nearchus (3.20.6). A bi-sexual response is implied in the picture of the ambivalent Gyges (*Odes* 2.5.20-4; cf. Lucilius 324-5). But the most interesting reference is to Horace's Ligurinus in *Odes* 4.1 – the boy whom at night he holds fast in his dreams, or follows as he speeds like a bird over the grass of the Campus Martius or through rolling waters, always unkind. From these few references we may conjecture (though of course there can be no actual proof) that Horace had some interest in boys, and that although it played no very significant part in his life he remained susceptible to their attractions. Our chief concern here, however, has been to see how love (of both kinds) is represented in the *sermones*, and to draw comparisons with the treatment encountered in the other satirists.

When Persius was about six, his father died; his step-father died a few years later. He grew up to be a good-looking, modest boy, with a gentle disposition. He lived a good, clean life, and showed exemplary devotion to his mother, sister and aunt. At sixteen he came under the influence of Cornutus. He had a filial regard for the historian Servilius Nonianus, and for ten years he saw a good deal of the Stoic Thrasea Paetus. Given these details from the *Life*, it is not surpising that there is a negligible amount of heterosexual material in the satires, and none that concerns Persius himself. All the more striking, then, that in addition to seven coarse lines in 4, in which an innocent sun-bather is abused as a pathic and an exhibitionist (35-41), there is an elaborate metaphor of homosexual corruption which recurs at several points in 1. A number of passages from the poem have been translated already and will not be repeated here. But it is desirable to look briefly at the background to what Persius is saying and at the way in which the sexual metaphor is developed.

We start with the fact of literary and rhetorical degeneration. What lay behind it? Velleius pointed out that the different genres quickly became exhausted as a result of emulation (1.17.6-7). Others blamed the wrong-headed ideas of teachers, students, or parents (Petronius, 1-4). Others again explained the decline in oratory in terms of political conditions: it had flourished in the rough and tumble of the free republic, but now led a more subdued existence under the empire; perhaps the price was worth paying (Tacitus, *Dial*. 36-40; Longinus, 44.2-3). But Persius agreed with those like Seneca, who maintained that an abandoned style was a sign of public luxury (*Epist*. 114.2-3). In 1 he does

[25] In *Epod*. 14, addressed to Maecenas, Horace compares his passion for Phryne to that of Anacreon for Bathyllus. Maecenas was warmly attached to a contemporary Bathyllus (Tacitus, *Ann*. 1.54), so this was a cheeky piece of innuendo on Horace's part.

not go further back to ask about the causes of luxury, but he may well have accepted Velleius' succinct account of the matter: 'The elder Scipio (Africanus) opened the way to Rome's power, the younger (Aemilianus) to her luxury' (2.1.1). Since he is concerned with literary taste and style, he does not dwell on the usual appurtenances of wealth, like houses, parks, fish-ponds, and antiques. He does draw attention to over-eating (31, 51, 53, 57) and expensive dining-couches (52-3). But his chief emphasis falls on the Romans' loss of virility.[26] This loss is seen in the popularity of sentimental elegies and epyllia (34, 51) about heroines like Phyllis, Hypsipyle, Callirhoe, and troops of Maenads; the only masculine subject is Attis – the boy who castrated himself. Elegy had always been associated with softness, tenderness, and charm. These qualities have now become rotten. A manly work like the *Aeneid* (*arma uirum*) is shunned – a thing which would never have happened if contemporary Romans had any trace of their fathers' virility (*testiculi uena ulla paterni* in v.103). Grand subjects are handled in the smoothest possible style (14, 63-8). Even forensic oratory is presented in trim antitheses (85-6). The reciters of these poems are described as effeminate in voice (17-18, 35, and perhaps 80), facial expression (the swooning eye of v.18), hair-style (*pexus* in v.15), posture (the drooping neck in v.98), dress (15 and 32) and jewelry (16). And the reaction they produce in the audience is analogous to the pleasure of a pathic (19-21, 82, 87). Even if we leave open the question whether the venerable demeanour in v.9 and the nuts in v.10 foreshadow the motif of perversion,[27] there can be no doubt that this motif is the central feature of the poem, producing an original blend of literary and moral criticism. There is nothing at all like it in the other satirists.

By joining up certain points in the *Life* (gentleness, modesty, devotion to female relatives, respect for Stoic elders) and adding in other points from the *Satires* (absence of girls, presence of imaginative attack on degeneracy written in terms of a homosexual metaphor) one might be tempted to hazard a psychological profile of Persius. There might be room in such a profile for his early teacher, the dissolute Remmius Palaemon (Suetonius, *Gramm.* 23). But even if one eschews that kind of speculation, it remains true that Persius is in some sense involved in the situation described in 1, because the satire concerns poetic taste, and he is a poet. When Juvenal describes the 'gay scene' in 2, however, he has no connexion with it of any kind. Such people make him want to leave Rome, and indeed seek refuge beyond the borders of the empire (1-2). That extreme reaction is prompted by feelings of loathing and disgust. And if it seems absurd that such feelings should be levelled at a tiny

[26] Cf. Seneca the elder (born *c.* 50 B.C.) in his *Contr.* 1, *praef.* 8; Seneca the younger, *Ep.* 114.22 and *NQ* 7.31.2-3.
[27] This is argued by Bramble, 142, but contested by Harvey.

sub-group in Roman society, the answer, it seems, is that it is *not* a tiny sub-group. Such creatures are everywhere. Every street is full of them (8-9). So the violent emotion and the heated rhetoric are appropriate responses to a peculiar kind of satiric vision – a vision which we are asked to accept as sane.

The poem has three movements. (1) An attack is launched against well-to-do Roman pathics who masquerade as Stoic moralists (1-63). (2) One of these, Creticus, is singled out, whose behaviour goes further: he wears diaphanous clothes, allegedly because of the heat, and he carries his hypocritical preaching into the law-courts, where he denounces immoral women (64-116). (3) Another rich and well-born Roman pathic, namely Gracchus, goes further still, contracting a homosexual marriage (117-48). This leads straight into some general and pessimistic reflections on the type of corruption described (149-70). There are important internal divisions. The opening assault is shared between the poet (1-35) and Laronia, who is no angel but is at least honest (36-63). The attack on Creticus, after describing his present behaviour (64-78), goes on to foretell how he will join a club of like-minded people (82-116). In v.143 we learn that Gracchus has so far demeaned himself as to appear in the arena. The sections are connected by various links (e.g. the denunciation of female immorality is foreshadowed in v.37, and Creticus' Stoicism is hinted at in v.77). The conclusion, namely that corruption is already beginning to spread throughout the empire, recalls the beginning, where the poet contemplates flight 'beyond the Sarmatians and the frozen ocean'. And throughout run the contrasting threads of manly past and degenerate present.

The total reversal which has taken place is conveyed in various ways. The most straightforward is a series of references to the stern old Romans of the past – the Curii and Scauri, Cato, and others. Behind them stand the mountain folk (74), the shepherds of Latium (127), the legion of Cremera and the lads who fell at Cannae (155). Such men are held up as *exempla* to shame the Romans of today. Then there is a sequence of antithetical juxtapositions, starting with *qui Curios simulant et Bacchanalia uiuunt* (3) 'those who affect the Curii's style and live like the Bacchae'. Another is the famous *quis tulerit Gracchos de seditione querentes?* (24), 'Who could stomach the sight of the Gracchi denouncing sedition?' Sometimes the effect is encapsulated in two words, as in *tristibus obscenis* (9) 'austere debauchees'. A further contributory technique is that of parody. Thus the pathic's hairy arms, which turn out to be deceptive, give the impression of an *atrocem animum* (12). This alludes to Horace's *atrocem animum Catonis* (*Odes* 2.1.24), 'Cato's inflexible will'. Or again, in the homosexuals' club one holds a mirror. As mirrors were made of bronze, this may have put Juvenal in mind of Virgil's line: *aere cauo clipeum, magni gestamen Abantis* (*Aen.* 3.286) 'a shield of convex bronze, borne by the mighty Abas'. The last phrase is then distorted into *speculum, pathici gestamen Othonis* (99) 'a mirror, [an article] borne by the pathic Otho'. Juvenal then added another phrase from the *Aeneid*. Virgil had described the spear brandished by Turnus as *Actoris Aurunci spolium* (*Aen.* 12.94) 'a trophy seized from Auruncan Actor'. This reappears unaltered in the satire, except that it now has a double meaning. If the first 'a' is thought of as being in the lower case, the phrase will mean 'an Auruncan actor', and the mirror will be a piece of loot extracted by an acquisitive 'beloved'.[28]

Another technique, used here and elsewhere to underline contemporary viciousness, is that of obscenity. It has been rightly pointed out by modern scholars (Courtney 45, Adams 221) that Juvenal does not employ certain basic crudities found in Horace and Martial, e.g. *futuo, cunnus, mentula*. It is also true that from time to time he used neutral terms like *coitus* (10.204) and even euphemisms like *facio* (7.240). Yet we should not on that account underrate his indecency. Take the use of *fossa* (2.10) = anus (used *pars pro toto* of a pathic). Adams observes: 'It is not unlikely that *fossa* ... was in use in the colloquial language' (86). It may well have been, but that does not make it polite. Or what of *podex* = anus? It occurs in two obscene poems of Martial (2.43, 6.37) and in Horace's disgusting eighth epode (6). Its appearance in Juvenal 2.12 is hardly a sign of his 'lexical mildness' (Adams 112, disagreeing with Courtney, who calls it 'essentially gross'). On two occasions Juvenal knowingly confuses micturition with female secretions (6.64, 11.170; cf. 1.39), a practice which Adams rightly calls 'crudely figurative' (142). Both *criso* and *ceueo* are classified by Adams with basic obscenities (2); and they both occur in Juvenal (6.322, 2.21, 9.40). Again, Juvenal sometimes uses a general and clean word in a special and indecent sense. A witty if improper example is *tenui rima* (3.97) 'narrow chink' used of the female genitalia; a revolting example is the use of *lambit* 'licks' in 2.49. Finally, a drastically obscene effect can be obtained simply by describing a certain kind of action in an uncompromisingly accurate way. Perhaps the most shocking instance of this is 9.43-4.

These, then, are the main stylistic methods which convey Juvenal's attitude. One might argue that such dislike and contempt would be unreasonable if the behaviour in question were involuntary. Juvenal seems half aware of the point when he identifies Peribomius as a special case:

[28] Lelièvre, 242, makes the interesting suggestion that the actor was Nero, citing Suetonius (*Otho* 2.2) who records the rumour of homosexual relations. We still have to explain *Aurunci*. The fact that Virgil's Turnus was in Nero's repertoire hardly seems relevant (Suetonius, *Nero* 54). It would have been better had he been in Otho's repertoire. But perhaps geography can help. Nero was born at Antium (Suetonius, *Nero* 6.1). As we move down the coastline of Latium from Antium we eventually reach the territory of the *Aurunci*. So could Nero be referred to as an Auruncan? The notion ought not to be ruled out, for in Juvenal's day readers would have been very hazy about the exact position occupied by those early people. The gain in satirical point is considerable.

                                   Peribomius, therefore,
is franker and more authentic. He, by his gait and expression,
proclaims his ailment. I accept he was fated to be like that.
Such people's candour calls for pity; their very disorder
secures indulgence (15-19).

By allowing these few exceptions (cf. Hispo in v.50) Juvenal implies that
the great majority of passive homosexuals were not born with such
propensities but acquired them; in which case either they individually or
society collectively must be held responsible. Clearly that is a very
important theoretical distinction, but in actual life Juvenal was no more
able to apply it than we are.[29] Perhaps that is why he fails to keep a firm
grip on it, and slides into the much easier distinction between open and
covert practitioners. Granted crypto-homosexuals were his theme; yet it
is plain that if they came into the open he would not like them any
better. Speaking of Gracchus' 'marriage', he says

            liceat modo uiuere, fient,
      fient ista palam, cupient et in acta referri

Give us a few more years, such things will be done in public –
yes, in public; and then they will want to appear in the papers! (135-6)

The discussion has brought us back to a general point which was
touched on in the Preface. It was suggested there that we should, and
probably do, read classical poetry through bi-focal lenses. Through one
pair of lenses we try to see the work in its original setting (political,
social, literary, and so on) and to gauge, as best we can, from the text how
the writer meant us to respond. Through the other lenses we view the
work in the larger perspective which we have available, judging it quite
consciously in the light of our own understanding and values. This
sounds less patronising if we admit that our understanding and values
may be modified by what we read.
    On the subject of this last chapter some important scholarly work has
been published in the last twenty years which could not readily have
appeared in English before – articles like that of M.K. Hopkins, books
like those of K.J. Dover and J.N. Adams. For the social scientist or
linguist a clinical, dispassionate, approach is *de rigueur*. Ancestral tabus
must be quietly discarded, and the evidence must be collected and
arranged to show that such-and-such behaviour was practised, and
such-and-such terms employed, by certain people in certain situations at
certain times. The student of literature will gratefully acknowledge such
information, for it enlarges and strengthens the foundation on which he
builds. But having learned, for instance, that a certain word is, or is not,

----

[29] There is still no consensus among scientists on the old question about the relative
importance of nature and nurture.

a basic obscenity, he must try to read it as the author intended. (It would surely be wrong to imagine that Persius or Juvenal expected his readers to greet every shocking passage with the same sophisticated yawn.) After trying to react in the appropriate way, a process which becomes more spontaneous as our control of the language improves, we can ask how far the poet's attitude is acceptable from our point of view. If we are Christians, we will condemn the Romans' sexual treatment of slaves, because it runs counter to our religion, and we will see it, at best, as the unavoidable consequence of a pagan culture. If we are not Christians, we may still deplore such treatment, because the girl or boy concerned was exploited as a 'sex-object', or because, contraception being rudimentary, such treatment must have led to abortion or infanticide, or to the rearing of a child who would eventually be sold on the slave-market. In the case of covert homosexuality, it is easy for someone with a temperamental aversion to join in Juvenal's ridicule and contempt. But then one must ask whether it is not precisely that contempt which forces such people into concealment. How far can such orientation be altered? And in the end what harm does it do?

Scholarly understanding and fair-minded criticism will prevent us from regarding the Roman satirists either as 'just like ourselves' (if they were, they would be too unremarkable to study) or as 'totally alien' (in which case we could not relate to them at all). In reading what they wrote so many centuries ago, *humani nil ... alienum puto* remains a good motto,[30] provided we remember that it has sombre, indeed appalling, implications which Terence's old busybody does not seem to have had in mind.

---

[30] 'I think nothing human is alien', Terence, *Heaut.* 77.

Appendix

Greek words in Lucilius, Category B

FISH OR SHELLFISH: *amia* (1221), *cephalaea acarnae* (51), *echinus* (1222), *helops* (1220), *maena* (1033), *murena* (340), *ostrea* (126), *peloris* (126), *polypus* (925), *purpura* (126), *sargus* (1220), *tunnus* (50).

VEGETABLES: *asparagi* (127, 986), *cyma* (986), *lapathus* (200), *ruta* (129).

OTHER FOOD: *obsonia* (1225), *placentae* (629).

UTENSILS: *cyathus* (977), *echinus* (1155), *oenophorum* (132).

DININGROOM: *triclinium* (228).

CURTAINS: *aulaea* (897).

CLOTHES: *clamides* (349), *paenula* (507).

SEAFARING: *anquina* (618), *catapirates* (1163), *carchesia* (620), *hypereticos celetes* (p. 421), *cercurus* (346), *guberna* (622), *mataxa* (1164), *pelagus* (498), *prora* (622).

SOLDIERING: *catapulta* (243), *exanclor* (1012), *pareutactoe* (349, 816). *Sarisa* (243).

HORSEMANSHIP: *cantherius* (101, 507), *postomis* (518).

MEDICINE: ἀπεψία (976), *cataplasma* (967), *gangrena herpestica* (52), *stomachus* (178).

GAMES AND ATHLETICS: *gymnasium* (688), *mechanicus* (1264), *naumachia* (489), *petaurum* (1264), *schema* (972), *stadium* (343), *trigonum* (211).

WEAVING: *gerdius, zonarius* (1054), *panus* (327).

TRADE AND MONEY: *medimnum* (581), *tesorophylax* (623), *thesaurus* (830).

LANGUAGE: *cacosyntheton* (389), *euphonus* (after 418), *soloecismus* (397), *syllaba* (369).

LITERATURE AND RHETORIC: *archaeotera* (411), *coragus* (456), *crisis* (417), *enthymema* (410), *epistula* (404), ἔπος (406), *exodium* (415), *hexameter* (235), *historia* (700), *pausa* (18), *poema* (403f.), *poesis* (405, 409), *schema* (416), θέσις (406), *tragicus* (504).

PHILOSOPHY: *atomos* (820), *eidola* (820), *philosophus* (821), *physicus* (676), *scole* (823).

MISCELLANEOUS: *cannabinus* (1919), ἐπίτευγμα (955), *ergastilus* (543), *mysterium* (673), *pessulus* (171), *thomix* (1219), *tyrannus* (835).

Abbreviations

AJAH	*American Journal of Ancient History*
AJP	*American Journal of Philology*
ANRW	*Aufstieg und Niedergang der römischen Welt*
BICS	*Bulletin of the Institute of Classical Studies*
CJ	*Classical Journal*
CP	*Classical Philology*
CQ	*Classical Review*
GL	*Grammatici Latini*, ed. H. Keil
GR	*Greece and Rome*
GRBS	*Greek, Roman, and Byzantine Studies*
HSCP	*Harvard Studies in Classical Philology*
ICS	*Illinois Classical Studies*
JRS	*Journal of Roman Studies*
LCM	*Liverpool Classical Monthly*
PCPS	*Proceedings of the Cambridge Philological Society*
Phil.	*Philologus*
Rh. Mus.	*Rheinisches Museum*
ROL	*Remains of Old Latin*, ed. E.H. Warmington
RSC	*Revista di Studi Classici*
TAPA	*Transactions ... of the American Philological Association*
UCPCP	*University of California Publications in Classical Philology*
WZ	*Wissenschaftliche Zeitschrift der Wilhelm-Pieck-Universität, Rostock*

Bibliography

The following list includes only items referred to in the text. For a full survey of recent work see W.S. Anderson, 'Recent work in Roman satire (1968-78),' *CW* 75 (1982), 273-99.

Adamietz, J.	*Untersuchungen zu Juvenal* (Wiesbaden, 1972)
Adams, J.N.	*The Latin Sexual Vocabulary* (London, 1982)
Ahl, F.M.	*Lucan: an Introduction* (Ithaca and London, 1976)
Anderson, W.S.	(1) 'Pompey, his friends, and the literature of the first century B.C.', *UCPCP* 19 (1963), 1-87
	(2) *Essays on Roman Satire* (Princeton, 1982)
Anonymous	editor of *D. Junii Juvenalis ... Satirae expurgatae* (London, 1784)
Astin, A.E.	(1) *Scipio Aemilianus* (Oxford, 1967)
	(2) *Cato the Censor* (Oxford, 1977)
Bailey, C.	*Epicurus* (Oxford, 1926)
Balsdon, J.P.V.D.	*Romans and Aliens* (London, 1979)
Bardon, H.	*La Littérature latine inconnue*, 2 vols. (Paris, 1952)
Bauman, R.A.	*The Crimen Maiestatis in the Roman Republic and Augustan Principate* (Johannesburg, 1967)
Beikircher, H.	*Kommentar zur VI Satire des A. Persius Flaccus* (Wien, Köln, Graz, 1969)
Bo, D.	(1) *Q. Horati Flacci Opera*, vol. 3 (Paravia, 1960)
	(2) *A. Persi Flacci Saturarum Liber* (Paravia, 1969)
Boissier, G.	*L'Opposition sous les Césars* (Paris, 1913)
Bonaria, M.	*Mimorum Romanorum Fragmenta* (Genova, 1955)
Boren, H.C.	'The urban side of the Gracchan economic crisis', in *The Crisis of the Roman Republic*, ed. R. Seager (Cambridge and New York, 1969), 54-66
Bowersock, G.W.	*Augustus and the Greek World* (Oxford, 1965)
Bradley, K.R.	*Suetonius' Life of Nero* (Bruxelles, 1978)
Bramble, J.C.	*Persius and the Programmatic Satire* (Cambridge, 1974)

Braund, S.H. and Cloud, J.D.	'Juvenal: a diptych', *LCM* 6 (1981), 195-208
Brink, C.O.	*Horace on Poetry* 1. *Prolegomena to the Literary Epistles* (Cambridge, 1963). 2. *The Ars Poetica* (Cambridge, 1971). 3. *Epistles, Book II* (Cambridge, 1982)
Briscoe, J.	'Supporters and opponents of Tiberius Gracchus', *JRS* 64 (1974), 125-35
Britannicus, J.	*Commentarii in Juvenalem* (Brixiae, 1501)
Broughton, T.R.S.	(1) *The Magistrates of the Roman Republic*, 2 vols. (New York, 1968)
	(2) 'Comment', in *The Crisis of the Roman Republic*, ed. R. Seager (Cambridge, 1969), 118-30
Brower, R.A.	*Alexander Pope: the Poetry of Allusion* (Oxford, 1959)
Brunt, P.A.	(1) 'The Equites in the Late Republic', in *The Crisis of the Roman Republic*, ed. R. Seager (Cambridge, 1969)
	(2) '*Amicitia* in the Late Roman Republic', *ibid.*
	(3) *Italian Manpower* (Oxford, 1971)
Cairns, F.	*Generic Composition in Greek and Roman Poetry* (Edinburgh, 1972)
Carcopino, J.	*Daily Life in Ancient Rome*, trans. E.O. Lorimer (London, 1941)
Charpin, F.	*Lucilius. Satires*, 2 vols. (Paris, 1978)
Christes, J.	*Der Frühe Lucilius* (Heidelberg, 1971)
Cichorius, C.	*Untersuchungen zu Lucilius* (repr. Zürich and Berlin, 1964)
Citroni, M.	*M. Valerii Martialis Epigrammaton Liber I* (Firenze, 1975)
Clausen, W.V.	*A. Persi Flacci et D. Iuni Iuuenalis Saturae* (Oxonii, 1959)
Cloud, J.D.	see Braund, S.H.
Cody, J.V.	*Horace and Callimachean Aesthetics* (Bruxelles, 1976)
Coffey, M.	(1) *Roman Satire* (London, 1976)
	(2) 'Turnus and Juvenal', *BICS* 26 (1979), 88-94
Cooper, Lane	*Concordance of the Works of Horace* (repr. Cambridge, 1963)
Courtney, E.	*A Commentary on the Satires of Juvenal* (London, 1980)
Crönert, G.	'Variae Lectiones', *Rh. Mus.* 65 (1910), 461-71
Crook, J.	*Consilium Principis* (Cambridge, 1955)
Daly, L.W.	'Roman study abroad', *AJP* 71 (1950), 40-58
Dalzell, A.	(1) 'C. Asinius Pollio and the early history of public recitation at Rome', *Hermathena* 86 (1955), 20-8
	(2) 'Maecenas and the poets', *Phoenix* 10

	(1956), 151-62
D'Arms, J.H.	*Commerce and Social standing in Ancient Rome* (Cambridge. Mass. and London, 1981)
De Decker, J.	*Iuuenalis Declamans* (Gand, 1913)
Dover, K.J.	*Greek Homosexuality* (London, 1978)
Dryden, J.	'A discourse concerning the origin and progress of satire', in *Essays of John Dryden*, ed. W.P. Ker (Oxford, 1900) vol. 2, 15-114.
Duckworth, G.E.	*The Nature of Roman Comedy* (Princeton, 1952)
Dudley, D.R.	*A History of Cynicism* (London, 1937)
Duff, A.M.	*Freedmen in the Early Roman Empire* (Oxford, 1928)
De Quesnay, I.M. Le M.	'Horace and Maecenas: the propaganda value of *Sermones* 1', in *Poetry and Politics in the Age of Augustus*, ed. A. Woodman and D. West (Cambridge, 1984)
Earl, D.C.	*The Political Thought of Sallust* (Cambridge, 1961)
Erskine-Hill, H.	*The Augustan Idea in English Literature* (London, 1983)
Ferguson, J.	*Juvenal: The Satires* (London and New York, 1979)
Fiske, G.C.	*Lucilius and Horace* (Madison, 1920)
Fraenkel, E.	review of Beckmann's *Zauberei und Recht in Roms Frühzeit* in *Gnomon* 1 (1925), 185-200
Frank, T.	*Vergil* (New York, 1922)
Fredericks, S.C.	see Ramage, E.S.
Garnsey, P.D.A.	'Where did Italian peasants live?', *PCPS* 25 (1979), 1-25
Garton, C.	*Personal Aspects of the Roman Theatre* (Toronto, 1972)
Gérard, J.	*Juvénal et la réalité contemporaine* (Paris, 1976)
Gifford, W.	*The Satires of D.J. Juvenalis* (London, 1802)
Goodyear, F.R.D.	*The Annals of Tacitus, Books 1-6*, vol. 2. (Cambridge, 1981)
Gordon, M.L.	'The nationality of slaves under the early Roman empire', *JRS* 14 (1924), 93-111
Gow, A.S.F. and Page, D.L.	*The Garland of Philip* (Cambridge, 1968)
Gratwick, A.S.	'Lucilius', in *The Cambridge History of Classical Literature*, vol. 2 (Cambridge, 1982), 162-71
Green, P.	*uvenal: The Sixteen Satires* (Harmondsworth, 1967)
Greenberg, N.A.	'The use of *poiema* and *poiesis*', *HSCP* 52 (1957), 263-89

Griffin, J.
'Augustan poetry and the life of luxury', *JRS* 66 (1976), 87-105

Griffin, M.T.
Seneca: a Philosopher in Politics (Oxford, 1976)

Griffith, J.G.
'Juvenal, Statius, and the Flavian establishment', *GR* 16 (1969), 134-50

Gruen, E.S.
Roman Politics and the Criminal Courts 149-78 B.C. (Cambridge Mass., 1968)

Guite, H.
'Cicero's attitude to the Greeks', *GR* 9 (1962), 142-59

Hagstrum, J.
The Sister Arts (Chicago, 1958)

Hallett, J.P.
'*Perusinae Glandes* and the Changing Image of Augustus', *AJAH* 2 (1977), 151-71

Halliwell, S.
'Ancient interpretations of ὀνομαστὶ κωμῳδεῖν in Aristophanes', *CQ* 34 (1984), 83-8

Hammond, M.
'Composition of the Senate, A.D. 68-235', *JRS* 47 (1957), 74-81

Hardie, A.
Statius and the Silvae (Liverpool, 1983)

Harvey, R.A.
A Commentary on Persius (Leiden, 1981)

Haupt, P.
'Abraham's bosom', *AJP* 42 (1921), 162-7

Heinsius, D.
Q. Horati Flacci Opera (Lugduni Batavorum, 1612)

Heinze, R.
see Kiessling, A.

Hennig, D.
'T. Labienus und der erste Majestätsprozess *de famosis libellis*', *Chiron* 3 (1973), 245-54

Herington, C.J.
'Senecan tragedy', in *Essays in Classical Literature* ed. N. Rudd (Cambridge and New York, 1972), 170-219

Highet, G.
Juvenal the Satirist (Oxford, 1954)

Hofmann, J.B.
*Lateinische Umgangssprache*³ (Heidelberg, 1951)

Hopkins, M.K.
'Contraception in the Roman Empire', *Comparative Studies in Society and History* 8 (1965-6), 124-51

Horsfall, N.
'Ad Juv. 1.40', *Mnemosyne* 28 (1975), 422

Hubbard, M.
see Nisbet, R.G.M.

Jahn, O.
Auli Persii Flacci Saturarum Liber (repr. Hildesheim, 1967)

Jenkinson, J.R.
Persius: The Satires (Warminster, 1980)

Jenkyns, R.
Three Classical Poets (London, 1982)

Jocelyn, H.D.
(1) 'Ennius, Varia 14 V²,' *CR* 15 (1965), 146-9
(2) *The Tragedies of Ennius* (Cambridge, 1967)
(3) 'The poet Cn. Naevius, P. Cornelius Scipio and Q. Caecilius Metellus', *Antichthon* 3 (1969), 32-47
(4) 'The ruling class of the Roman Republic and Greek philosophers', *Bulletin of the John Rylands Library* 59 (1976-7), 323-66

Jones, B.W.
Domitian and the Senatorial Order, The American Philosophical Society (1979)

232   *Bibliography*

Jones, C.P.
(1) 'Towards a chronology of Plutarch's works', *JRS* 56 (1960) 61-74
(2) *Plutarch and Rome* (Oxford, 1971)
(3) *The Roman World of Dio Chrysostom* (Harvard, 1978)

Kelly, J.M.
Roman Litigation (Oxford, 1966)

Kenney, E.J.
(1) 'The first satire of Juvenal', *PCPS* 8 (1962), 29-40
(2) 'Books and readers in the Roman world', in *The Cambridge History of Classical Literature*, vol. 2 (Cambridge, 1982), 3-32

Kiessling, A.
*Q. Horatius Flaccus, Satiren*⁶, erneuert von Richard Heinze (Berlin, 1957)

Klingner, F.
Q. Horati Flacci Opera (Lipsiae, 1959)

Knoche, U.
Roman Satire, trans. E.S. Ramage (Bloomington and London, 1975)

Knox, B.M.W.
'Silent reading in Antiquity', *GRBS* 9 (1968), 421-35

Körte, A.
(1) 'Augusteer bei Philodem', *Rh. Mus.* 45 (1890), 172-7
(2) *Menandri Quae Supersunt, Pars Altera* (Lipsiae, 1959)

Krenkel, W.A.
(1) 'Zur literarischen Kritik bei Lucilius', repr. in *Die Römische Satire*, ed. D. Korzeniewski (Darmstadt, 1970), 161-266
(2) *Lucilius: Satiren* 2 vols. (Berlin, 1970)
(3) 'Zur Biographie des Lucilius', *ANRW* 1.2 (1972), 1240-59
(4) *'Pueri Meritorii'*, *WZ* 28 (1979), 179-89

LaFleur, R.A.
(1) 'Artorius and Catulus in Juvenal 3', *RSC* 22 (1974), 5-9
(2) '*Amicitia* and the unity of Juvenal's first book', *ICS* 4 (1979), 158-77

Lelièvre, F.J.
'Juvenal: two possible examples of wordplay', *CP* 53 (1958), 241-2

Lenel, O.
Das Edictum Perpetuum (repr. Leipzig, 1956)

Lubinus, E.
D. Iunii Iuvenalis Satyrarum Libri V (Hanoviae, 1603)

McGann, M.J.
(1) *Studies in Horace's First Book of Epistles* (Bruxelles, 1969)
(2) 'The three worlds of Horace's *Satires*', in *Horace*, ed. C.D.N. Costa (London, 1973), 59-93

MacMullen, R.
Roman Social Relations (New Haven and London, 1974)

Maidment, K.J.
'The later comic chorus', *CQ* 29 (1935), 1-24

Malcovati, H.
(1) *Imperatoris Caesaris Augusti Operum Fragmenta*,⁴ (Paravia, 1962)
(2) *Oratorum Romanorum Fragmenta*,⁴ vol. 1 (Paravia, 1976)

Mancinelli, A.
Iuvenalis Satyrae (Venetiis, 1492)

Manfredini, A.D.	*La Diffamazione Verbale Nel Diritto Romano*, vol. 1 *Età Repubblicana* (Milano, 1979)
Mariotti, I.	*Studi Luciliani* (Firenze, 1960)
Marmorale, E.V.	*Giovenale*² (Bari, 1950)
Marx, F.	*C. Lucilii Carminum Reliquiae*, 2 vols. (Lipsiae 1904)
Mason, H.A.	'Is Juvenal a classic?' in *Critical Essays in Roman Literature: Satire*, ed. J.P. Sullivan (London, 1963)
Momigliano, A.	'Nero,' *Cambridge Ancient History*, vol. 10, ch. 21, 702-42
Morel, W.	*Fragmenta Poetarum Romanorum* (Stuttgart, 1963)
Morford, M.	(1) 'Juvenal's thirteenth satire', *AJP* 94 (1973). 26-36 (2) 'Juvenal's fifth satire', *AJP* 98 (1977) 219-45
Munro, H.A.J.	'Another word on Lucilius', *Journal of Philology* 8 (1879), 201-25
Newman, J.K.	*The Concept of Vates in Augustan Poetry* (Bruxelles, 1967)
Nisbet, R.G.M.	'Persius', in *Critical Essays in Roman Literature: Satire*, ed. J.P. Sullivan (London, 1963)
Nisbet, R.G.M. and Hubbard, M.	*A Commentary on Horace's Odes*, Book 1 (Oxford, 1970), Book 2 (Oxford, 1978)
Petrochilos, N.	*Roman Attitudes to the Greeks* (Athens, 1974)
Pleket, H.W.	'Domitian, the Senate, and the Provinces', *Mnemosyne* 14 (1961), 296-315
Plescia, J.	'The development of *iniuria*', *Labeo* 23 (1977), 271-89
Pollitt, J.J.	*The Art of Rome* (Eaglewood Cliffs, New Jersey, 1966)
Quinn, K.	'The poet and his audience in the Augustan age', *ANRW* II.30.1. 76-180
Ramage, E.S, Sigsbee, D.J. and Fredericks, S.C.	*Roman Satirists and their Satire* (Park Ridge, New Jersey, 1974)
Ramsay, G.G.	*Juvenal and Persius*, Loeb Translation (London, 1918)
Raschke, W.	'The early books of Lucilius', *JRS* 69 (1979), 78-89
Reckford, K.J.	'Horace and Maecenas', *TAPA* 90 (1955), 195-208
Reynolds, R.W.	'The adultery mime', *CQ* 40 (1946), 77-84
Robinson, R.P.	'Valerius Cato', *TAPA* 54 (1923), 98-116
Rogers, R.S.	'A Tacitean pattern in treason-trials', *TAPA* 83 (1952), 279-311
Ruckdeschel, F.	*Archaismen und Vulgarismen in der Sprache*

des Horaz (repr. Hildesheim, 1972)

Rudd, N.
(1) 'Had Horace been criticised? a study of *Serm*. 1.4', *AJP* 76 (1955), 165-75
(2) *The Satires of Horace* (Cambridge, 1966)
(3) *Lines of Enquiry* (Cambridge, 1976)

Ruperti, G.A.
D. Iunii Iuuenalis Satirae XVI, 2 vols. (Lipsiae, 1819)

Saller, R.P.
(1) *Personal Patronage Under the Early Empire* (Cambridge, 1982)
(2) 'Martial on patronage and literature', *CQ* 33 (1983) 246-57

Scarborough, J.
Roman Medicine (London, 1969)

Scott, K.
'The political propaganda of 44-33 B.C.', *Memoirs of the American Academy in Rome* 11 (1933), 1-49

Seager, R.
'*Amicitia* in Tacitus and Juvenal', *AJAH* 2 (1977), 40-50

Serafini, A.
Studio sulla satira di Giovenale (Firenze, 1957)

Shackleton Bailey, D.R.
(1) 'Stray lights on Lucilius', *CJ* 76 (1980-81), 117-18
(2) *Profile of Horace* (London, 1982)

Sherwin-White, A.N.
The Letters of Pliny (Oxford, 1966)

Sigsbee, D.L.
see Ramage, E.S.

Skutsch, O.
Studia Enniana (London, 1968)

Skydsgaard, J.E.
'Non-slave labour in rural Iraly during the Late Republic', in *Non-Slave Labour in the Greco-Roman world*, ed. Peter Garnsey, *PCPS* Suppl. vol. 6 (1980), 65-72

Smith, R.E.
'The law of libel at Rome', *CQ* 1 (1951), 169-79

Starr, C.G.
'Epictetus and the tyrant', *CP* 44 (1949), 20-9

Sullivan, J.P.
(1) ed. *Critical Essays on Roman Literature: Satire* (London, 1963)
(2) 'Martial's sexual attitudes', *Phil.* 123 (1979) 288-302

Syme, R.
(1) *The Roman Revolution* (repr. Oxford, 1960)
(2) *Tacitus*, 2 vols. (Oxford, 1958)
(3) *Ten Studies in Tacitus* (Oxford, 1970)
(4) *History in Ovid* (Oxford, 1978)
(5) 'Juvenal, Pliny, Tacitus', *AJP* 100 (1979), 250-78

Tate, J.
'Cornutus and the poets,' *CQ* 23 (1929), 41-5

Terzaghi, N.
(1) *C. Lucili Saturarum Reliquiae*,[3] I. Mariotti adiuuante (Firenze, 1966)
(2) *Lucilio*[2] (Torino, 1944)

Thylander, H.
Etude sur l'épigraphie latine (Lund, 1952)

Townend, G.B.
'The literary substrata to Juvenal's satires', *JRS* 63 (1973), 148-60

Toynbee, J.M.C.
'Dictators and philosophers in the first century A.D.', *GR* 13 (1944), 43-58

Treggiari, S.
(1) *Roman Freedmen During the Late Republic* (Oxford, 1969)
(2) 'Intellectuals, poets, and their patrons in the first century B.C.', *Classical News and Views* 21 (1977), 24-9
(3) 'Lower-class women in the Roman economy', *Florilegium* 1 (1979), 65-86

Van Geytenbeek, A.C.
Musonius Rufus and the Greek Diatribe, trans. B.L. Hijmans (Utrecht, 1963)

Warmington, E.H.
Remains of Old Latin, 4 vols. Loeb Translation (repr. 1979)

Waters, K.
(1) 'The character of Domitian', *Phoenix* 18 (1964), 49-77
(2) 'Traianus Domitiani continuator', *AJP* 90 (1969), 385-405

Watson, A.
Law Making in the Later Roman Republic (Oxford, 1974)

Weinbrot, H.W.
Augustus Caesar in 'Augustan' England (Princeton, 1978)

West, M.L.
Iambi et Elegi Graeci (Oxonii, 1971)

White, P.
(1) 'The friends of Martial, Statius, and Pliny, and the dispersal of patronage', *HSCP* 79 (1975), 265-300
(2) '*Amicitia* and the profession of poetry in Early Imperial Rome', *JRS* 68 (1978), 74-92
(3) 'Positions for poets in Early Imperial Rome', in *Literary and Artistic Patronage in Ancient Rome*, ed. B.K. Gold (Austin, 1982), 50-66

Wiedemann, T.
Greek and Roman Slavery (London, 1981)

Wiesen, D.
'Juvenal and the intellectuals', *Hermes* 101 (1973), 464-83

Wimmel, W.
Kallimachos in Rom (Wiesbaden, 1960)

Wirszubski, C.
Libertas (Cambridge, 1968)

Wiseman, T.P.
'*Pete nobiles amicos*: poets and patrons in Late Republican Rome', in *Literary and Artistic Patronage in Ancient Rome*, ed. B.K. Gold (Austin, 1982)

Wolff, C.
Bisexuality (London, 1979)

Yavetz, Z.
'The living conditions of the urban plebs', in *The Crisis of the Roman Republic*, ed. R. Seager (Cambridge, 1969), 162-79

Index of names

Accius, 4, 8, 42, 166
Adamietz, J., 158
Adams, J.N., 34, 198, 199, 223, 224
Ahl, F., 63
Albucius, 48, 163, 169, 206, 217
Alpinus, 16
Anderson, W.S., 33, 34
Antony, 52, 53, 54, 55, 70, 134
Apuleius, 218
Archias, 132
Archilochus, 51, 165, 199
Aristophanes, 5, 42, 49, 122, 181
Arnobius, 56
Astin, A.E., 2, 49, 50, 163, 170
Augustine, 40
Augustus, 51-62, 64, 67, 70, 80, 94, 120,
    134, 171, 176

Balsdon, J.P.V.D., 170
Bardon, H., 16
Barea Soranus, 63-5, 69, 79
Bauman, R.A., 62
Beikircher, H., 144
Bo, D., 68, 92, 173
Boissier, G., 191-2
Bonaria, M., 15
Boren, H.C., 127
Boswell, J., 11
Bowersock, G., 175
Bramble, J.C., 23, 108, 221
Braund, S., 155
Brink, C.O., 9
Briscoe, J., 49
Britannicus, J., 28, 68
Broughton, T.R.S., 127
Brower, R., 61
Brunt, P.A., 127, 128, 134
Brutus, 51, 63, 65-6, 81

Caecilius, 173, 207
Caesar, 52-3, 110, 134
Cairns, F., 38
Callimachus, 90-1, 95, 172, 179, 181
Calvinus, 36-7, 112

Calvus, 16, 24, 171-2
Canidia, 14, 57
Carcopino, J., 195
Cassius Dio, 72
Catius, 14, 19, 57, 95, 159, 168
Cato the censor, 48, 92, 162, 170, 173,
    184, 191, 193, 205, 222
Cato, M. Porcius, 33, 63, 65-6, 182
Cato, Valerius, 116, 172
Catullus (the poet), 16, 24, 116, 171-2,
    181, 196, 205, 209, 211
Catullus (friend of Juvenal), 38
Charpin, F., 45
Christes, J., 45
Chrysippus, 25, 62-3, 182, 186-7
Cicero, 9, 13-14, 27, 33, 40-1, 48, 83-4,
    89-90, 92, 99-100, 108, 114, 118,
    129-32, 135, 139, 164, 171, 173, 176,
    178, 207, 217
Cichorius, C., 2, 44, 46-9
Citroni, M., 216
Clitomachus, 45, 164
Cloud, J.D., 155
Cody, J.V., 91
Coffey, M., ix, 2, 71, 74
Columella, 133, 145, 193-4
Cornutus, 22, 62-3, 68-9, 105, 122,
    143-4, 182, 212, 220
Cotta, L. Aurelius, 47, 50, 206
Courtney, E., 32, 38, 70-1, 196, 223
Crassus, L. Licinius, 3, 129, 163
Crispinus (Stoic preacher), 14-15, 26-7,
    54
Crispinus (friend of Domitian), 31, 77,
    112, 151, 157
Crönert, G., 166
Crook, J., xii, 76

Daly, L., 163
Dalzell, A., 117
D'Arms, J., 127
Davus, 26, 94, 98, 134, 200, 213
De Decker, J., 33-4, 111
Democritus, 136, 151, 177-8

Index of passages quoted

(pages of this book are in **bold type**)